CHEMISTRY
FOR
TOXICITY
TESTING

CHEMISTRY FOR TOXICITY TESTING

Edited by

C.W. Jameson

Head, Chemistry Section/Program Resources Branch
National Institute of Environmental Health Sciences (USDHHS)
Research Triangle Park, North Carolina

Douglas B. Walters

Head, Chemical Health and Safety Section/
    Program Resources Branch
National Institute of Environmental Health Sciences (USDHHS)
Research Triangle Park, North Carolina

BUTTERWORTH PUBLISHERS
Boston • **London**
Sidney • **Wellington** • **Durban** • **Toronto**

Library of Congress Cataloging in Publication Data
Main entry under title:

Chemistry for toxicity testing.

  Bibliography: p.
  Includes index.
  1. Toxicity testing. 2. Chemistry, Analytic. I. Jameson, C.W.
II. Walters, Douglas B.
RA1199.C48 1984   615.9′07   83–19031
ISBN 0–250–40547–4

Butterworth Publishers
80 Montvale Avenue
Stoneham, MA 02180

10 9 8 7 6 5 4 3 2 1

Printed in the United States of America

To Brenda and C.W.,
the most important people in my life.

CONTENTS

THE EDITORS

C.W. JAMESON

C.W. Jameson, a research chemist at the National Institute of Environmental Health Sciences (USDHHS) in Research Triangle Park, North Carolina, is the Acting Chief for the Program Resources Branch and is also head of the Chemistry Section of that branch. He received his Ph.D. from the University of Maryland, specializing in the synthesis and photochemistry of aliphatic amides and imides and the interaction of nuclear magnetic resonance shift reagents with substrates in solution. He has been an active participant in the National Institutes of Health's Carcinogenesis Testing Program since 1976.

Since joining the National Institute of Environmental Health Sciences, he has assumed responsibility for the chemistry aspects of the testing and research programs of the Toxicology Research and Testing Program. In addition, Dr. Jameson has served as program leader for chemistry in the Department of Health and Human Service's National Toxicology Program since its inception. In this position, he has developed chemistry standards for toxicity studies that have been widely accepted as an integral part of many toxicology testing programs.

Dr. Jameson is currently an active member of the Division of Analytical Chemistry of the American Chemical Society, serving as a member of the division's Committee on Regulatory Affairs. He has lectured throughout the United States and is the author or coauthor of numerous publications.

DOUGLAS B. WALTERS

Douglas B. Walters is head of the Chemical Health and Safety Section for the Program Resources Branch at the National Institute of Environmental Health Sciences (USDHHS) in Research Triangle Park, North Carolina. He is the former chief of the safety office and the former technical programs manager of the Laboratory of Environmental Chemistry at the National Institute of Environmental Health Sciences. His Ph.D. was earned at the University of Georgia concentrating on the analytical chemistry of metal-complex interactions using NMR spectroscopy and organophosphorus synthesis. Until 1977 he was an active researcher with the USDA's Tobacco and Health Program specializing in the fractionation, characterization, and bioassay of cigarette smoke.

Since joining National Institute of Environmental Health Sciences, he has been involved in diverse projects which apply chemistry principles to a broad range of environmental health and safety concerns. Included in these areas are the design of high-hazard chemistry laboratories, establishment of a chemical repository with associated analytical and synthetic support, implementation of a comprehensive health and safety program, and foundation of health and safety guidelines and requirements for various types of toxicology studies. Dr. Walters' work covers a range of areas of interest including: design of specialty equipment and facilities for chemical containment; application of human factors engineering to chemical health and safety; chemical control and management of environmental quality, health and safety in multidisciplinary operations; and use and application of chemical health and safety information. He has organized, developed, and implemented an internationally recognized program in chemical health and safety for the National Toxicology Program which utilizes interdisciplinary knowledge of chemistry, industrial hygiene, and toxicology as applied to problems of environmental concern.

Dr. Walters is the current chairman and past secretary of the Division of Chemical Health and Safety of the American Chemical Society (ACS). He is the past chairman of the Northeast Georgia Section of the ACS and was appointed by the National ACS headquarters from 1973 to 1978 as ACS science advisor to U.S. Senator Herman Talmadge and U.S. Congressmen Robert G. Stephens and Doug Barnard, all of Georgia. He has lectured throughout the United States and is the author or coauthor of numerous publications, including 17 book chapters.

Dr. Walters has edited the unique two-volume set *Safe Handling of Chemical Carcinogens, Mutagens, Teratogens and Highly Toxic Substances*, and serves on the editorial board of the *International Journal of Chemical Health and Safety* and the *Handbook of Environmental Chemistry: Chemical Waste* volume.

THE CONTRIBUTORS

Duane R. Boline
Radian Corporation
Austin, Texas

V.F. Boyd
Litton Bionetics
Kensington, Maryland

Richard D. Brown
Midwest Research Institute
Kansas City, Missouri

Bruce A. Burgess
E.I. du Pont de Nemours & Co., Inc.
Haskell Laboratory for Toxicology
and Industrial Medicine
Newark, Delaware

Carlos A. Castro
Midwest Research Institute
Kansas City, Missouri

James M. Cholakis
Midwest Research Institute
Kansas City, Missouri

John R. Decker
Battelle Pacific Northwest
Laboratories
Richland, Washington

Robert T. Drew
Brookhaven National Laboratory
Upton, New York

J.M. Fitzgerald
Litton Bionetics
Kensington, Maryland

Daniel L. Geary
Bushy Run Research Center
Export, Pennsylvania

Charles K. Grieshaber
National Toxicology Program
Research Triangle Park,
North Carolina

Jack H. Hagensen
Midwest Research Institute
Kansas City, Missouri

C. Tucker Helmes
SRI International
Menlo Park, California

C.W. Jameson
National Toxicology Program
Research Triangle Park
North Carolina

Larry H. Keith
Radian Corporation
Austin, Texas

David P. Kelly
E.I. du Pont de Nemours & Co., Inc.
Haskell Laboratory for Toxicology
and Industrial Medicine
Newark, Delaware

George W. Klein
Bushy Run Research Center
Export, Pennsylvania

Gustav O. Kuhn
Midwest Research Institute
Kansas City, Missouri

Trent R. Lewis
National Institute for Occupational
   Safety and Health
Cincinnati, Ohio

A.G. Manus
Litton Bionetics
Rockville, Maryland

Owen R. Moss
Battelle Pacific Northwest
   Laboratories
Richland, Washington

Evelyn A. Murrill
Midwest Research Institute
Kansas City, Missouri

Stephen S. Olin
Tracor Jitco, Inc.
Rockville, Maryland

Patricia A. Papa
SRI International
Menlo Park, California

John J. Rollheiser
Midwest Research Institute
Kansas City, Missouri

Linda M. Scheer
Carltech Associates, Inc.
Rockville, Maryland

Bruce A. Schworer
Midwest Research Institute
Kansas City, Missouri

Caroline C. Sigman
SRI International
Menlo Park, California

David H. Steele
Midwest Research Institute
Kansas City, Missouri

Kathleen M. Stelting
Midwest Research Institute
Kansas City, Missouri

Joseph E. Tomaszewski
National Toxicology Program
Bethesda, Maryland

Douglas B. Walters
National Toxicology Program
Research Triangle Park
North Carolina

Ralph J. Wheeler
Gulf South Research Institute
New Iberia, Louisiana

Carrie E. Whitmire
National Institutes of Environmental
   Health Sciences
Research Triangle Park,
   North Carolina

Edward J. Woodhouse
Midwest Research Institute
Kansas City, Missouri

PREFACE

Evaluation of chemicals for their toxic potential plays an important part in protecting man's environment. Currently much effort is being exerted through government, academia, and private industry in this area by establishing toxicity testing programs. Any testing or research program for environmental chemicals requires a chemistry support program capable of handling a wide variety of materials. The chemicals tested for toxicity can vary from highly volatile, nonpolar organics to nonvolatile polar organometallics and inorganics. Analysis of this broad range of materials requires the skills and knowledge of highly trained personnel with a broad theoretical background and practical experience with sophisticated analytical instrumentation. Chemistry capabilities need to be provided for procurement, chemical analysis, analytical methods development, purification, and synthesis of test chemicals. These capabilities must provide for analysis of bulk chemicals, as well as chemicals in test vehicles, methods development for quality assurance, purity and stability evaluations (for both bulk chemical and chemical/vehicle mixtures), and special studies for the analysis of chemical residues in body tissues and fluids.

The origin of this book lies with the formation of the National Toxicology Program, which was established by the Secretary of the Department of Health, Education and Welfare (now DHHS) in November 1978. This Program joined the toxicology testing efforts of the National Institutes of Health's National Institute of Environmental Health Sciences and National Cancer Institute, the Food and Drug Administration's National Center for Toxicological Research, and the Center for Disease Control's National Institute for Occupational Safety and Health. The broad scope of this Program is to consolidate the Department's activities in toxicological testing of chemicals of public concern and to develop and validate new and better test methods. This Department-wide effort provides information about potentially toxic chemicals to regulatory and research agencies and strengthens the scientific bases.

The need for such a Program evolved from increasing scientific, regulatory, and public concerns over the human health effects of environmental chemicals. Many increases in human diseases can be related to chemical exposure. Thus, decreasing and controlling such exposure should prevent many human diseases.

This book is an outgrowth of the knowledge and experience gained through the many research and testing activities of the National Toxicology Program. Chapters are included to describe analytical chemistry requirements for many aspects of in vivo toxicity studies. They provide information on studies using various methods of dose administration including dosed feed, dosed water, gavage, skin painting, and inhalation.

The book is divided into four parts, which focus on the main areas of analytical chemistry involvement in a toxicity testing program. Part I describes general chemistry considerations for any in vivo toxicity study. The chapters present an overview of the analytical chemistry requirements for toxicity testing. Also included are structure-activity predictions of the carcinogenicity of chemicals, as well as practical experience with testing commercial-grade chemicals and chemical/vehicle mixing and analysis problems associated with testing chemicals at a testing laboratory.

Part II covers dosage mixing and analysis of chemicals for a toxicity study. This part contains an informative chapter on methods development for mixing chemicals in rodent feed. Also included are chapters on the formulation of insoluble and immiscible test agents in liquid vehicles, analysis of dosed feed samples, and stability determinations for chemical/vehicle mixtures.

Inhalation toxicology presents an interesting and complex challenge to the chemist. Part III describes chemical inhalation studies and the approaches used to adequately conduct such studies. In addition to an overview of inhalation toxicology, this part contains chapters on methods for generating and monitoring test atmospheres, detecting degradation products in inhalation test atmospheres, and monitoring for both intentional and unintentional test chemical release during an inhalation study.

The last part of the book deals with chemistry data and their evaluation. It contains chapters focusing on data evaluation and management, evaluation of dosage analysis data from a problem-solving point of view, inventory management, and data storage for chemicals used in coded toxicity testing. Finally, the effect of Good Laboratory Practices on chemistry requirements for toxicity testing is discussed.

The chapters in this book are written by authorities in the field who represent an extensive cross-section of knowledge in the many aspects of chemical toxicity studies. Many disciplines are involved, illustrating the difficulties of a field that encompasses a diversity of expertise.

The chapters in this book are adaptations of presentations from the symposium on Chemistry and Safety for Toxicity Testing of Environmental Chemicals, presented at the 183d national meeting of the American Chemical Society in Las Vegas, Nevada, in March 1982.

The goal of any chemistry-support resource for toxicity studies is to better define the chemicals being investigated and to aid in interpreting how the test chemical effects the test systems. It is hoped that by better defining the actual test material, the interpretation of the final results of an animal toxicity study will be facilitated.

I am grateful to the contributors, whose combined expertise made this book possible. I also thank Thomas Goehl and Christine Davies for their valuable suggestions and constructive criticism throughout the writing of this book. The assistance and patience of Bonnie Davis in clerical support of this undertaking is very gratefully acknowledged.

PART I

General Chemistry Considerations

CHAPTER 1

Analytical Chemistry Requirements for Toxicity Testing of Environmental Chemicals

C.W. Jameson

National Toxicology Program, P.O. Box 12233,
Research Triangle Park, North Carolina 27709

Our environment is made up of a large number of natural products, as well as an ever-increasing number of synthetic chemicals. Chemical contamination has been steadily increasing for the last 150 years or more, and since World War II, man-made pollution has also increased. Nearly 60,000 chemicals currently are used in commerce in the United States, and humans are exposed in varying degrees to most of them. Although the majority of these chemicals are not hazardous to humans, many have expressed concern that the toxic potential of these substances needs to be assessed.

Casarett and Doull's Toxicology defines toxicity as "the capacity of a substance to produce injury to a living organism" and toxicology as "the study of the adverse effects of chemicals on living organisms"[1]. It is clear that a central element of toxicology is the delineation of the safe use of chemicals. Testing the toxic potential of chemicals to which humans are exposed both voluntarily and involuntarily (for example, through pesticides, air pollutants, and industrial chemicals) is receiving increased attention from the federal government through the National Toxicology Program (NTP).

The NTP was formed in 1978 as a Department of Health and Human Services (DHHS) cooperative effort to coordinate and manage the Department's programs to develop the scientific information necessary to protect the health of the American public from exposure to hazardous chemicals. The goals of the NTP include an expansion of the toxicological profiles of chemicals nominated and tested by the Program, to develop and begin to validate a series of tests and protocols more appropriate for regulatory needs, and to establish and use a coordinated communications network to collect, evaluate, and disseminate toxicological information. This chapter will discuss how chemistry is involved as an integral part of the toxicological evaluation of chemicals as it relates to the support of NTP programs. These requirements could easily be expanded to include any type of toxicity testing program.

PROTOCOL DEVELOPMENT

Chemistry is an essential part of any toxicity study from its beginning to its completion. In the NTP, once a chemical has been selected for study, toxicity testing is initiated by developing a protocol for the study to determine the toxic end point—carcinogenicity, teratogenicity, and so forth. The chemist assists in the experimental design by providing information about a chemical's physical state, its chemical reactivity, or the appropriateness (from a chemistry standpoint) of the route of administration. Once the actual testing protocol is established, information as to the proper choice of test material is also required. The factors that may be included concern the various grades of test material available, different impurity profiles expected from different manufacturing processes, and appropriateness of a salt form versus the parent compound. The requirements for a particular testing facility may also be determined by the chemist. These may be as simple as a chemical fume hood to as complex as a high-hazard laboratory. Facility requirements are covered in more detail in *Safety Concerns for Toxicity Testing* [2].

CHEMICAL PROCUREMENT

Once the study protocol has been established, chemical procurement can be initiated. Before making the selection of test material, one has to consider such things as rationale for testing, the chemical's various uses and grades and how these relate to why it is being studied, and the various manufacturing processes and which one is most widely used. The selection should be such that it reflects the majority of potential human exposure. The chemical properties of the test material often dictate the route of administration; for example, feed studies require stable, free-flowing solids or nonvolatile liquids, and drinking water studies require water-soluble materials. Study considerations also play a major role in procurement of the test chemical. Dose levels as well as the number and species of test animals must be estimated in order to calculate the amount of test chemical required for the study.

In general, the material obtained for a toxicity study should be representative of the product to which the populations at risk are exposed. Most chemicals obtained for test in the NTP are unformulated, technical-grade products. Formulated products are avoided where possible to minimize the number of components in the test material while still providing an evaluation of the chemical (including impurities) to which people are most likely to be exposed. If, however, the chemical is being tested primarily because of an interest in its molecular structure or because it is an impurity in a commercial product, a pure form of the chemical is obtained because it is more appropriate for study.

If possible and practical, any chemical obtained for toxicity studies should be procured in a single batch. Thus dose levels must be estimated before any studies are performed. The estimates can be based on toxicity information available in the literature. If no information is available on the specific test chemical, estimates can be made based on structure activity considerations of similar compounds. If a chemical is unstable, if it is very expensive, or if there is insufficient literature on its toxicity to estimate dose levels, then multiple smaller batches can be procured at appropriate intervals.

The amount of test chemical required for a study is based on the estimated dose levels. Once dose levels have been estimated, the general equations shown here can be used to calculate the quantity of test chemical required for the study:

amount of chemical = # of animals × dose level (mg/ kg body weight)
× average body weight (kg) × # of dosing days

or

amount of chemical = # of animals × dose level (concentration in vehicle)
× average daily consumption (g) × # of dosing days

The concentration of the test chemical in the vehicle usually is based on a standard amount of vehicle administered to the test animal on a daily basis (for example, a Fischer 344 rat eats approximately 15 g of feed a day). The toxicologist usually expresses dose levels in terms of mg of test chemical per kg of test animal body weight. This value has to be converted to concentration in the vehicle based on arbitrarily selected standard amounts of vehicle normally administered to or consumed by the test animals on a daily basis. The NTP uses the following criteria for estimating dose concentrations. It is assumed that the Fischer 344 rat used in the NTP toxicity studies consumes 15 g of feed and 20 ml of water a day. The B6C3F1 hybrid mouse used in toxicity studies is assumed to eat 5 g of feed and drink 7 ml of water a day. For gavage or direct-stomach intubation studies, the Fischer rat is administered 5 ml of dosing solution per kilogram of body weight, and the B6C3F1 mouse is administered 10 ml of dosing solution per kilograms body weight. NTP skin-painting studies require that a constant volume of 0.2 ml of dosing solution be administered to the Fischer rat and 0.1 ml of dosing solution be administered to the B6C3F1 mouse.

CHEMICAL ANALYSIS

Once test material is procured, a number of operations are performed. Figure 1–1 shows the tasks performed on the test chemical at various stages of a toxicity study. The tasks outlined in this figure pertain specifically to the NTP's carcinogenesis testing program but are applicable to other toxicity testing programs. The tasks include both bulk chemical and chemical/ vehicle analysis. A series of bulk chemical identity, purity, and stability analyses should be performed prior to the actual animal studies. Every batch of chemical tested in the NTP's carcinogenesis testing program is first analyzed to confirm its identity and ensure that it is of acceptable purity.

Bulk Chemical Analysis

The initial analytical work on a chemical has a number of objectives.

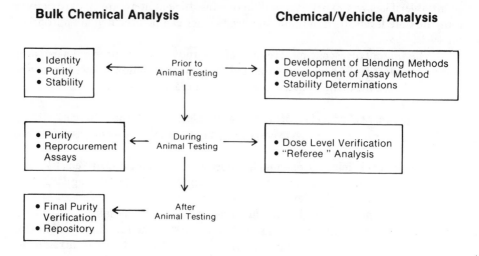

Figure 1-1. Flow of analytical chemistry tasks required for a toxicity study.

1. *To ensure that the batch is homogeneous.* Solids and liquids should be inspected visually for apparent inhomogeneity in color or texture. Solids may have to be mixed by shaking or rotating in the original container, or they may have to be put through a mechanical blender. Liquids can be mixed in their original containers or, if in multiple containers, combined, mixed, and repackaged in appropriate containers. These methods have been checked and found effective for a number of chemicals by comparative analysis of samples taken from several different points in the batch.

2. *To determine the range of particle sizes of solids.* It may be important to determine the particle size range for powdered solids. This is necessary for both dosed feed and inhalation studies. Ideally, for feed studies, the particle size range of the chemical to be mixed in feed for dosing should be similar to that of rodent meal to facilitate mixing and avoid gradual reseparation of chemical from feed after mixing (see Chapter 5). For inhalation studies, particle size is very important to ensure that the test material can be properly dispersed as a solid aerosol and be absorbed in the lungs of the test animal (see Chapter 12). If particle size is found to be unacceptable, grinding by an appropriate method will be necessary.

3. *To confirm the identity of the chemical.* A wide range of routine analytical methods should be applied to confirm that the material procured is in fact the correct test chemical. The NTP has selected methods to provide complementary information including:

- Physical properties
    Appearance
    Melting point/ boiling point
    Density
    Optical rotation

- Spectroscopy
  Infared
  Ultraviolet/visible
  Nuclear magnetic resonance
  Mass
  Atomic absorption
  Emission

Different structural features are revealed by each method, and all are considered important in confirming that the material tested is the correct chemical. The data and spectra of the test material are compared to literature values, if available, for conformation.

4. *To estimate the purity of the chemical.*   The following routine purity assays are performed, where appropriate, by the NTP:

- Elemental analysis
- Water analysis
- Titrimetry
- Chromatography
  thin layer
  vapor phase
  high-performance liquid
  gc/mass spectroscopy

An evaluation of whether the purity of a test material is acceptable for study must be made. In most NTP studies, the criterion of purity is that a technical grade chemical be representative of the commonly marketed product (before formulation) and meet the manufacturer's own specifications. Pharmaceuticals are confirmed as meeting USP [3] or NF [4] specifications. Food additives are checked against selected Food Chemical Codex [5] specifications when available.

The most commonly used methods for estimating purity are vapor-phase chromatography or high-performance liquid chromatography, thin-layer chromatography, and elemental analysis. If functional groups are present that can be titrated, purity is estimated by this analysis method. Water content is established by either the Karl Fischer method [6] or weight loss on drying. Quantitative spectrometry is sometimes useful, particularly nuclear magnetic resonance for hydrogen containing chemicals with impurities greater than 1%.

For the NTP, absolute purity of the test chemical is not normally determined as part of the primary analysis, although it may be required in special cases. The objectives of most toxicity studies generally do not demand a knowledge of the chemical's absolute purity. In addition, pure reference standards are not available for many industrial and environmental chemicals, making absolute purity determinations very difficult, if not impossible.

One rule of thumb followed in NTP studies is that if the test material meets the manufacturer's specifications for purity, it is used in toxicity studies with no further action to identify impurities. However, if there is a major impurity—$\geq 1\%$—the NTP will routinely identify and quantitate it. Also in several instances it may be important to identify and quantitate minor impurities —for example, when a chemical is suspected of containing a known carcinogenic or highly toxic impurity such as chlorinated dibenzodioxins in chlorinated phenols.

5. *To estimate the long-term stability of the test chemical.* As part of any standard protocol for the analysis of test chemicals, its long-term stability should be determined. The NTP's protocol for this study requires storage for a 14-day period at four temperatures (-20, 0, 25, and $60°$ C). Typically purities are compared chromatographically against an internal reference standard. The chromatograms are monitored for the appearance or disappearance of impurity peaks. The elevated temperature data are used to estimate long-term stability to aid in setting storage conditions for the chemicals.

6. *To perform studies and develop methods for mixing and analysis of chemical/vehicle mixtures.* In addition to the analysis performed on the bulk chemical itself, considerable effort is required for demonstrating that a vehicle is appropriate for administering (dosing) a test chemical and assuring that dosage mixtures are homogeneous and stable. The approach the NTP uses for its carcinogenesis testing program, outlined as follows, includes methods development work for the preparation of protocols for mixing chemicals with the administration vehicle used in toxicity tests:

- Acute
    Mixing protocol at $2 \times LD_{50}$
- Subchronic
    Mixing protocol at $10 \times MTD$
    Homogenity studies
    Handling and storage protocol
- Chronic
    Mixing protocol at MTD
    Homogenity studies
    Stability studies
    Handling and storage protocol

For an effective study, the chemical must be homogeneously mixed with the vehicle for administration, and such a mixture should be both chemically and physically stable. Protocols are developed for mixing chemicals with selected liquids at twice the LD_{50} level for acute gavage studies. Protocols are also developed for mixing chemicals at estimated chronic levels with the appropriate vehicle (feed, water, corn oil, and so on). Feed mixtures and other chronic chemical/vehicle mixtures that are not solutions are tested for homogeneity by sampling at various locations of the mixture and then analyzed. The procedure usually involves isolation of the test chemical by extraction followed by spectroscopic or chromatographic analysis of the extract. In addition, a study to determine the stability of the chemical/vehicle mixes is carried out. The protocol for this stability determination is dependent on the route of administration of the test chemical (see Chapter 8). Gas and high-performance liquid addition, a study to determine the stability of the chemical/vehicle mixes is carried out. The protocol for this stability determination is dependent on the route of administration of the test chemical (see Chapter 8). Gas and high-performance liquid chromatographic methods of analysis are preferred techniques for analyzing stability samples because of their ability to separate complex mixtures efficiently. The data obtained from these stability studies are used to estimate the storage life of the chemical/vehicle mixture and the conditions under which it should be stored to minimize decomposition. Mixing protocols with specific details are issued to enable investigators to produce homogeneous, physically stable chemical mixes for toxicity studies.

Any good toxicity study should include a requirement that the bulk test material be monitored for stability and that dose levels used during animal testing be verified by chemical analysis. The NTP requires that any batch of test chemical that is used for extended periods be rechecked for purity routinely. The objective of this bulk chemical reanalysis is to demonstrate that the test material as received and stored by the testing laboratory remains identical to that received and analyzed prior to the start of a study. The most efficient method for determining stability is to maintain a stable standard to be used for comparison with the stored bulk test material. The NTP requires that standard samples of the bulk test material be pulled on receipt at the test laboratory. These samples are stored at –20° C or lower. The purity of the test material is then checked at specified intervals for the duration of the toxicity studies. These purity determinations require that the analysis of the bulk test material and the reference standard be run in tandem. This protocol allows the bulk purity to be compared to that of the reference standard from the same batch. The bulk reanalysis involves at least two methods, which are chosen to be appropriate for the test material as well as suspected degradation products.

Dosage Mixture Analysis

Quality control checks of dosage preparation procedures are also a routine requirement for NTP studies. A good example of what these requirements entail would again be the NTP's carcinogen testing program. The testing program can be broken down into three phases that are run in series. The first phase is a 14-day repeated dose study. During this study, one sample of each dose level is mixed and analyzed in duplicate to demonstrate the efficacy of the mixing procedure and the analytical method. The analytical method used for this routine analysis should be a simple and effective method that does not involve unacceptably high background interferences from the vehicle matrix. The methods most often used by the NTP include spectroscopic or chromatographic analysis of extracts of the chemical/vehicle mixtures. (Actual analytical methods are discussed in Chapters 7 and 8.) In addition, samples of the dosage preparation are pulled from the animal room during the actual dosing procedure and analyzed in duplicate to confirm dose concentration and ensure the mixtures are being handled properly in the animal rooms.

The second phase of the testing program is the 13-week study. Samples of the initial, middle, and final dosage preparation at each dose level are pulled and analyzed in duplicate, again to demonstrate the efficacy of the mixing and analytical methods. If feed is used as the vehicle of administration, a homogeneity study is conducted at this stage to demonstrate that the blending procedure is producing a homogeneous blend at the highest and lowest dose levels. Samples are taken from various locations of the blender, and analysis is performed in duplicate to verify uniform distribution of the test material in the feed. Animal room samples are again pulled and analyzed to ensure proper handling during the dosing procedure.

The final phase of the testing program is the 104-week chronic study. For this study at each dose level, the initial set of dosage preparations is analyzed in duplicate to verify concentration. Thereafter these analyses are carried out for each dose level on the average of every eighth dosage preparation. As with the previous two phases, animal room samples are pulled and analyzed for the initial set of dose preparations and randomly thereafter during the study.

As part of a quality assurance program, the NTP has established a chemical/ vehicle referee analysis program for the testing program. This referee program was established to check the mixing efficacy at the testing laboratories, as well as their analysis of the dosage mixtures. For this program, samples of the same dosage mixtures are analyzed at both the bioassay testing laboratory and at an analytical resource lab, and the results are compared. In this fashion, a record is kept of how well the testing laboratories are preparing and analyzing dosage mixtures. The referee laboratory analyses provide an independent check on the dose levels administered, as well as a check on the validity of analytical results obtained at the testing laboratory and verification of the performance of the dosage analysis method at the dose levels selected for the study.

Control Material Analysis

Another important aspect of any toxicity study is the monitoring of vehicle and control materials to ensure they do not contain any contaminants that may compromise a study. Feed should be monitored to ensure that the proper levels of essential nutrients, minerals, and vitamins are present and that it does not contain contaminants, such as pesticides, aflatoxins, and heavy metals. If corn oil is used, it should be routinely monitored for the presence of peroxide. Drinking water should be analyzed at least annually to demonstrate that it meets U.S. Environmental Protection Agency (EPA) drinking water standards. Other materials such as bedding and skin paint solvents also should be routinely monitored to ensure that they meet study specifications. Materials such as feed, corn oil, drinking water, bedding, and solvents used for skin-paint studies are routinely monitored by the NTP to ensure that they contain no toxic impurities and meet Program specifications.

Special Analysis

Along with the required routine analysis of bulk chemicals and chemical/vehicle dosage mixtures, there is the possibility that nonroutine analyses may be required to better define the test material or help interpret how the chemical is affecting the test system. These nonroutine analyses can include identification and quantitation of impurities, methods development for analysis of chemicals in body fluids and tissues, tissue-residue analysis, synthesis, and/or purification of test materials and development of industrial hygiene and pollution monitoring techniques. The following are examples of several nonroutine analyses performed in support of the NTP's Carcinogen Testing Program.

Impurity Identification

An interesting example of a special study performed in support of an NTP study was the determination of a major impurity in a sample of chloramphenicol sodium succinate obtained for carcinogenesis testing. Analysis of the test material by both thin layer chromatography and high-performance liquid chromatography indicated it contained a large impurity, approximately 16%. A literature reference [7] indicates that two molecular forms of chloramphenicol succinate (open chain and cyclic) can exist in equilibrium (Figure 1–2). The large impurity observed by both thin layer and high performance liquid chromatography was identified as the cyclic form of chloramphenicol sodium succinate by matching R_f values (TLC) and retention times (HPLC) and spiking with solutions of a USP chloramphenicol standard (HPLC) after hydrolysis of the succinate ester. In addition, based on the chemical/vehicle analyses of the feed mixes of chloramphenicol sodium succinate, the stability of both the linear and cyclic forms in feed was determined. The analytical procedure included extraction of dosed feed mixes with acetonitrile: acetic acid (99.1) and analysis of the extract by HPLC. The results of the stability study, presented in Table 1–1, show that after seven days at room temperature in a rat cage, there is an overall loss of 3.4%. The majority of this loss is due to the instability of the cyclic form when mixed in feed. Based on this study, a special handling protocol for the dosed feed mixture was recommended.

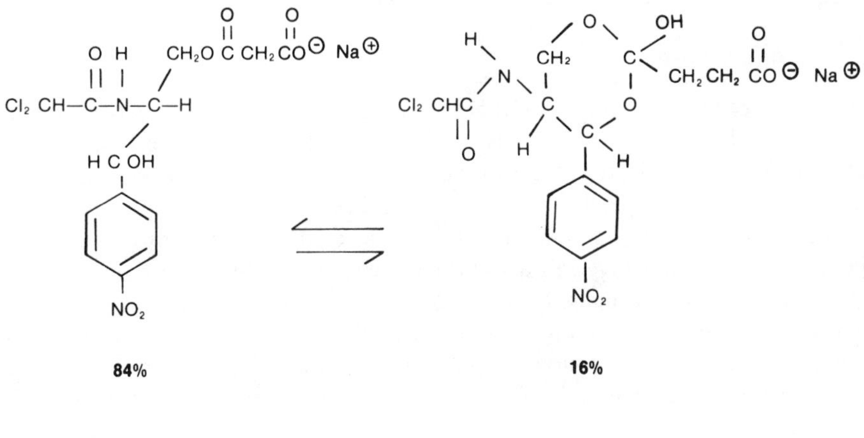

Figure 1-2.   Chloramphenicol sodium succinate.

Table 1-1.   Feed Stability Study

Storage Conditions	Stability of Major Component, %	Stability of Minor Component, %	Overall % Loss of Chemical
0 time	99.0	100.0	0
3 days (cage, 25° C)	98.5	94.7	1.3
7 days (cage, 25° C)	97.1	88.4	3.4
7 days (sealed, 25°C)	96.1	86.7	4.5
7 days (sealed, 5° C)	98.4	98.0	0.9
14 days (sealed, 25° C)	94.6	77.6	7.3
14 days (sealed, 5°C)	97.6	97.9	1.6

Body Fluid Analysis

Another interesting example of a special study was the development of an analytical method for the analysis of β-naphthylamine in rat urine. The NTP was studying N-phenyl-β-naphthylamine, which was reported in the literature [8] to be metabolized by dogs and humans to β-naphthylamine, a known carcinogen. In order to address this possibility, it was necessary to develop a simple method for quantitation of β-naphthylamine in rat urine at levels of 100 ppb or above in the presence of possible N-phenyl precursor. The basis of the workup procedure was that β-naphthylamine is very soluble in toluene and only slightly soluble in water. The pH of the urine samples was adjusted to 9 with sodium carbonate (10%), and an aliquot was forced through a small C_{18} Sep-Pak column (Waters Associates) and the eluent discarded. The column was then washed with distilled water. Toluene was used to pull the β-naphthylamine off the column. After concentrating the toluene wash, it was analyzed by gas chromatography using a thermionic specific detector. Figure 1–3 shows the chromatograms of a β-naphthylamine standard in toluene, an unspiked rat urine sample, and an aliquot of rat urine spiked with 1 μg of β-naphthylamine. This method gave a recovery from spiked samples of $92 \pm 4\%$ with a detection limit significantly less than the required 100 ppb.

Chemical Purification

Purification of test materials is another special requirement of an analytical chemistry resource. The NTP wanted to study C.I. Direct Blue 15 (Figure 1–4). The test material was provided by the Dye Environmental Toxicology Organization (DETO) as a representative composite dried press cake. Due to the synthetic process for this dye, a significant amount of sodium chloride was contained in the press cake. This high salt content could adversely affect the toxicity studies by causing an electrolyte imbalance in the test animals. In order to avoid this, the material was purified by placing the test material in dialysis tubing and submerging the tubing in circulating deionized water for 24 hr, followed by a change of water and resubmersion for an additional 16 hr (see Chapter 3). On completion of the dialysis, the contents of the

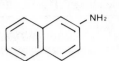

β- Naphthylamine

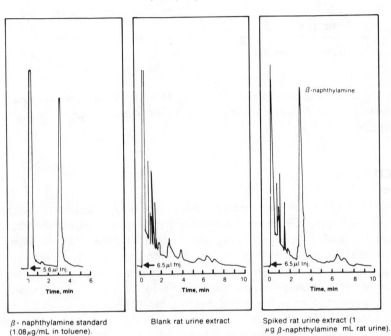

β- naphthylamine standard   Blank rat urine extract   Spiked rat urine extract (1
(1.08 μg/mL in toluene).   μg β-naphthylamine mL rat urine).

Column: 3% SP2100-DB on 100/120 Supelcoport; 1.8 m X 2mm i.d.; glass. Detector: thermionic
specific, 250°C. Carrier gas: N_2, 30 cc/min. Inlet: 200°C. Column oven: 145°C.
Sensitivity: 4 X 10^{-12} AFS.

Figure 1-3. β-Naphthylamine study chromatograms.

Figure 1-4. C.I. Direct Blue 15.

Table 1-2. Results of Desalting C.I. Direct Blue 15 Test Sample

C.I. Direct Blue 15	Before Desalting	After Desalting
Elemental analysis (for chloride)	24.75%[a]	4.19%[a]
Water analysis (Karl Fischer titration)	7.28	9.83

[a]As sodium chloride.

tubes were dried by heating at 110° C for 16 to 24 hrs until the material appeared dry by visual inspection. As Table 1-2 shows, this procedure decreased the salt content to an acceptable level.

CONCLUSION

The goal of this overview chapter was to discuss the NTP's chemistry requirements for toxicity testing, requirements that could easily be adapted to other toxicity testing program. The goal of the analytical chemistry resource for the NTP is to better define the chemicals being tested by the Program. This includes not only the analysis of the original test chemicals but also the analysis of chemical/vehicle mixtures administered to the test animals and special analyses to help interpret how the chemical may be affecting the test system. It is hoped that by better defining the actual test material and its interaction with administration vehicles and test animals, the interpretation of the final results of the animal studies will be facilitated.

REFERENCES

1. Doull, J., C.D. Klaassen, and M.O. Amdur. *Casarett and Doull's Toxicology: The Basic Science of Poisons,* 2nd ed. (New York: Macmillan, 1980).
2. Walters, D.B. and C.W. Jameson, Eds. *Safety Concerns for Toxicity Testing* (Boston, Mass.: Butterworth Publishers, 1984).
3. *The United States Pharmacopeia, Twentieth Revision* (Rockville, Md.: United States Pharmacopeial Convention, 1980).
4. *The National Formulary,* 15th ed. (Rockville, Md.: United States Pharmacopeial Convention, 1980).
5. *Food Chemicals, Codex,* 3rd ed. (Washington, D.C.: National Academy Press, 1981).
6. Fischer, K.Z. *Angew. Chem.* 48:394 (1935).
7. Sandmann, B.J. *Dissertation Abstracts Int. B.,* no. 69–12, 410 (1969).
8. NIOSH Current Intelligence Bulletin. "Metabolic Precursors of a Known Human Carcinogen, Beta-Naphthylamine," December 17, 1976.

CHAPTER 2

Structure-Activity Prediction of the Carcinogenicity of Chemicals

C. Tucker Helmes
Director, Biological and Environmental Chemistry
Department, SRI International, 333 Ravenswood
Avenue, Menlo Park, California 94025

Caroline C. Sigman
Director, Chemical-Biological Information
Program, SRI International, 333 Ravenswood
Avenue, Menlo Park, California 94025

Patricia A. Papa
Chemist, Chemical- Biological Information Program,
SRI International, 333 Ravenswood Avenue,
Menlo Park, California 94025

The principles of chemistry have contributed many advances to our knowledge of carcinogenesis, particularly with respect to the identification, structure elucidation, metabolism, and mechanism of action of chemical carcinogens. With the accumulation of this knowledge, certain relationships between chemical structure and carcinogenic activity have been established and used as a basis in attempts to predict the carcinogenicity of untested chemicals. For example, a large number of polycyclic aromatic hydrocarbons [1] and aromatic amines [2] were tested and are now known to be carcinogenic because the rationale for testing them was based largely on structure-activity theory. The studies by Van Duuren and coworkers [3] of bis(chloromethyl)ether and epichlorohydrin provide further examples of chemicals that were examined for potential carcinogenicity because of suspicion based on structure-activity relationships. These two industrial chemicals first were shown to be carcinogenic in laboratory animals and subsequently were shown to be human carcinogens.

This project has been funded in part with federal funds from the Department of Health and Human Services under contract numbers N01-CP-33285 and N01-CP-95607. We are indebted to Susan Stachon for her excellent typing skills.

Not all sources agree that sufficient evidence is available to classify epichlorohydrin as a human carcinogen[4].

The purpose of this chapter is to demonstrate the valuable role that structure-activity relationships may play in the study of chemical carcinogenesis, particularly with respect to analyzing the current state of known structural information about chemical carcinogens and predicting the possible carcinogenicity of untested chemicals.

RATIONALE

The rationale for structure-activity prediction of the carcinogenicity of chemicals perhaps may be viewed best from the perspective of the universe of existing chemicals. Over 5.7 million unique chemical substances are registered in the files of Chemical Abstracts Service [5], yet there may be potential human exposure to only about 66,000 chemicals. This number is likely to be an overstatement, but it is an estimate that includes chemicals on the Toxic Substances Control Act (TSCA) Inventory[6], as well as chemicals regulated as pesticides [7], drugs [8], food additives [9], and cosmetics[10] (see Table 2-1).

Most of these chemicals have not been tested adequately for carcinogenicity, and so, by contrast, the number of chemicals known to be carcinogenic is quite small. This number varies according to the source of information, but currently SRI International has a data base[11] that contains 345 carcinogenic chemicals according to reports published in the open literature. Consideration of these numbers helps one to appreciate the contribution that structure-activity prediction could make in any effort to establish research priorities and to rank untested chemicals according to suspected carcinogenic activity.

The role of structure-activity comparisons in assessing the possible carcinogenicity of chemicals can be envisioned as the first component of a tiered testing system for carcinogens of the type that has been proposed by a number of workers in the field of cancer research, such as Van Duuren[3] and Weisburger and Williams[12]. In this system, structure-activity prediction is followed, in order, by short-term tests in vitro (e.g., mutagenicity), the standard, long-term toxicity test in animals, and finally, to confirm carcinogenicity in humans, epidemiological studies. The large number of untested chemicals that have been introduced into the potential human environment and the high cost of a single animal toxicity test, now estimated to be as high as

Table 2-1.   Data on Existing Chemicals with Potential Human Exposure

Chemical Type	Number
TSCA inventory	~55,000
Pesticides	~ 1,500
Drugs	> 4,000
Food additives	~ 2,600
Cosmetics	~ 3,000
Total	~66,000

$500,000 per chemical[12], make such a stepwise system the most prudent approach to carcinogen hazard assessment.

The usefulness of structure-activity prediction is best illustrated by the following examples:

- The National Cancer Institute (NCI)/National Toxicology Program (NTP) Carcinogenesis Testing Program uses structure-activity relationships to assign priorities in the chemical selection process[13].
- The Interagency Testing Committee (ITC) uses structure-activity among other criteria to establish testing priorities for the Environmental Protection Agency (EPA) as required by TSCA[14].
- The analysis of structure-activity relationships may serve as a basis to evaluate the potential hazards associated with the large number of new, untested chemicals that are being introduced into the human environment by occupational exposure, industrial use, consumer products, drugs, food, air, or water.
- The interpretation of results from animal carcinogenicity experiments often may be strengthened by consideration of the degree to which the observed activity of the chemical conforms to the behavior expected of it according to structure-activity theory.

METHODOLOGY

In developing a structure-activity methodology for predicting carcinogenicity, certain requirements should be met to ensure that the approach is scientifically meaningful:

- Structures of the known chemical carcinogens are required to identify the various chemical structure features associated with carcinogenic activity.
- A model for mechanism of action is essential to provide a unifying concept for the many chemicals of diverse structural types that exhibit carcinogenic activity.
- Understanding pathways of carcinogen metabolism helps to predict whether a chemical of unknown carcinogenicity will be metabolized by similar pathways and hence will be operative according to the unifying concept of mechanism of action.
- A data base containing a sufficient number of chemicals that have been tested adequately for carcinogenicity according to standard, generally accepted protocols is needed so that structural correlations can be established to distinguish between carcinogenic and noncarcinogenic compounds.

A variety of chemicals, belonging to several different chemical classes, are known to be carcinogenic in animals or humans. Among the classes of known chemical carcinogens shown below are alkylating and acylating agents:

Direct Acting	*Indirect Acting*
Alkyl sulfates and sulfonates	Polycyclic aromatic hydrocarbons
Epoxides	Aromatic amines and nitros
Lactones	N-Nitroso compounds
Haloalkyl ethers	Hydrazines and triazenes
Nitrogen and sulfur mustards	Halogenated hydrocarbons
Acyl halides	Pyrrolizidine alkaloids
	Aflatoxins
	Other carcinogens

These agents are referred to as direct-acting carcinogens [15] because they interact with target tissue directly without the need for metabolic activation. Most classes of chemical carcinogens do require metabolic activation to a reactive species and are referred to as precarcinogens or indirect-acting carcinogens [15]. Structures representative of the classes of chemical carcinogens just listed are provided in Figure 2–1, along with the structures of several other carcinogens, to illustrate the diversity of chemical structure among known carcinogens.

A common feature between these diverse structural types of known carcinogens is believed to be their mechanism of action. The unifying concept is that most chemical carcinogens act as electrophiles to interact covalently with nucleophilic sites in nucleic acids, proteins, or other cellular macromolecules of the target tissue [16]. Most chemical carcinogens are not electrophiles themselves but must be activated by metabolism to a reactive electrophilic species referred to as the "ultimate" carcinogen [16]. The direct-acting carcinogens appear to be exceptions to the requirement for metabolism.

The concept of the formation of electrophilic species underlies most attempts at developing structure-activity relationships for carcinogens. Currently these attempts have led to the following conclusions:

- Chemical structure can be a predictor of carcinogenic activity but only within the limitations of current knowledge of the ultimate forms of chemical carcinogens and structural requirements for metabolic activation.
- So far, only a few structure-activity principles have been established that are generally applicable to all, or even some, of the various classes of chemical carcinogens.
- Structure-activity predictions about the probability of certain chemicals being carcinogenic are most reliable within classes of chemicals that have been well studied for carcinogenicity.

The ultimate utility and success of chemical structure as a predictor of carcinogenic activity depend on the availability of sufficient empirical data to permit conclusions about associations between structural features or functional groups and carcinogenicity and to provide more specific knowledge about metabolism and the formation of ultimate carcinogens within various chemical classes and across different animal species, target sites, and routes of exposure.

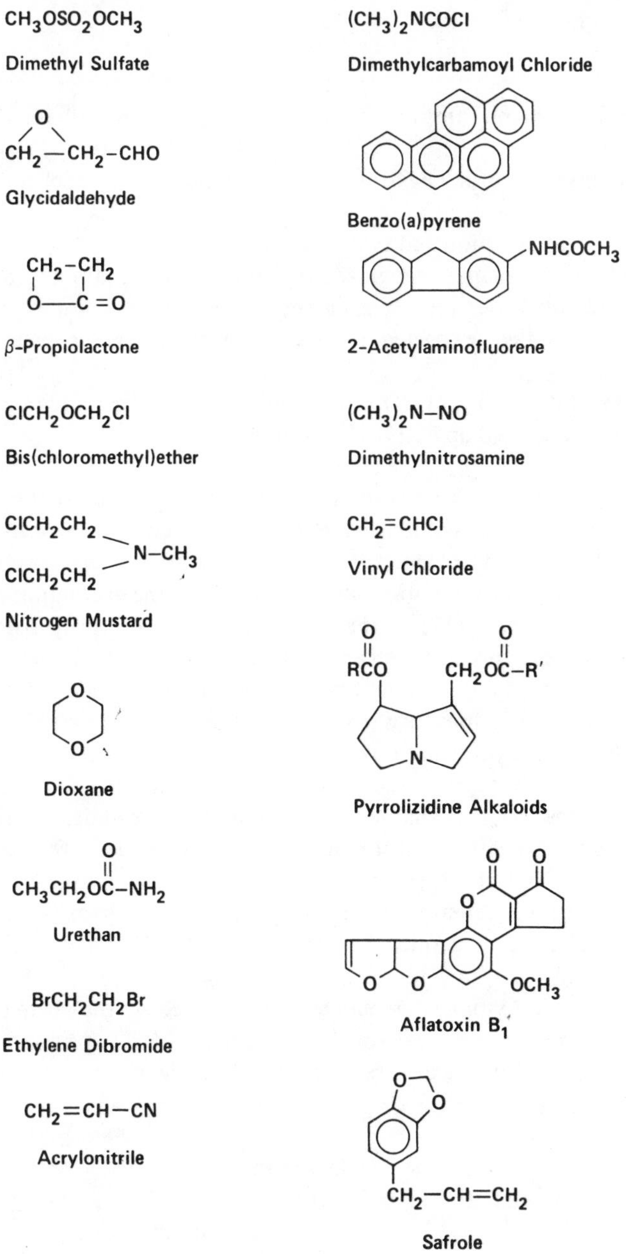
CH3OSO2OCH3
Dimethyl Sulfate
(CH3)2NCOCl
Dimethylcarbamoyl Chloride
CH2—CH2-CHO
Glycidaldehyde
Benzo(a)pyrene
NHCOCH3
β-Propiolactone
2-Acetylaminofluorene
ClCH2OCH2Cl
Bis(chloromethyl)ether
(CH3)2N–NO
Dimethylnitrosamine
ClCH2CH2
N–CH3
ClCH2CH2
Nitrogen Mustard
CH2=CHCl
Vinyl Chloride
RCO
CH2OC–R′
Dioxane
Pyrrolizidine Alkaloids
CH3CH2OC–NH2
Urethan
OCH3
BrCH2CH2Br
Aflatoxin B1
Ethylene Dibromide
CH2=CH–CN
Acrylonitrile
CH2–CH=CH2
Safrole

Figure 2-1. Representative structures of known carcinogens.

PRACTICAL APPLICATIONS

We have approached the study of structure-activity relationships among chemical carcinogens using a methodology based on the concept of a structure-activity tree:

- Systematic method for assessing possible carcinogenicity of chemicals prior to testing.
- Based on expert opinion and evaluation of published data.
- Basic units are principal, recognized classes of chemical carcinogens.
- Nodes are subclasses representing specific structural features or functional groups that reflect expected differences in carcinogenic behavior among chemicals.
- Estimates of strength of evidence and probability of being carcinogenic.
- Maintained and used on PROPHET computer system.

The structure-activity tree is seen ultimately as a tool that would provide a systematic method for assessing the possible carcinogenicity of chemicals prior to testing. It is intended to reflect meaningful associations between chemical structure and carcinogenic activity according to the opinions of experts and the evaluation of published data. The original version [17] of the tree consisted of the principal, recognized classes of chemical carcinogens such as the polycyclic aromatic hydrocarbons, aromatic amines, N-nitroso compounds, and various alkylating agents. It was designed to aid in establishing priorities for the selection of chemicals for carcinogenesis testing when combined with information on relative human exposure ranking.

Development of the structure-activity tree has continued so that its basic units are subdivided into subclasses that we refer to as nodes. The nodes represent specific structural features or functional groups associated with known carcinogenic activity and therefore may reflect expected differences in carcinogenic behavior among chemicals. In addition, estimates of the strength of evidence associated with chemicals having the particular structural characteristics of a node and of the probability of those chemicals being carcinogenic are being developed.

The structure-activity tree is maintained and used by the chemical structure analysis and data management capabilities of the PROPHET computer system [18, 19]. Sixteen classes of chemicals are represented on the current structure-activity tree:

Alkyl halides	Quinolines
Vinyl halides	Acridines
Acyl halides	Polycyclic N-heterocycles
Aryl halides	Benzofurans
Alkyl sulfates/Sulfonates	Dioxanes
3-Atom heterocycles	Polycyclic aryl compounds
Lactones	Hydrazines
Aryl amino/nitro/azo compounds	N-Nitroso compounds

These include several categories of direct-acting carcinogens such as the alkyl and acyl halides, the alkyl sulfates and sulfonates, and the various strained-ring compounds. Also included are classes of chemical carcinogens requiring metabolic activation such as the vinyl halides, aromatic amines and related compounds, polycyclic aromatic compounds, and N-nitroso and related compounds. Most of our work so far has focused on development of the organohalide and aromatic amine components of the activity tree.

To illustrate the construction of the tree, schematic representations of the alkyl halides and aromatic amines classes are shown in Figures 2–2 and 2–3. The alkyl halides class is subdivided into nodes and subnodes for simple haloalkanes, nitrogen and sulfur mustards, haloethers, and aromatic alkyl halides.

The aromatic amines class includes two major categories: (1) nodes representing the single, aromatic ring amines and related compounds (these include the anilines and extended anilines such as biphenylamines, methylene (bis)anilines, and stilbenamines) and (2) nodes for the fused-ring amines including the fluorenamines and naphthylamines. Other nodes included on the aromatic amines portion of the tree but not shown in Figure 2–3 are amino/nitro 5-member ring heterocycles (for example, the nitrofurans), and aromatic aminoazo compounds, including the azo dyes.

To illustrate the operation of the structure-activity tree as it now stands and to test its validity as a classification scheme for structural characteristics of known carcinogens, we have used it to perform an analysis of a computerized data base of known carcinogens. This data base [11], developed in part under our contract to the NCI Office for Environmental Cancer, contains data on 345 chemicals classified as carcinogenic on the basis of criteria and definitions established in collaboration with NCI for the evaluation of published test results. Chemicals in the data base come from several sources, including technical reports of the NCI/NTP Carcinogenesis Testing Program [20], monographs published by the International Agency for Research on Cancer (IARC) on the evaluation of the carcinogenic risk of chemicals to humans [21], surveys of carcinogens in air [22] and drinking water [23] that we have compiled as part of our contract with NCI, and studies of various chemical classes that we have prepared for NCI's chemical selection process [24]. The data base contains computer-searchable elements, such as chemical name, CAS registry number, and structure, that facilitate comparisons between chemical structure and carcinogenic activity across various species, routes of administration, or target sites.

Details of this analysis for the alkyl halides portion of the activity tree are shown in Tables 2–2 and 2–3. First, the distribution of known carcinogens among the various nodes of the alkyl halides class is shown in Table 2–2. Of particular interest is the bias of our data base toward chemicals classified by the activity tree as haloalkanes. This reflects not only the structural characteristics of known carcinogens but also the ability of the activity tree to discriminate among halogenated hydrocarbons of various structural types.

A closer look at the alkyl halides analysis reveals that several of the thirty-seven chemicals in this category also can be assigned to other classes and nodes on the structure-activity tree (see Table 2–3). Specifically, there are five chemicals that can

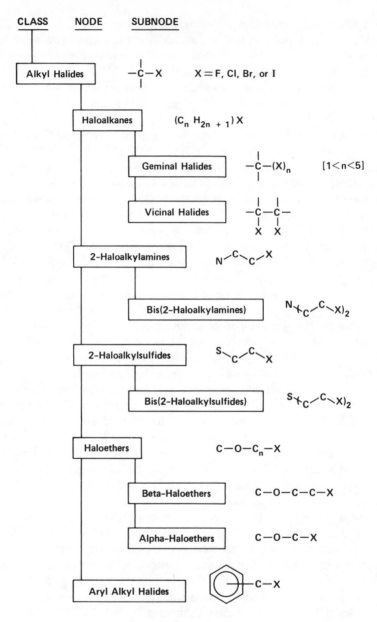

Figure 2-2. Structure-activity tree for alkyl halides.

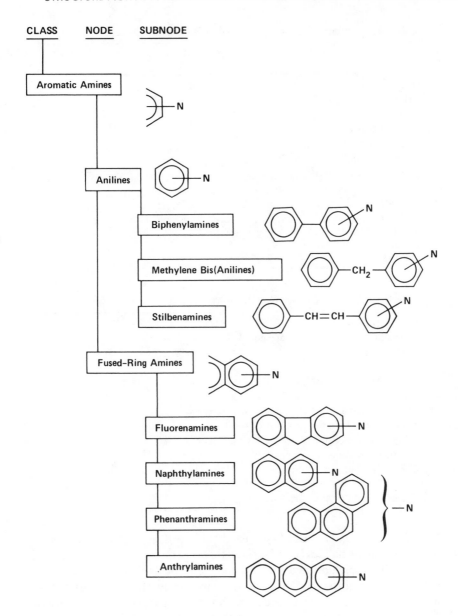

Figure 2-3.   Structure-activity tree for aromatic amines.

Table 2-2.   Activity Tree Analysis of Alkyl Halide Carcinogens

Class/Node

Alkyl halides (37)
  Haloalkanes (25)
    gem-haloalkanes (11)
    vic-haloalkanes (14)
  2-haloalkylamines (4)
    bis-2-haloalkylamines (2)
  2-haloalkylsulfides (0)
    bis-2-haloalkylsulfides (0)
  Haloethers (2)
    beta-haloethers (1)
    alpha-haloethers (1)
  Aryl alkyl halides (6)

Note: Number of carcinogens appears in parentheses.

Table 2-3.   Summary of Alkyl Halides Analysis

Number classified: 37
Other activity tree classes represented
  Vinyl halides (5)
  Aromatic halides (2)
  Epoxides (3)
  Aromatic amines/nitros (3)
Significant unclassified chemical structure groups
  Polychlorinated alicyclics (for example, chlordane, heptachlor)
  Halomethanes (for example, $CHCl_3$, CH_3I)
Gaps in knowledge
  Fluorides, iodides, bromides
  Haloalkanes where n >2
  Benzylic halides, mustards, haloethers

be classified as vinyl halides (for example, dieldrin and heptachlor), two chemicals classified as aromatic halides (DDT is one), three chemicals that can be classified as epoxides (such as epichlorohydrin), and three chemicals that can be classified as aromatic amines or nitro compounds (for example, trifluralin, a fluorinated tertiary aromatic amine and dinitrotoluene derivative). There are two significant groups of alkyl halide carcinogens in our data base that were not classified distinctly by the activity tree: eight polychlorinated alicyclics (for example, chlordane and heptachlor) and six halomethanes (chloroform and methyl iodide are two of them). The number of carcinogens falling into these groups suggests that new nodes should be designed to account specifically for these structural features.

One of the benefits of the structure-activity tree methodology is that it helps to identify gaps in our knowledge of carcinogenicity. Within the limits of our data base,

Table 2–4.   Activity Tree Analysis of Aromatic Amine/Nitro Carcinogens

---

Class/Node

Aryl amino/nitro/azo compounds (57)
  Single-ring amino/nitro compounds (44)
    Anilines and heterocyclic analogs (43)
      Biphenylamines and heterocyclic analogs (5)
      Methylene bis (anilines) and heterocyclic analogs (4)
      Stilbenamines (0)
    Amino/nitro 5-member ring heterocycles (1)
      Nitrofuryl compounds (0)
        5-nitro-2-furyl compounds (0)
          5-nitro-2-furyl-2-thiazolyl compounds (0)
  Fused-ring amino/nitro compounds (12)
    Naphthylamines and heterocyclic analogs (7)
      Amino/nitro quinolines (0)
        Amino/nitro quinoline N-oxides (0)
    Fluorenamines and heterocyclic analogs (0)
    Anthrylamines and heterocyclic analogs (3)
    Phenanthramines and heterocyclic analogs (0)
  Aryl azo compounds (5)
    Phenylazoanilines and heterocyclic analogs (2)
    Azotoluenes and heterocyclic analogs (0)

Note: Number of carcinogens appears in parentheses.

there is a lack of adequate carcinogenicity test data on alkyl fluorides, iodides, and, to a lesser extent, alkyl bromides; haloalkanes of all types where the number of carbons is greater than two; and benzylic halides, mustards, and haloethers.

An examination of the aromatic amino/nitro class on the activity tree (see Table 2–4) reveals that the distribution of known carcinogens is heavily weighted in favor of the single, aromatic ring compounds and derivatives. By contrast, we have fewer heterocycles and fused-ring compounds represented.

As with the alkyl halides, many of the aromatic amines and nitros also can be assigned to other classes and nodes on the activity tree (see Table 2–5). Three chemicals can be classified as alkyl halides (for example, trifluralin); eleven chemicals as aromatic halides (for example, o-chloronitrobenzene); one chemical (3-amino-9-ethylcarbazole) as a nitrogen heterocycle; two chemicals as N-nitroso compounds (for example, N-nitrosodiphenylamine); and one chemical (phenylhydrazine) as a hydrazine.

It appears from our analysis that new nodes should be constructed to accommodate the structural features represented by single, aromatic ring nitro compounds and amino- or nitro-substituted anthraquinones. These two groups were not classified distinctly by the activity tree. The gaps in knowledge that have been identified by the aromatic amines/nitros analysis of our data base include fused-ring compounds and amino- and nitro-substituted aromatic heterocyclics.

Table 2-5.   Summary of Aromatic Amines/Nitros Analysis

Number classified: 57
Other activity tree classes represented
  Alkyl halides (3)
  Aromatic halides (11)
  N-Heterocycles (1)
  N-Nitroso compounds (2)
  Hydrazines (1)
Significant unclassified chemical structure groups
  Single, aromatic ring nitro compounds (11)
  Amino- or nitro-substituted anthraquinones (3)
Gaps in knowledge
  Fused-ring compounds
  Amino- and nitro-substituted aromatic heterocycles

FUTURE DEVELOPMENTS

The development and operation of the structure-activity tree methodology has demonstrated its potential for application to several practical situations. It has been used to analyze a data base of known carcinogens. It provides a classification scheme and index of the structural information known about chemical carcinogens. It may be used to evaluate trends or patterns that may exist between chemical structure and specificity for target tissue, route of exposure, and animal species. Activity tree analysis serves to identify structural requirements for carcinogenicity within specific chemical classes that may aid in understanding mechanism of action, gaps in knowledge, and areas of the tree that need refinement based on evaluation of additional data or on reclassification of chemical structure characteristics. Finally, the tree currently cannot be considered a completely validated predictor of carcinogenic activity. It does provide, however, a systematic, computerized framework for analyzing the structures of chemicals of unknown activity in terms of a schematic representation of the structural requirements that have been established for known chemical carcinogens.

The future development of the structure-activity tree methodology will entail several tasks. We plan further expansion and refinement to improve the classification of structural features associated with differences in expected carcinogenicity represented by the various nodes. Mutagenicity data and, within certain nodes, the application of quantitative structure-activity relationships are expected to aid in the refinement process. The activity tree now does not classify the structures of chemicals that may be operative by epigenetic or other mechanisms that serve to enhance the carcinogenesis process as in the phenomena of tumor promotion or cocarcinogenesis. The development of nodes representing the structural characteristics of these types of agents is planned. Structure-activity tree methodology is envisioned as an essential component of a resource in predictive toxicology, which we see as a comprehensive approach to assessing the suspected hazard associated with a particular chemical or group of chemicals. This approach entails literature searching, data evaluation, consideration of exposure conditions, and structure-activity prediction.

The ultimate objectives of predictive toxicology are to develop recommendations for further testing needs, if any, and to make decisions about the feasibility of continued development or use of the particular chemical(s) in question. We look forward to opportunities to refine further and test the structure-activity tree technique by applying predictive toxicology to any data base or list of chemicals that may either be of scientific interest or pose potential problems in terms of use, environmental distribution, or human exposure in general.

SUMMARY

A variety of chemicals, belonging to several different chemical classes, are known to be carcinogenic in animals or humans. Chemical structure can be a predictor of carcinogenic activity within the limitations of current knowledge of the ultimate forms of chemical carcinogens and of the structural requirements for metabolic activation. The role of structure-activity comparisons is envisioned as the first component of a tiered testing system for carcinogens that also includes short-term tests in vitro, long-term toxicity testing in animals, and epidemiological studies. A systematic method for assessing the possible carcinogenicity of chemicals prior to testing is based on the concept of a structure-activity tree, which serves as an index of known chemical structure features associated with carcinogenic activity. The basic units of the tree are the principal, recognized classes of chemical carcinogens that are subdivided into subclasses known as nodes according to specific structural features that may reflect differences in carcinogenic potential among chemicals in the class. An analysis of a computerized data base of known carcinogens is being performed using the structure-activity tree in order to test the validity of the tree as a classification scheme and to evaluate trends or patterns that may exist between chemical structure and specificity for target tissue, route of administration, and animal species. Practical applications of the structure-activity tree depend on its eventual validation as a predictor of carcinogenic activity. Further expansion and refinement of the tree is under way, with emphasis on improvement of the classifications of chemical substructures and on incorporation of more knowledge on mechanism of action of diverse environmental chemicals.

REFERENCES

1. Dipple, A. "Polynuclear Aromatic Carcinogens," in *Chemical Carcinogens, ACS Monograph 173,* C.E. Searle, Ed. (Washington, D.C.: American Chemical Society, 1976), pp. 245–314.
2. Clayson, D.B. and R.C. Garner. "Carcinogenic Aromatic Amines and Related Compounds," in *Chemical Carcinogens, ACS Monograph 173,* C.E. Searle, Ed. (Washington, D.C.: American Chemical Society, 1976), pp. 366–461.

3. Van Duuren, B.L. "Prediction of Carcinogenicity Based on Structure, Chemical Reactivity and Possible Metabolic Pathways," *J. Environ. Pathol. Toxicol.* 3:11-33 (1980).

4. Althouse, R., L. Tomatis, J. Huff, and J. Wilbourn. *IARC Monographs on the Evaluation of the Carcinogenic Risk of Chemicals to Humans: Chemicals and Industrial Processes Associated with Cancer in Humans,* Supplement 1 (Lyon, France: International Agency for Research on Cancer, 1979), pp. 16, 33.

5. "CAS ONLINE," Chemical Abstracts Service (Columbus, Ohio: February 15, 1982).

6. "Toxic Substances Control Act Chemical Substances Inventory: Cumulative Supplement," Office of Toxic Substances, U.S. Environmental Protection Agency (July 1980).

7. EPA, personal communication (February 1982).

8. FDA, Department of Adverse Reactions to Drugs, personal communication (February 1982).

9. Senti, F.R. "Food Additives and Food Safety," *Ind. Eng. Chem. Prod. Res. Dev.* 20(2):237–246 (1981).

10. Estrin, N.F., Ed. *CTFA Cosmetic Ingredient Dictionary,* 2nd ed. (Washington, D.C.: Cosmetic, Toiletry and Fragrance Association, 1977).

11. Jaffer, J.P., V.J. McGovern, D. Lent, L. Kanerva, E.M. Knowlton, P.A. Sullivan, C.T. Helmes, and C.C. Sigman. "Data Base of Carcinogens, Mutagens, and Tumor Promoters and Cocarcinogens," SRI International, developed for the National Cancer Institute under Contract No. N01-CP-95607 (February 1982).

12. Weisburger, J.H. and G.M. Williams. "Carcinogen Testing: Current Problems and New Approaches," *Science* 214:401–407 (1981).

13. Kraybill, H.F. "Approaches of the NCI," in *Proceedings of the Second FDA Office of Science Summer Symposium* (Rockville, Md.: Food and Drug Administration, 1978), pp. 216–220.

14. "Initial Report of the TSCA Interagency Testing Committee to the Administrator, Environmental Protection Agency," EPA 560-10-78/001 (Springfield, Va.: National Technical Information Service, January 1978).

15. Weisburger, J.H., and G.M. Williams. "Chemical Carcinogens," in *Casarett and Doull's Toxicology: The Basic Science of Poisons,* 2nd ed., J. Doull, C.D. Klaassen, and M.O. Amdur, Eds. (New York: Macmillan, 1980), pp. 84–138.

16. Miller, E.C. "Some Current Perspectives on Chemical Carcinogenesis in Humans and Experimental Animals: Presidential Address," *Cancer Res.* 38(6):1479–1496 (1978).

17. Dehn, R.L. and C.T. Helmes. "An Automatic Procedure for Assessing Possible Carcinogenic Activity of Chemicals Prior to Testing," Stanford Research Institute Report, prepared for the National Cancer Institute under Contract No. N01-CP-33285 (June 1974).

18. Raub, W.F. "The PROPHET System and Resource Sharing," *Fed. Proc.* 33:2390-2392 (1974).

19. Hollister, C. and J.J. Wood. *Users' Manual for the PROPHET System* Version 3.6. (Cambridge: Bolt Beranek and Newman, 1978).

20. National Cancer Institute/National Toxicology Program. "Carcinogenesis Technical Report Series," U.S. Department of Health and Human Services. (Springfield, Va.: National Technical Information Service). Continuing series.

21. *IARC Monographs on the Evaluation of the Carcinogenic Risk of Chemicals to Humans.* (Lyon, France: International Agency for Research on Cancer). Continuing series.

22. Helmes, C.T., D.L. Atkinson, J. Jaffer, C.C. Sigman, K.L. Thompson, M.I. Kelsey, H.F. Kraybill, and J.I. Munn. "Evaluation and Classification of the Potential Carcinogenicity of Organic Air Pollutants," *J. Environ. Sci. Health,* A17(3):321–389(1982).

23. Helmes, C.T., C.C. Sigman, S. Malko, D.L. Atkinson, J. Jaffer, P.A. Sullivan, K.L. Thompson, E.M. Knowlton, H.F. Kraybill, J. Hushon, and N. Barr. "Evaluation and Classification of the Potential Carcinogenicity and Mutagenicity of Chemical Biorefractories Identified in Drinking Water," First Report, U.S. Department of Health and Human Services (February 1981).
24. Helmes, C.T., V.A. Fung, B. Lewin, K.E. McCaleb, S. Malko, and A.M. Pawlovich. "A Study of Aromatic Nitro Compounds for the Selection of Candidates for Carcinogen Bioassay," *J. Environ. Sci. Health* A17(1):75–128 (1982).

CHAPTER 3

Problems of Testing Commercial-Grade Chemicals

Edward J. Woodhouse, Evelyn A. Murrill, Kathleen M. Stelting, and Richard D. Brown
Midwest Research Institute, 425 Volker Boulevard, Kansas City, Missouri 644110

C.W. Jameson
National Toxicology Program, P.O. Box 12233, Research Triangle Park, North Carolina 27709

Commercial-grade chemicals are elected for toxicity testing in the National Toxicology Program (NTP) because of their potential health hazard to the human population. Criteria for chemical selection include the production levels of the chemical, major uses of the chemical, type and breadth of potential human exposure, chemical structural relationship to known carcinogens, and availability of toxicological information.

Typically, commercial chemicals selected for toxicity testing represent a wide range of chemical types and uses; they include solvents, food additives, cosmetics, drugs, dyes, pigments, catalysts, and a myriad of other chemicals incorporated into products responsible for significant exposure to the public and/or workers producing or handling the material. In this chapter we discuss the procurement of such chemicals for NTP toxicity studies, the chemical analyses conducted on them, and some of the problems involved in such analyses.

CHEMICAL PROCUREMENT

Once a commercial-grade chemical is approved for testing by the NTP, the most appropriate material for testing must be identified. First, the chemical procured must be representative of the product used by the exposed population. In this regard, the be representative of the product used by the exposed population. In this regard, the major uses of the material determine whether the chemical should be tested as an unformulated technical substance or as a particular formulation. Finally, the production-treatment processes used by the manufacturers or sources of the product must be considered because they ultimately determine the composition of the commercial product.

Once the appropriate material has been selected and a supplier identified, the procurement process for the test chemical should ensure that a typical lot of the product is secured in an amount sufficient for the entire toxicity test, unless otherwise dictated by stability considerations. Procurement of the test chemical in several lots is normally avoided because successive lots may have different impurity profiles and the availability of successive lots may not coincide with the test schedule. In addition, multiple procurements require duplication of analytical work.

CHEMICAL ANALYSIS

Chemical analysis is conducted on commercial-grade chemicals for the National Toxicology Program at Midwest Research Institute (MRI), the analytical chemistry resource contractor, to establish the following:

1.   Conformance to NTP specifications with regard to the major component and any impurities anticipated from the production process.
2.   Agreement between MRI analytical data and that of the manufacturer for the typical lot procured.
3.   Identification of the major components in complex synthetic mixtures and natural products.
4.   Determination of the impurity profile of the material, with identification and quantitation of impurities present at significant levels (i.e. $> 1\%$).
5.   Identification of storage conditions required to prevent decomposition of the material during the toxicity testing period.

To accomplish these goals, a wide range of analytical techniques is employed. These include methods to identify and accurately quantitate the major component and impurity profiling techniques designed to detect other components, such as known or suspect toxins or carcinogens or inorganic salts, which might compromise the toxicity test.

Specific techniques used depend on the nature of the test compound and any suspected impurities, but typically they include elemental analysis; thin-layer chromatography (TLC), gas chromatography (GC), or high performance liquid chromatography (HPLC); nuclear magnetic resonance (NMR), infrared (IR), and ultraviolet (UV)/visible spectroscopy; measurement of physical constants; and organic functional group titrations. More specialized methods such as GC/MS (gas chromatography and mass spectrometry) are used as circumstances warrant. Corroborative analyses are done to minimize the effect of individual method bias on the final assessment of purity.

The results of chemical characterization used by the NTP for toxicity testing are often more extensive than the analytical data available from the manufacturer, whose analyses are largely quality control oriented. Frequently, thorough evaluation of the data is necessary to provide a final statement of purity and an impurity profile consistent with all the data and to reconcile MRI's results with those of the manufacturer.

PROBLEMS IN CHEMICAL ANALYSES

Based the NTP's experience in analyzing a large number of commercial-grade chemicals, the major problems associated with this type of analysis can be classified into four categories:

1. Determination of specific impurities.
2. Identification of major components in incompletely characterized materials.
3. Reconciliation of analytical results with those obtained by the manufacturer.
4. Determination of a complete impurity profile for a commercial-grade material.

Determination of Specific Impurities

The determination of specific impurities in commercial-grade chemicals involves the quantification of substances anticipated from the production and distribution process. Such impurities may include synthesis starting materials, intermediates or by-products, formulation additives or stabilizers, and degradation products.

The determination of chlorinated impurities in pentachlorophenol (PCP) illustrates this type of analysis. Pentachlorophenol is a chemical widely used in large quantities as a wood preservative. Because of its economic and toxicological importance, PCP was procured in several different grades from the major manufacturers. The various grades of the compound were analyzed to compare the levels of several known or suspected impurities, including synthesis by-products such as chlorinated diphenyl ethers, chlorinated higher phenols, and the highly biologically active chlorinated dibenzodioxins and dibenzofurans, as depicted in Figure 3-1. The compound commonly called dioxin (2,3,7,8-tetrachlorodibenzodioxin) was of particular concern since it is among the more toxic compounds known and could therefore profoundly affect bioassay studies.

A column chromatographic method was used for preseparation of the dioxins and furans from PCP. Pentachlorophenol (5.0 g) was dissolved in benzene (50.0 ml). An aliquot (10.0 ml) of this solution was placed on a column containing 40 ml Fisher Adsorption A-50, 80-200 mesh, deactivated with 5% water. The column was eluted with benzene and the first 115 ml of eluent collected. This eluent was concentrated on a steam bath to approximately 4 ml in a Kuderna-Danish concentrator fitted with a three-ball Snyder column. The concentrate was further evaporated under nitrogen to 0.50 ml. An aliquot (0.40 ml) of this solution was placed on a microcolumn containing dry ICN Aluminum Oxide W 200 basic, activity grade Super I (1.0 g). The column

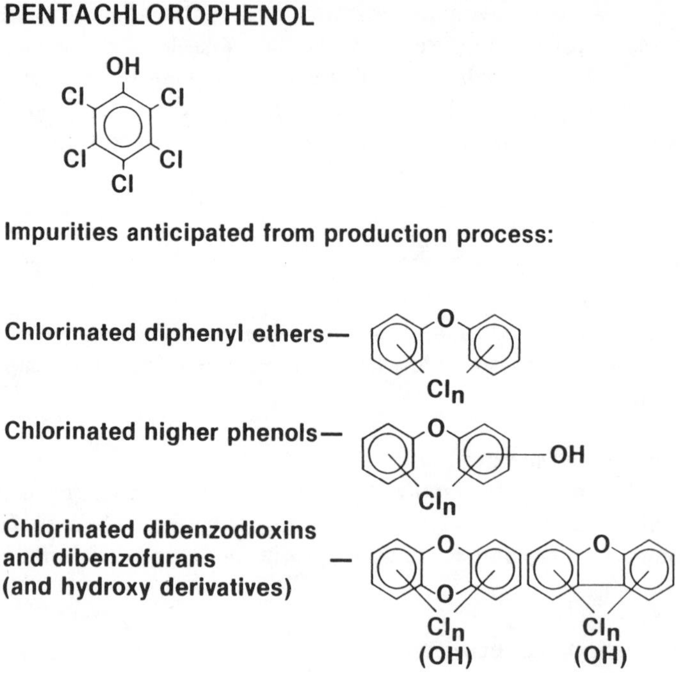

PENTACHLOROPHENOL

Impurities anticipated from production process:

Chlorinated diphenyl ethers—

Chlorinated higher phenols—

Chlorinated dibenzodioxins
and dibenzofurans
(and hydroxy derivatives)   —

Figure 3-1.   Pentachlorophenol and suspected impurities.

was eluted with an 8.0 ml portion, followed by elution with two 1.0 ml portions of 2% methylene chloride in hexane. The column was then eluted with a 5.0 ml portion, followed by a 1.0 and a 4.0 ml portion of 50% methylene chloride in hexane. The fraction consisting of the first 5.0 ml of the 50% methylene chloride in hexane was believed to contain the chlorinated dibenzodioxins and chlorinated dibenzofurans and was collected in a 10 ml volumetric flask, evaporated to dryness under a gentle stream of nitrogen, and diluted to volume with benzene. All other fractions were collected in septum vials. The tenth ml of the 2% methylene chloride in hexane fraction and the sixth ml of the 50% methylene chloride in hexane fraction (bracketing the fraction of interest) were evaporated to dryness under a gentle stream of nitrogen and reconstituted with 1.0 ml of benzene. The chlorinated dibenzodioxins and chlorinated dibenzofurans were found by GC to be contained solely in the first 5.0 ml of the 50% methylene chloride in hexane elution. A spiked sample and a spiked blank containing aliquots (5.0 ml) of a solution containing octachlorodibenzodioxin (61.32 μg/ml in benzene) were also chromatographed using the same procedure as described to confirm 100% recovery.

Capillary GC/MS was then employed to resolve and identify the various isomers of chlorinated dioxins and furans and to quantitate several of these compounds. The chlorinated impurities sought and quantitated include: 2,3,7,8-tetrachlorodibenzodioxin, hexachloro-, heptachloro-, and octachlorodibenzodioxins and furans. GC/MS profiles, as depicted in Figure 3-2 for PCP (DP-2), were obtained for all

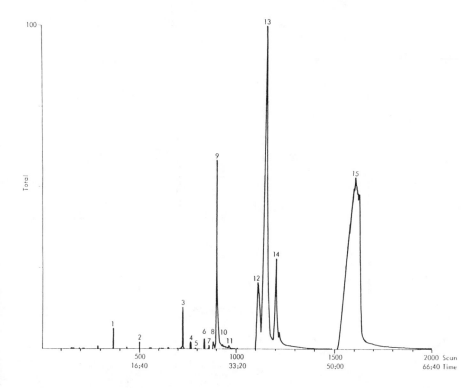

Figure 3-2. GC/MS profile of pentachlorophenol (DP-2) impurities from column eluent. Instrument: Finnigan 4000 mass spectrometer interfaced directly to a Finnigan 9610 gas chromatograph. Data processed by an INCOS 2300 data system. Gas Chromatography Parameters: Injector temperature—250°C; Column—Capillary, 30 m × 0.25 mm ID, glass, coated with SP-2100 (Grade AA, J&W Scientific, Inc.); Carrier gas—Helium; Carrier gas linear velocity—25 cm/sec; Program—60°C for 2 min, then 60 to 250°C at 10°C/min; Injection mode—Splitless (30 sec); Solutions injected—2 μl of a concentrated pentachlorophenol extract (2.0 ml concentrated to 25 μl under a stream of nitrogen). Mass Spectrometer Parameters: Transfer line temperature—300°C; Mass spectrometer temperature—280°C; Scan times—Up, 1.90 sec; Top, 0.00 sec; Down, 0.00 sec; Bottom, 0.10 sec; Electron energy— 70 eV; Electron multiplier voltage— -1750 v; Preamplifier sensitivity—10^{-8}; Scan range—200 to 510 amu. Peak identification: 1,2—Unidentified; 3,4—Hexachlorohydroxybiphenyl; 5— Unidentified; 6,7—Heptachlorohydroxybiphenyl; 8—Hexachlorodibenzofuran; 9—Hexachlorodibenzofuran and Hexachlorodibenzodioxin, 99.8:0.2; 10,11—Hexachlorodibenzodioxin; 12—Heptachlorodibenzofuran; 13—Heptachlorodibenzofuran and Heptachlorodibenzodioxin, 96:4; 14—Heptachlorodibenzodioxin; 15—Octachlorodibenzofuran and Octachlorodibenzodioxin, 65:35.

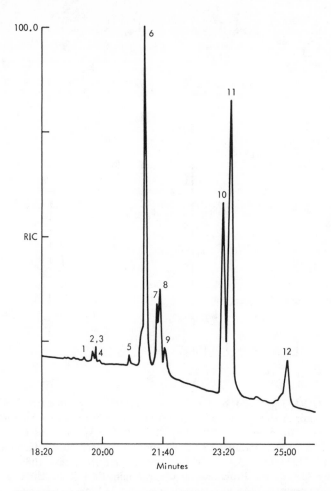

Figure 3-3. GC/MS profile of pentachlorophenol (DP-2) impurities derivatized with diazomethane. Instrument: Finnigan 4000 mass spectrometer interfaced via a single stage glass separator to a Finnigan 4610 gas chromatograph. Data processed by a Finnigan 2300 data system. Gas Chromatography Parameters: Injector temperature—300°C; Column—15 m SE-54 WCOT capillary, 0.25 mm ID; Carrier gas—Helium; Carrier flow rate—1 ml/min; Injection mode—Splitless (30 sec); Program—100°C for 1 min, then 8°C/min to 260°C and hold; Solutions injected—2 μl of 5.0% (w/v) solutions of PCP (derivatized). Mass Spectrometry Parameters: Separator transfer line—280°C; Ionizer temperature—280°C; Manifold temperature—100°C; Electron energy—70 eV; electron multiplier voltage— -1850 V; Pre-amplifier sensitivity—10^{-7}; Scan range—90 to 525 m/e, 2.5 sec scan. Peak identification: 1—Octachlorodiphenyl ether; 2,3,4—Heptachloromethoxydiphenyl ether; 5,6,7,8—Octachloromethoxydiphenyl ether; 9—Hexachloromethoxydibenzofuran; 10,11—Nonachlorometh-oxydiphenyl ether; 12—Heptachloromethoxydibenzofuran.

grades of PCP examined. Peaks representing mixtures of furans and dioxins were assigned weight % values for the two compounds using mass spectral intensity values of ions in the molecular ion cluster for each compound. Quantitation was achieved using the capillary GC system with standards. When standards of specific individual isomers were not available, it was assumed that the detector response for all isomers of a given compound was identical.

Other classes of impurities quantitated in PCP were the so-called higher phenols and chlorinated diphenyl ethers. The nonvolatile phenolic impurities were derivatized with diazomethane. Duplicate 10 ml solutions of 5.0% (w/v) pentachlorophenol in HPLC-quality tetrahydrofuran containing 0.1% (w/v) dichlorodibenzodioxin internal standard were prepared. The internal standard was added as a 1.0 ml spike from a 1.0% dichlorodibenzodioxin solution prior to dilution of the sample. The solutions were transferred to amber vials (with Teflon®-lined septa) and stored at –20° C. A portion (1.0 ml) of each solution was transferred to a 5 ml amber vial and the solvent evaporated under a stream of nitrogen. Diazomethane solution (1.0 ml, diethyl ether solution, prepared from alkaline N-methyl-N-nitro-N-nitrosoguanidine) was then added, and the vials were sealed. After 1 hr at room temperature, an additional 1.0 ml of diazomethane solution was added, and the vials were resealed and allowed to stand for an additional hour. The solvent was then evaporated under nitrogen, and the residue was taken up in 1.0 ml THF for analysis. Freshly derivatized solutions were prepared immediately prior to each analysis, although there was no evidence of sample instability. The residues were identified by capillary GC/MS. GC/MS profiles, as depicted in Figure 3-3 for PCP (DP-2), were obtained for all grades of PCP examined. Quantitation was achieved by comparison of sample and standard selected ion intensities.

Four commercial samples of PCP were analyzed: a technical-grade PCP obtained from Monsanto Industrial Chemical Company, PCP (DP-2) and PCP (EC-7) from Dow Chemical Company, and a pure-grade PCP from Aldrich Chemical Company. The results of the analyses are shown in Table 3-1. Typically, 2,3,7,8-tetrachlorodibenzodioxin was found to be present at levels less than 1 ppm. Other chlorinated dibenzodioxins and furans ranged in concentration from < 1 ppm to 1700 ppm. Hydroxychlorinated dibenzodioxins and furans ranged from < 1000 ppm to over 6000 ppm, and other chlorinated higher phenols and diphenyl ethers ranged from < 1000 ppm to over 50,000 ppm. These kinds of analyses are most useful in determining which commercial source of PCP should be used for carcinogenesis bioassay testing. In this case, comparative toxicity studies are being run on the technical and EC-7 grades.

Identification of Major Components in Incompletely Characterized Materials

Many chemicals procured for bioassay studies are actually complex mixtures that have not been completely characterized because the end use of the compound in commerce or industry does not require complete characterization. This category

Table 3–1. Summary of Impurities Found in Four Grades of Pentachlorophenol

Sample		Impurities Present (ppm)			
	2,3,7,8-TCDD	Other Chlorinated Dibenzodioxins	Chlorinated Dibenzofurans	Hydroxychlorinated Dibenzodioxins/ furans	Chlorinated Higher Phenols and Diphenyl Ethers
PCP (technical)	<0.9	1,702	142	6,300	55,800
PCP (DP-2)	<0.04	201	505	3,800	36,700
PCP (EC-7)	<0.04	1.4	0.28	<1,000	<1,000
PCP ("Pure")	<0.08	<1.0		3,300	3,100

includes both synthetic materials (such as dyes and pigments) and natural products (for example, β-cadinene). Prior to toxicity testing, the identity and concentration of the components of these mixtures must be determined to the fullest extent possible within the constraints of available methods, time, and expense.

The complexity of this problem for synthetic materials is illustrated by the analysis of the high molecular weight dyes, Direct Blue No. 15 and Acid Red No. 114, the structures of which are depicted in Figure 3–4. Dye materials are among the most difficult commercial chemicals to analyze because the synthetic processes yield a complex mixture of chemically similar compounds, organic and inorganic compounds are intentionally added to achieve desired properties, and standards are not available for most of the suspected impurities.

Because of the difficulties, definitive purity values and quantitation of impurities, while possible, is not cost-effective. However, it is still possible within existing time constraints to assess purity ranges and general structural characteristics of the impurities through the use of less elaborate analytical methods.

Elemental analysis data are useful for obtaining the inorganic salt content. HPLC, using multiple wavelength detection and programmed solvent elution, provides a useful (and fairly well-resolved) impurity profile. This method obviously cannot be used for quantitation without standards, but comparison of data at multiple detection wavelengths does allow some assessment of the structures of the impurities (for example, presence or absence of the azo groups) as well as an estimate of the

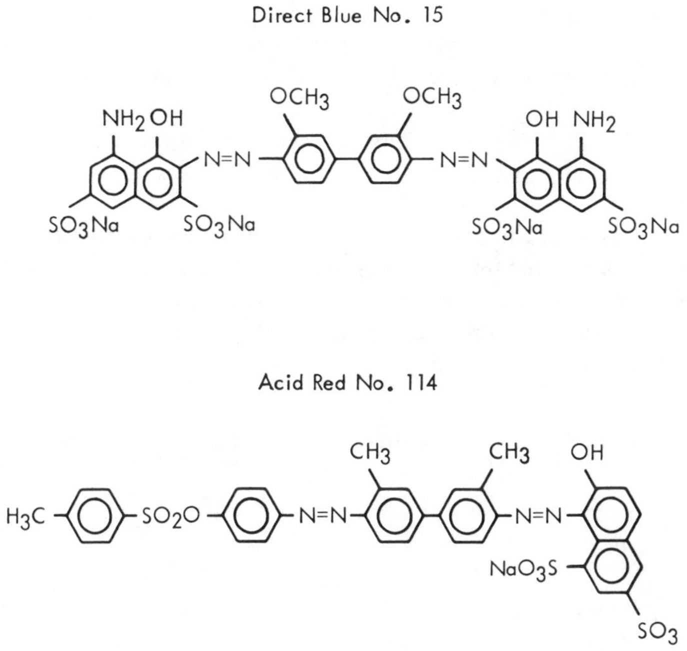

Figure 3–4. Structure of high molecular weight dyes.

number of impurities present. Reductive titration of azo groups can also be used to ascertain maximum purity values.

After careful interpretation of the data obtained from multiple analyses of the dye, a report is prepared containing an estimate of total inorganics (including water), tentative identification and quantitation of inorganic species, total orga- ics and an estimate of the ratio of organic impurities to the major component, quantitation of specific impurities against standards, and as confident a statement as possible about the identity of the major components. Any more than this requires much more extensive work and expense and generally yields limited information.

The commercial formulations of Direct Blue No. 15 and Acid Red No. 114 were found to contain too many inorganics to be suitable for bioassay. Press cakes, the materials produced before final formulation, were therefore procured and analyzed. Elemental analyses for sodium, sulfur (total), sulfur (ionic), and chlorine, combined with Karl Fischer analysis for water, indicated as shown in Table 3–2 that the press cakes for both Direct Blue No. 15 and Acid Red No. 114 also contained too much salt for use in bioassay studies. The organic content of the two dye press cakes was only 68% and 78%, respectively, with the major organic component estimated by HPLC to be only 35% and 62%, respectively. Therefore desalting procedures were developed based on dialysis to produce materials more suitable for bioassay.

Samples of the dyes (200 g) were transferred to 60 cm lengths of 3.0 in. flat-width dialysis tubing, which had been boiled for 75 min and rinsed with deionized water prior to use. Approximately 200 ml of deionized water was added to each tube; the tubing was knotted, and the contents were kneaded to form a slurry. The dialysis tubes were then submerged in 55 gal. of deionized water for 24 hr. During the process, a peristaltic pump was used to circulate the water around the tubing. A water change (150% turnover) was made at the end of 24 hr, and dialysis was continued for an additional 16 hr.

On completion of the dialysis, the contents of the tubes were transferred to Pyrex drying pans and heated at 110°C until the samples appeared dry by visual inspection (16 to 24 hr).

The batches of desalted material recovered from the dialysis were combined and processed in a ball mill for ~ 4 to 8 hr to reduce particle size to less than 60 mesh. The samples were then sealed in double plastic bags and kneaded for about 10 min to homogenize. As shown in Table 3–2, the final products contained much less salt than the press cakes, with corresponding increases in the organic constituents present.

Table 3–2. Analytical Summary for Direct Blue No. 15 and Acid Red No. 114

	Inorganics	Organics
Direct Blue No. 15		
Press cake	25% NaCl 7% water	68% (major component ~35%)
Desalted Press cake	4% NaCl 10% water	86% (major component ~60%)
Acid Red No. 114		
Press cake	15% NaCl 7% water	78% (major component ~62%)
Desalted Press cake	<1% NaCl 4% water	96% (major component ~77%)

These materials were considered suitable for bioassay. The major organic component in the desalted dyes still only represented about 70% and 80% of the total organics for Direct Blue No. 15 and Acid Red No. 114, respectively, as illustrated in the HPLC chromatograms shown in Figures 3-5 and 3-6.

Natural product mixtures (such as β-cadinene) are more amenable to characterization by classical methods. β-cadinene is a terpenoid natural flavoring agent to which there is a wide exposure in the population.

Spectroscopy and other analyses indicated that the sample was, as expected, probably a mixture of β-cadinene, other cadinene isomers, and other terpenoid compounds. The most important analytical method used to characterize this compound was capillary GC, which detected over twenty impurities of concentrations between 1

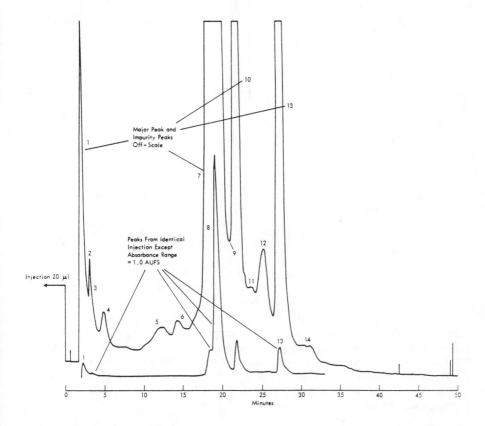

Figure 3-5. High performance liquid chromatographic profile of desalted Direct Blue No. 15 at 546 nm. Direct Blue No. 15, 0.9968 mg/ml in Solvent A. Column: Altex Ultrasphere ODS, 5 μm, 4.6 × 250 mm I.D. Solvents: A—Water containing 0.1% v/v triethanolamine, 10% v/v methanol, and the pH adjusted to 7.2 with 55% v/v phosphoric acid in water; B—Methanol containing 0.1% v/v triethanolamine with volume of 55% v/v phosphoric acid in water identical to that used for the adjustment of Solvent A. Solvent Program: 10 to 55% B linearily in 30 min. Flow Rate: 1.0 ml/min. Detection: 546 nm Absorbance Units Full Scale (AUFS).

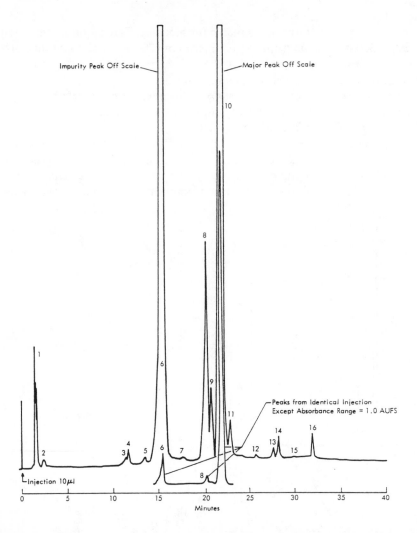

Figure 3–6. High performance liquid chromatographic profile of desalted Acid Red No. 114 at 546 nm. Acid Red No. 114, 0.35 mg/ml in methanol. Column: Supelco Supelcosil LC-18-D8, 150 × 4.6 mm ID. Solvents: A—Aqueous pH 7.41 buffer containing 10% v/v methanol; B—Methanol containing pH 7.41 buffer and 10% v/v water. Solvent Program: Linear solvent gradient 40 to 100% B in 30 min. Flow Rate: 1.0 ml/min. Detection: 546 nm, 0.05 Absorbance Units Full Scale (AUFS).

and 11% relative to the major component. The major peak comprised only 61% of the total chromatogram area, as shown in Figure 3–7.

Capillary GC/MS was conducted, and the reconstructed ion chromatogram depicted in Figure 3–8 resembled the flame ionization chromatogram closely. Of the thirty-four peaks observed, twenty-three had the same molecular ion as β-cadinene, and the remainder had masses very near β-cadinene and fragmentation peaks characteristic of sesquiterpenoids.

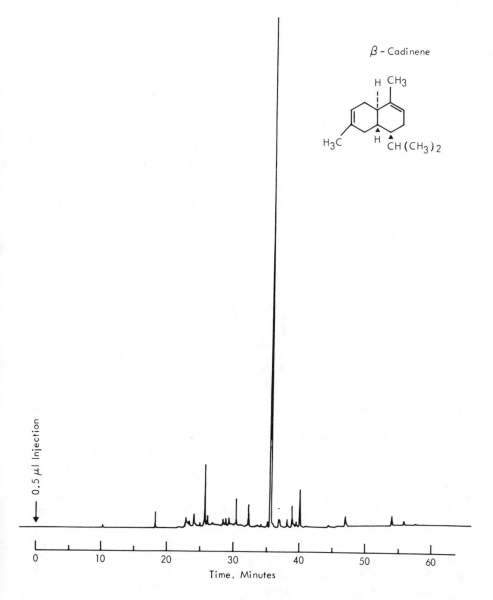

β - Cadinene

Figure 3-7. Capillary gas chromatogram of β-cadinene. Instrument: Varian 3700. Column: Capillary; 60 m × 0.25 mm ID; glass; coated with Carbowax 20 M. Detector: Flame ionization. Carrier gas: Nitrogen; 10 cm/sec. Inlet temperature: 250° C. Column oven temperature: 125 to 175° C, 1°/min. Detector temperature: 250° C. Splitter flow rate: 400 cc/min. Sensitivity: 16 × 10^{-12} AFS.

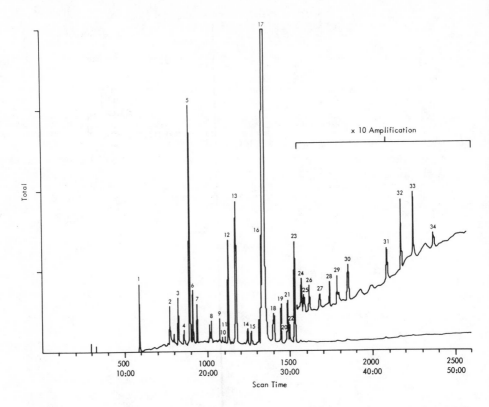

Figure 3–8. Reconstructed ion chromatograph of β-cadinene. Instrument: Finnigan 4000 mass spectrometer interfaced via a single-stage glass jet separator to a Finnigan 9610 gas chromatograph. Data handled by an INCOS 2300 data system. Gas Chromatography Parameters: Injector temperature—250°C. Column: Capillary, 60 m × 0.25 mm I.D., glass; coated with Carbowax 520M. Carrier Gas: Helium. Carrier Flow Rate: 16 cm/sec. Program: 125 to 175°C at 1°C/min. Inlet Splitter Flow Rate: 100 cc/min. Sample Injected: 0.25 μl of neat β-cadinene. Mass Spectrometry Parameters: Transfer line—275°C; Separator—300°C. Scan Range: 10 to 475 amu. Scan Times (sec): Up—1.10; Top—0.00; Down—0.00; Bottom—0.10. Electron Energy: 70 eV. Electron Multiplier Voltage: –1,600 V at 10^{-8} sensitivity.

Reconciliation of Analytical Results with Those Reported by the Manufacturer

When differences between observed analytical data and those of the manufacturer's typical lot analysis occur, the manufacturer is contacted so that the conditions and constraints of the analytical methods can be compared. In the majority of these cases, the manufacturer's quality-control analyses provide an incomplete representation of the purity of the material, and the more extensive data obtained by the NTP complete the analytical picture, providing a better basis for interpretation. Occasionally dis-

ALLYL ISOVALERATE

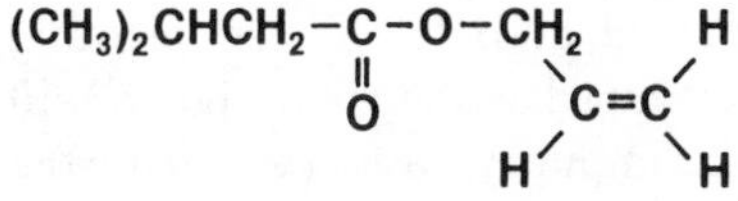

$$(CH_3)_2CHCH_2-\overset{\underset{\displaystyle O}{\|}}{C}-O-CH_2 \quad \overset{H}{\underset{H}{\diagdown}}C=C\overset{\diagup}{\underset{\diagdown H}{}}$$

MANUFACTURER: 99% purity—based on ester hydrolysis and titration of isovaleric acid

NTP: 80% purity—16% free acid (titration before hydrolysis)
80% allyl isovalerate ⎤
4% impurities ⎦ G.C.

Figure 3-9.   Summary of analyses of allyl isovalerate.

crepancies can be traced to the use of inappropriate methodology by the manufacturer.

In the case of allyl isovalerate, 99% pure food grade chemical was ordered. Analysis of the chemical received, primarily by GC, ester hydrolysis, and free acid titration, indicated, as shown in Figure 3-9, that the compound was only 80% pure; the material was found to contain 16% free acid, with the remaining 4% impurities detected by GC. Subsequent communication revealed that the manufacturer's claim of 99% purity was based on an ester hydrolysis alone, with no correction for the unusually high acid content present prior to hydrolysis. The compound was returned, and a new batch meeting the specified 99% major component was procured for toxicity testing.

Determination of a Complete Impurity Profile

A decision to identify and quantitate impurities detected during impurity profiling is made on the basis of their estimated concentration or as a consequence of positive toxicity test data.

The analysis of 4,4'-diamino-2,2'-stilbenedisulfonic acid (amsonic acid) is an example of impurity determination based on the

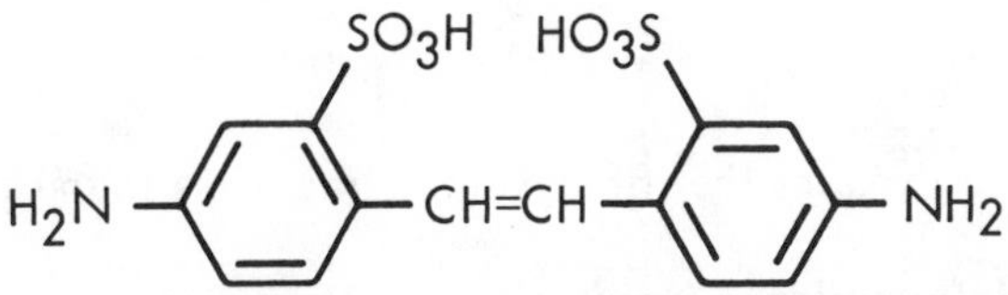

$$H_2N-\underset{SO_3H}{\text{⬡}}-CH=CH-\underset{HO_3S}{\text{⬡}}-NH_2$$

concentration criterion. Preliminary HPLC data for this compound indicated an impurity that varied in size relative to the major peak area (0.01 to 40%) at detection wavelengths of 340 nm and 254 nm. Although differences in molar absorptivity with wavelength often cause differences in concentrations estimated from HPLC peak areas, discrepancies of this magnitude must be resolved prior to toxicity testing.

In the case of amsonic acid, an HPLC system providing optimal separation of the peaks of interest was developed as shown in Figure 3–10 from a system used for initial impurity profiling. The impurity was isolated from the sample by multiple collections of the HPLC effluent, concentrated by evaporation, and reinjected. The results indicated that the isolated impurity was > 99% pure.

The sample was introduced into a mass spectrometer by direct inlet techniques because of the presence of paired ion solvents in the isolated fraction and the probable polar nature of the impurity, as indicated by the need for a paired ion system to obtain column retention during the HPLC analysis.

The reconstructed ion chromatogram showed three compound peaks, unresolved from each other. The first two appeared to be due to the quarternary amine solvent. The third peak, which was also dominated by ions produced by the fragmentation of tributylamine, contained additional ions in the high mass range. With the exception of mass 242, these high mass fragments, although not abundant, were very diagnostic and indicated that the impurity was an isomer of ethylenedianilinesulfonic acid, probably 4,4′-ethylenedianiline-2-sulfonic acid, which would be

expected to have a higher absorbance at 254 nm than at 340 nm.

The high mass range ions observed and possible fragment structures are shown in Table 3–3. The presence of the butyl ether group in these fragments is explained by the decomposition of the ion pair in the heated inlet according to the following reaction:

This reaction also explains the tributylamine fragments found in the compound spectrum.

Using this information in conjunction with the previously determined titration and elemental analysis data, the impurity was estimated to be present in the sample at a level of approximately 16%.

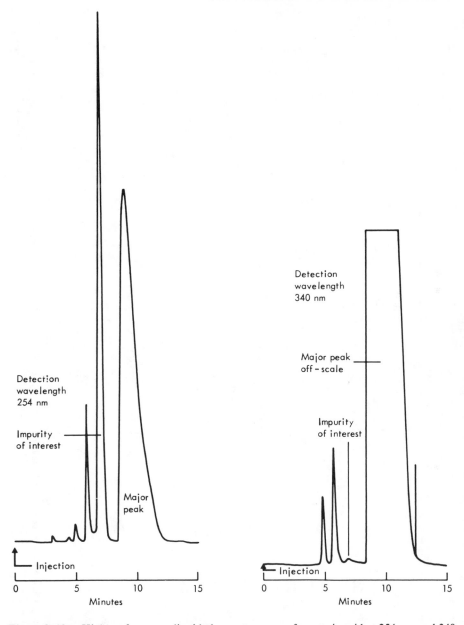

Figure 3-10. High performance liquid chromatograms of amsonic acid at 254 nm and 340 nm. Solvent Delivery System: Pumps—Waters 6000A; Programmer—Waters 660. Detector: Waters 440. Injector: Waters U6K. Detection: Ultraviolet, 254 and 340 nm. Column: Waters μBondapak C_{18}; 300 × 7.8 mm I.D. Solvent system: A—0.005 M aqueous tetrabutyl-ammonium hydroxide, adjusted to pH 7.4 with 1% phosphoric acid; B—0.005 M tetrabutyl-ammonium hydroxide in methanol, with volume addition of 1% phosphoric acid identical to Solvent A. Solvent ratios: A—80%; B—20%. Flow rate: 4.0 ml/min. Sample injected: 2 ml (5 × 0.4 ml) of a saturated solution of 4,4'-diamino-2,2'-stilbenedisulfonic acid in 0.005 M aqueous tetrabutylammonium hydroxide.

Table 3-3.   Assignment of High Mass Ions on Mass Spectrum of Amsonic Acid Impurity*

M/e	Fragment
347	H_2N—⟨⟩—C(CH₃)₂—⟨⟩—NH ; O=S=O ; O—Butyl (structure, +)
317	M/e 347—OCH₂
243	H_3C—⟨⟩—NH₂ ; O=S=O ; O—Butyl (+)
242	H_2C—⟨⟩—NH₂ ; O=S=O ; O—Butyl (+) (rearrangement ion)
211	H_2N—⟨⟩—C(CH₃)₂—⟨⟩—NH₂ (+)
179	⟨⟩—C(CH₃)₂—⟨⟩—NH₂ (+)

*Instrument: Varian MAT CH4-B mass spectrometer. Data handled by an INCOS 2300 data system. Electron energy: 70 eV. Scan range: 30 to 600 AMU. Scan times (sec): Up—4.25; Top—0.25; Down—0.75; Bottom—0.75. Accelerator Voltage: 3,000 v. Trap current: 40 μa. Electron multiplier voltage: 2.1 kv. Sample introduction: Temperature programmed direct inlet.

CONCLUSION

The examples discussed in this chapter represent but a few of the instances encountered by MRI in its analytical support programs for the NTP programs which test the toxic potential of environmental chemicals. We hope these examples have shown some of the problems in characterizing commercial-grade chemicals and in providing data on such chemicals to allow determination of their suitability for toxicity testing.

CHAPTER 4

Chemical/Vehicle Mixing and Analysis Problems at a Bioassay Laboratory

Ralph J. Wheeler

Gulf South Research Institute,
P.O. Box 1177, New Iberia, Louisiana 70560

Since 1970, sixty compounds have been placed on test by Gulf South Research Institute (GSRI) for the National Cancer Institute (NCI) and/or the National Toxicology Program (NTP) to determine their tumorigenic activity in laboratory rats and mice. These chemicals include twenty-nine pesticides, four positive control carcinogens, eight chlorinated hydrocarbons, four common laboratory solvents, three natural products, seven surfactants, two dyes, a drinking-water disinfectant, a curing agent for fiberglass, and a fungicide used by the army to treat shoes. These compounds were tested using one of four routes of administration: dosed feed, dosed drinking water, dermal absorption, or oral gavage.

DOSAGE PREPARATION

Dosages were prepared by mixing the test chemical with the appropriate vehicle on a weekly basis using procedures developed by GSRI or an NCI/NTP analytical contractor. A stainless-steel Hobart® mixer or Patterson-Kelly® (PK) twin shell blender was used in the preparation of dosed feed mixes. Glass containers with vortex mixers or magnetic stirrers were used for dosage mixtures being administered orally or dermally as a liquid. Table 4–1 shows the materials tested by the various routes.

Between 1970 and 1975, all of the chemicals on test were pesticides that were administered as dosed feed. Aliquots of these chemicals were dissolved in 50 ml of acetone and added to the appropriate amount of animal feed in a stainless-steel mixing bowl. Corn oil (2% wt/wt) was added to the diet prior to mixing as a dust suppres-

GSRI wishes to acknowledge the support of this work by the National Cancer Institute and the National Toxicology Program through their prime contract with Tracor Jitco, Inc.

Table 4-1.   Chemicals Tested at GSRI

Compounds administered in dosed feed

Amitrol	Picloram
Saffrole	Heptachlor
2 AAF	Azinphos-methyl
Aldrin	Phosphamidon
Dieldrin	Parathion
Photodieldrin	Lindane
Chlordane	Captan
Endrin	Chlorothalonil
Dichlorovos	Toxaphene
Chloramben	Tetrachlorovinphos
Dimethoate	Chlordecone
Maloxon	Aldicarb
Malathion	Coumaphos
Fenthion	Fluometuron
Diazinon	Atrazine
Sodium 2-ethylhexyl sulfate	Sodium dodecyl sulfate
Dodecyl alcohol ethoxylated	Xylene sulfonic acid
Castor oil	Gilsonite
Manganese sulfate	Anilazine

Compounds administered in drinking water
  t-Butyl alcohol
  Sodium fluorescein
  Chloramine

Compounds administered by gavage[a]
  Methylene chloride (corn oil)
  Vinylidene chloride (corn oil)
  Tetrachloroethane (corn oil)
  Pentachloroethane (corn oil)
  Tetrachloroethylene (corn oil)
  1,1,1-Trichloroethane (corn oil)
  Trichlorfon (water)
  Maleic hydrazide/DEA (water)
  Diethanolamine (water)
  Pyridine (water)
  Tetrahydrofuran (water)
  Ethylene glycol monoethyl ether (water)

Compounds administered by skin paint
  Coconut oil/DEA[a] (deionized water)
  Oleic acid/DEA[b] (95% ethanol)
  Lauric acid/DEA[b] (95% ethanol)
  p-Nitrophenol (acetone)
  Witch hazel (deionized water)
  Glutaraldehyde (deionized water)
  1,2-Epoxyhexadecane (acetone)

2-Butanone peroxide (dimethyl phthalate)
7,12-Dimethylbenz(a)anthracene (acetone)

---

[a]Vehicle is shown in parentheses.
[b]DEA-diethanolamine condensate.

sant. This was mixed at low speed for 30 min using a Hobart Institutional Food Mixer. Control feed was mixed using 50 ml acetone and 2% wt/wt corn oil.

Dosed Feed Analysis

Analyses were performed on every eighth mix of each dose level. Standard pesticide residue extraction methodologies, as modified at GSRI, were employed. Because of the relatively high concentrations of test chemical, it was generally necessary to dilute the extracts rather than concentrate, as is usually the case for a standard pesticide-residue analysis method. During this period, 93.5% of the dosages analyzed were within the required ± 10% of the theoretical concentration.

Chemical volatility and reactivity were problems encountered during this period. To decrease the volatility of dichlorvos, the mixes were frozen, and fresh feed was given out daily. Anilazine (dyrene) was found to react with the thiol containing amino acids in the feed resulting in an apparent half-life of 24 hr. The reaction was retarded by freezing these mixes and supplying fresh dosed feed on a daily basis.

After 1975, the NCI assigned the development of mixing and analysis methodologies for the bioassay program to an analytical contractor, and the use of stainless-steel twin shell blenders for the diet preparations was mandated. The blenders chosen by GSRI were 8 and 16 qt size PK blenders with intensifier and/or liquid dispersion spin bars that operate in the mixer at its rotational axis.

Feed Blending

There is a critical mixing time for each chemical-feed mixture with the PK blenders. Mixing beyond that time will tend to concentrate the minor constituent into one of the upper arms of the blender. This time is somewhat dependent on the nature of the material—its particle size if solid or its viscosity if a liquid. As an example, dodecyl alcohol ethoxylated (Siponic L7-90) was supplied by the NCI as a 90% aqueous solution of high viscosity. Homogeneity studies were performed on 1.2% (vol/wt) mixtures of this compound using the PK blender. Samples were collected from top left, top right, and bottom of the PK blender for feed mixes mixed under the following conditions: 15 min mix with intensifier bar; 60 min mix with intensifier bar; a mix using bar for 5 min then 10 min without the bar; and finally a premix prepared in the Hobart blender followed by a 30 min mix in the PK blender using the intensifier bar. The samples were all analyzed in duplicate. The results appear in Table 4–2. Thus the

Table 4-2.   Results of Homogeneity Study of Dodecyl Alcohol
Ethoxylated/Feed Blends

		Concentration		
Position	15 Min	60 Min	5 Min On/ 10 Min Off	30 Min
TR	1.892%	1.045%	1.092%	1.272%
TL	1.335	1.781	1.210	1.222
B	0.722	1.215	0.104	1.190

optimum mixing time for this material was determined to be 30 min after using a premix.

The PK blender requires a minimum void space of 40% for efficient mixing. This allows all of the material to turn over in a single revolution of the mixer. An objection to the use of the PK blender is based on the narrow loading range of the mixer (60% ± 10%). Loads outside these limits could result in poor mixing. The narrow range results in either waste from overmixing or a loss of time due to having to mix more than one batch.

An 8 qt mixer must be loaded with 4.25 kg of feed. A test group of fifty mice will require approximately 1.75 kg dosed feed per week, which results in a waste of about 2 kg feed per week. If the males and females are receiving the same concentration of material in their diet, the waste is reduced to less than 1 kg. The 16 qt PK blender requires 8.25 kg of feed for proper mixing. A group of fifty male and fifty female rats receiving the same concentration will consume about 15 kg per week. Thus it is necessary to make two mixes, with a waste of approximately 2 kg.

Dosage Solution Preparation

The dosage mixtures in nonfeed vehicles were prepared on a weight/volume or volume/volume basis in glass containers and stirred vigorously with a magnetic or vortex stirrer. With the exception of careless mislabeling of solutions, there have been remarkably few problems with these materials.

Dosage Solution Analysis

The diversity of the materials has presented somewhat of an analytical challenge. Methods range from the direct ultraviolet (UV) measurements, which were used for witch hazel and p-nitrophenol, to argentometric titration for glutaraldehyde and treatment with BSTFA or $POCl_3/PCl_5$ followed by gas chromatography analysis for some of the fatty acid/DEA compounds.

Three compounds have been administered in the animals drinking water (see Table 4-1). Chloramine is one of the more interesting materials and one that presents the biggest challenge. It is used or planned for use in many cities as a replacement for chlorine for disinfecting city water supplies because it reportedly does not cause the formation of as many trihalomethane compounds. This material is not commercially available and must be generated in situ on a daily basis because it is not very stable. The material is generated by preparing a known solution of chlorine water by bubbling chlorine gas through a $Na_2CO_3/NaHCO_3$ buffer solution and titrating with $Fe(NH_4)_2(SO_4)_2$ standard solution and diethylphenylene diamine (DPD) indicator and adding to it a calculated solution of NH_4OH. The material is then titrated using DPD indicator to determine the amount of chloramine and dichloramine present.

Studies run using this material at concentrations ranging from 25 to 1400 ppm indicated it was very unstable, especially at the higher concentrations. Bubbles formed on the surface of the glass, and analyses after 18 hr showed losses up to 40%. A series of studies was run to determine the effect of a number of parameters on the stability of the material: acid washed versus buffer washed versus regular washed glassware; type of bottle cap, Teflon versus rubber versus plastic; physical treatment, undisturbed versus gentle airstream versus shaking; the effect of pouring versus siphoning; colored versus clear glass and the effect of head space. The results of the analyses showed that losses were greatly reduced by washing the glassware with buffer solution, siphoning rather than pouring, and handling as gently as possible. Using these precautions, it has been possible to reduce 24 hr losses to the range of 2.5 to 11% for chloramine concentrations up to 400 ppm.

Chloramine-dosed water from bottles returned from the animal rooms is analyzed monthly to determine the loss of chloramine for that 24-hr period and to determine the level of trihalomethanes formed during the period. In all cases, trihalomethanes have been less than 1 ppb.

PERSONNEL

The dosage/diet preparation technician fills one of the most critical positions in the testing laboratory. A careless or inadvertent mistake by this person could fault a half-million dollar study. GSRI recently had a bad experience when a dosage preparation technician mislabeled vehicle control material intended for a skin-paint study, and the vehicle control animals for a gavage study mistakenly received acetone. Fortunately, the animal care technician stopped dosing when the animals were observed to be reacting to the control material compound, but not before 50 vehicle control animals from that study died. A review indicated that two bottles (male and female) for that particular day were the only ones mislabeled and that those were the only vehicle control solutions prepared that day. Furthermore, it was found that standard operating procedures (SOPs) had not been followed. The SOPs required that all dosages for a given study be prepared together. Because of the consequences of the mistake, the dosage preparation technician was replaced.

It is difficult to recruit, train, and hold qualified persons in this position for several reasons. Most young B.S.-level persons consider the work too menial and the working conditions less than ideal. Also, persons in this position are vulnerable in terms of potential exposure to possible carcinogens or teratogens. Dosage preparation technicians are required to wear disposable protective suits, air-supplied hoods, and must work in pairs. Along with semiannual physical exams, these precautions provide for protection. However, most applicants are young and recent college graduates. The potential exposure hazards are compounded if the females are taking oral contraceptives or if they become pregnant. There is also a risk that a young male's sperm could be damaged.

SUMMARY

The majority of our problems have arisen from two sources: the nature of the test material and personnel. Trade-offs have been made on program requirements to satisfy and solve the material problems. The personnel problems generally evolve around carelessness and/or the ability to recruit, train, and keep well-qualified persons in a critical job.

PART II

Dosage Mixing and Analysis

CHAPTER 5

Methods Development for Mixing Chemicals in Rodent Feed

Gustav O. Kuhn, John J. Rollheiser, and Bruce A. Schworer
Midwest Research Institute, 425 Volker Boulevard,
Kansas City, Missouri 64110

C.W. Jameson
National Toxicology Program, P.O. Box 12233,
Research Triangle Park, North Carolina 27709

Frequently chemicals under study for their toxicological effect on animals are incorporated into feed for dose administration. Investigators prefer this method of dosing animals primarily for its convenience, lower labor requirements, and similarity to human exposure conditions. When this route of administration is employed, obtaining accurately dosed, homogeneous chemical-feed blends is a major concern for the investigator. This chapter considers some of the key factors that influence homogeneity and describes a series of mixing experiments conducted with dosed feeds. The objective of the studies was to develop a simple procedure for producing consistently homogeneous feed blends with the wide variety of chemicals used in studies conducted for the National Toxicology Program (NTP).

FACTORS AFFECTING FEED BLEND HOMOGENEITY

The attainment of a state of apparent homogeneity in a feed blend (that is, a minimum measurable variation in dose concentration between any two sampling points) is influenced by a variety of factors. One of the most important of these is the particle

Special thanks are extended to Lorren Kurtz, Tom Dux, Ted Harrison, and Sue Ann Scheppers for performing the many assays for these studies. The assistance of Kathleen Stelting and Evelyn Murrill in technical review and editing, and statistical interpretation of the results also is gratefully acknowledged.

size of the chemical. Other factors, such as screen profile of the feed, method of blend preparation, and, to a lesser extent, dose concentration, play significant roles in obtaining homogeneous blends. Methods used for sampling and analysis of feed blends also can influence the interpretation of results from homogeneity studies. The following sections present a discussion of these factors and describe feed mixing experiments in which some of these factors were studied.

Chemical Particle Size

An inverse relation would be expected between chemical particle size and homogeneity, whereas dose concentration and homogeneity would be directly related. In actual practice, however, dose concentration is generally fixed within relatively narrow limits for the toxicity study, and chemical particle size plays a dominant role in determining the degree of homogeneity that is possible.

A simple model crystal was used to establish optimum particle size criteria for dosing feed at various levels. The model system (Figure 5–1) assumed a simple rectangular prism shape, with a two-to-one length-to-width ratio. A density of 1.4 g/cc, which is typical for many organic chemicals, also was assumed.

Using the model, weights of individual crystals and numbers of crystals per milligram of chemical were calculated for crystals with widths corresponding to sieve openings for various U.S. Standard (USS) sieves. The calculated values are shown in Table 5–1. The values in Table 5–1 apply only to chemicals with the same crystalline form as the model. If the length-to-width ratio were changed from two-to-one to three-to-one, or if a different crystalline form or density were assumed, the crystals-

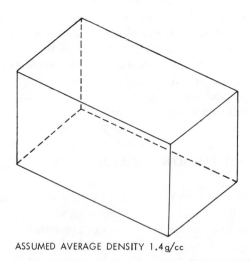

ASSUMED AVERAGE DENSITY 1.4 g/cc

Figure 5–1.   Crystal model.

Table 5-1.   Model Crystal Size-Weight Relationships

Sieve No./Opening (mm)	Single Crystal Weight, Mg	Calculated Crystals per Mg
18/1.00	2.8	0.36
35/0.50	0.35	2.9
40/0.42	0.21	4.8
50/0.30	0.076	13.2
70/0.21	0.026	38.5
100/0.15	0.0095	106
140/0.105	0.0032	308
200/0.074	0.0011	881
270/0.053	0.0004	2,500

per-milligram values shown in the table could be less than one-half the values shown. Also, since no lot of chemical is all one screen size, the actual number of crystals per milligram is a weighted average value depending on the screen analysis profile for that chemical.

Values in Table 5-1 are presented from a different perspective in Table 5-2, which shows the number of particles of chemical calculated to be present in one gram of feed at various dose concentrations when chemicals of different particle sizes are used for dosing. Although calculated values in Tables 5-1 and 5-2 represent optimistic estimates and can be expected to vary significantly if conditions are changed, they were useful in formulating tentative particle size criteria for assuring acceptable homogeneity at various dose concentrations.

These criteria, known in this laboratory as the 99% rule (see Table 5-3), define recommended maximum particle sizes for chemicals used in dosing feed at various concentrations. The table shows, for example, that an investigator dosing feed at the ~ 0.1% level should use chemical with at least 99% passing a USS No. 70 sieve. Table 5-2 shows that chemicals with this particle size will provide 46 particles per g of feed.

Table 5-2.   Number of Crystals per Gram of Feed

Sieve No./Opening (mm)	0.001% Dose	0.01% Dose	0.1% Dose	0.5% Dose
18/1.00		0.04	0.4	2
35/0.50	0.03	0.3	3	15
40/0.42	0.05	0.55	5.5	27
50/0.30	0.13	1.3	13	65
70/0.21	0.46	4.6	46	230
100/0.15	1.0	10.5	105	525
140/0.105	3.5	35	350	1,750
200/0.074	8.4	84	840	4,200
270/0.053	28.6	286	2,860	14,300

Table 5–3. Particle Size Selection Criteria (Minimum % Chemical Required to Pass USS Sieve)

USS Sieve No.	Dose Concentration				
	>0.5%	~0.5%	~0.1%	~0.01%	~0.001%
35	99%				
40		99%			
70			99%		
100				99%	
200					99%

In reality, because chemicals ground to pass a No. 70 sieve normally will contain substantial amounts of material finer than this size, the actual number of particles present will be considerably greater than this value, and producing blends with no more than 1 to 2% variability in dose concentration theoretically should be possible. If, however, a coarser chemical were used (for example, chemical just passing a USS No. 40 sieve), feed dosed at the 0.1% level would contain an estimated 5 to 6 particles per g. In this example, variations of 1 crystal per gm would cause a 16 to 20% variation in dose concentration, which exceeds allowable limits (± 10% of target concentration) specified by the NTP.

Feed Characteristics

The physical state of the feed used to prepare dosed feed blends can have a significant effect on homogeneity, as well as lead to inhomogeneity by sifting during subsequent handling of the dosed feed. Since NIH-07 Rat and Mouse Ration is used widely in

Table 5–4. NIH-07 Feed Physical Data: Typical Screen Analysis

USS Sieve No.	% Retained
16	2.8
20	9.2
30	6.3
40	21.3
60	27.6
80	15.6
100	16.4
PAN	0.8
Total	100.0

Note: Loose bulk density = 0.616 g/ml; packed bulk density = 0.772 g/ml; flow cone angle = 56–60°.

many NTP programs, this feed was examined for physical characteristics that can affect homogeneity. Results of physical measurements made on a typical lot of NIH-07 feed are shown in Table 5–4.

Perhaps of greatest significance are the relatively fine particle size profile and large flow cone angle exhibited by this feed. Relative to the preparation of dosed feeds, these characteristics present both advantages and disadvantages. The data in Table 5–4 indicate that NIH-07 feed has good holding power, that is, it will allow a minimum of sifting out of added chemicals during normal handling. The relatively high flow cone angle indicates that the feed has poor slip characteristics, which tends to make mixing with chemicals difficult. This latter characteristic is especially important when preparing mixes in V-type blenders, which depend on slip for much of their mixing action.

Dose Concentration

The production of homogeneous blends would be expected to be more difficult at low dose levels; however, results obtained in this study and subsequent experience with other low dose level blends prepared for toxicity studies indicate that the procedure developed in this study produces homogeneous blends, even at very low (e.g., ppb) dose levels. Figure 5–2 illustrates a typical homogeneity-concentration relationship. Maximum homogeneity is obtained as dose concentrations approach 100% chemical. As the dose concentration is decreased through the range normally employed in toxicity studies (10%–0.0001%), Figure 5–2 shows that a relatively high degree of homogeneity can still be expected.

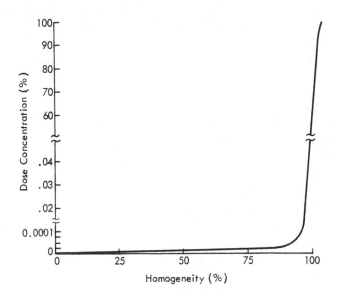

Figure 5–2.   Homogeneity-concentration relationship.

At some unspecified concentration (typically well below the 0.0001% level) apparent homogeneity is seen to fall rapidly, due primarily to factors other than mixing that affect the measurement of homogeneity. Some of these are sample size used for analysis and sensitivity of the analytical method. Theoretically the point of least homogeneity occurs where only one particle of chemical is present in the blend; however, if a sufficient number of particles can be provided and a sensitive analytical method is available, homogeneous mixes can be produced and confirmed, even at very low dose levels. Laboratories in many NTP programs currently produce homogeneous feed blends at 1 ppb dose levels.

PRELIMINARY MIXING STUDIES

To develop a protocol for making homogeneous feed blends, preliminary mixing studies were conducted using a model mixing system to test the effects of varying mixing parameters on blend homogeneity. The goal of these studies was to develop a simple mixing procedure that could be applied to the broad range of chemicals under study by the NTP and which would consistently yield blends with a high degree of homogeneity with a minimum of time and effort for the investigator.

Table 5–5 shows the equipment and conditions used for these initial mixes. Rotenone was chosen as one of the dosing chemicals for the preliminary study because its strong ultraviolet (UV) absorption ($\epsilon = 18{,}300$ at 294 nm) provided the high detectability required for good measurement of inhomogeneity in feed blends. This characteristic also made analysis of a large number of samples possible by a rapid spectrophotometric method.

Preliminary mixing studies with rotenone were conducted by varying mixing times, changing the order of charging the blender, and studying use of the intensifier bar during mixing. When mixing conditions had been tentatively optimized with rotenone, the procedure was evaluated with 4-hydroxyacetanilide at the 2% dose level and with sodium aluminosilicate at the 5% level. These chemicals extended the

Table 5–5.   Preliminary Mixing Studies

Equipment
   Patterson-Kelly Twinshell® blender with pin-type intensifier bar
Conditions
   Batch size, 1500 g
   Premix size, 200 g
   Mixer rotation rate, 20 rpm
   Intensifier bar speed, 3300 rpm
Vehicle
   NIH-07 feed
Chemicals
   Rotenone, 0.05% level
   4-Hydroxyacetanilide, 2% level
   Sodium aluminosilicate, 5% level

performance evaluation for the mixing method over a 100-fold dose concentration range with chemicals of significantly different densities (1.23 to 2.61 g/cc) and crystalline shapes representative of the broad range of chemicals tested by the NTP. It was felt that a method capable of producing homogeneous mixes with these extremes in dose concentration and physical characteristics probably could be broadly applicable to chemicals for the NTP.

Once these mixing parameters had been tentatively defined, the general applicability of the procedure was confirmed in extended mixing studies with eight liquid and twenty-two solid chemicals.

Feed Blending Procedures

1. *Premix preparation, solid chemicals:* Individual feed blends tested for homogeneity in the preliminary phase of the mixing study were prepared from 200 g premixes produced as illustrated in Figure 5–3. The required weight of chemical for a 1500 g feed blend was transferred to a 600 ml stainless-steel beaker and intimately mixed by spatula with an equal amount of feed. More feed was added and mixed in, each time doubling the weight of the mixture until the total 200 g premix had been made.

The importance of obtaining an intimate, thoroughly dispersed blend of the chemical with feed in the first step of the premix preparation cannot be overemphasized. Some chemicals that are supplied as finely ground powders by the manufacturer frequently tend to agglomerate into relatively firm masses during storage of the bulk chemical. If these masses are not completely crushed in the first step of making a premix, they usually will not be crushed in subsequent blending operations and will cause significant variability in final dosed feed blends. Occasionally it may be necessary to grind the chemical with feed in a mortar in the initial premix preparation step to ensure uniform distribution in the blend.

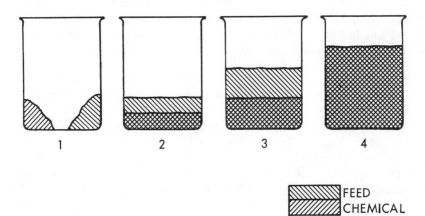

FEED
CHEMICAL

Figure 5–3.   Premix preparation.

Blends to be dosed at low concentrations ($< 0.01\%$) with solid chemicals may require use of a modified premix preparation procedure. For these premixes, the required weight of chemical is mixed thoroughly with small amounts (~ 1 g) of feed flour (feed screened through a USS No. 100 sieve) until ~ 10 g of mixture is obtained; then the premix is completed as described above.

Dusty or fluffy chemicals may require a larger premix (up to 25% of total blend weight, depending on dose level) in order to obtain a premix with satisfactory physical characteristics (low dustiness, free flowing). Sodium aluminosilicate evaluated at the 5% level in the preliminary studies was an example of such a change in premix size. This chemical required an increase in premix weight to 400 g for addition to the 1500 g feed blend. As a general rule, premixes should contain at least 50% feed diluent by weight to obtain adequate distribution of the chemical in the final feed blend. Premixes should never constitute less than 10% of the total blend weight.

2. *Premix preparation, liquid chemicals:* Experimental work conducted with liquid chemicals showed that premixes with feed required a slightly modified procedure from that used for solid chemicals. For these mixes, a quantity of feed equal to about four times the weight of chemical needed for the batch was first placed in a stainless-steel beaker; the required weight of chemical was then absorbed onto the feed. The agglomerates of feed and chemical were thoroughly rubbed out against the side of the beaker with a spatula. More feed was added in increments of 50 to 100 g and mixed in until the desired final weight of premix was reached. The importance of eliminating feed-chemical agglomerates in the initial mix cannot be overemphasized.

Premixes containing small amounts of liquid chemicals (< 1 g) for making feed blends at low dose concentrations required a special preparation procedure. A modified procedure was required because feed particles coated with a liquid chemical behave like single crystals of chemicals in a blend. If relatively coarse feed particles are coated with a small amount of liquid chemical, frequently too few particles of feed are coated to obtain adequate distribution (and therefore homogeneity) in the blend. This condition is tantamount to using coarse granular chemicals for dosing feed at low concentrations.

In order to ensure a sufficient number of coated feed particles for blends at low dose concentrations, the small weight of liquid chemical used is first absorbed onto feed flour and then blended with additional feed. The following procedure has been used successfully with liquid chemicals:

1.   Accurately weigh the required amount of liquid chemical for the batch into a 150 ml beaker.
2.   Weigh an amount of feed needed for the premix in a separate beaker.
3.   Transfer ~ 100 g of the feed to a USS No. 100 sieve and shake until ~ 10 g of feed flour has been collected.
4.   Add ~ 1 g of the feed flour to the beaker containing chemical and mix intimately by spatula. Continue adding 1 to 2 g increments of flour with mixing after each addition until the mixture weight is ~ 10 g.

5.   Transfer the mixture to a larger beaker and add the coarse fraction reserved on the screen in increments of 25 to 50 g, mixing after each addition.

6.   Add the remaining feed and mix thoroughly.

Liquid chemicals added to feed at dose concentrations above 2% usually required larger premixes (> 15% of total blend weight) to obtain reasonably free-flowing and nonsticky premixes. Premixes constituting as much as 25 to 30% of the total blend weight generally were required for liquid chemicals added to feed at concentrations up to 5% by weight.

3. *Blender charging:*   During the preliminary mixing studies with rotenone, 4-hydroxyacetanilide, and sodium aluminosilicate, several methods of introducing the chemical into the blender were tested. A premix of the chemical with feed was prepared initially and added either all into the bottom of the blender, all into one shell, or loaded sandwich style, as shown in Figure 5-4. From these experiments it was determined that sandwich-style charging gave the best homogeneity in the shortest mixing time.

To prepare the blends in sandwich style, about half of the feed required for the batch was placed evenly in the bottom of the blender (see Figure 5-4). The premix was then added in roughly equal portions to both blender shells and spread evenly over the feed. Residual premix in the beaker was purged by stirring 100 or 200 g of feed (depending on premix size) in the beaker and transferring this purge feed to the

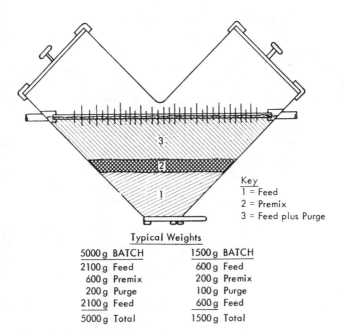

Key
1 = Feed
2 = Premix
3 = Feed plus Purge

Typical Weights

5000 g BATCH	1500 g BATCH
2100 g Feed	600 g Feed
600 g Premix	200 g Premix
200 g Purge	100 g Purge
2100 g Feed	600 g Feed
5000 g Total	1500 g Total

Figure 5-4.   Blender charging.

blender. The balance of the feed required to complete the batch was finally layered over the premix, and the ports were sealed prior to mixing.

The batch sizes shown in Figure 5-4 are maximum weights recommended for charging Patterson-Kelly Twinshell® blenders of 4 qt and 8 qt capacity. Since the primary mixing action of this type of blender depends on slipping action and NIH-07 feed exhibits relatively poor slip characteristics, filling this type of machine above the optimum load level results in a sharp decrease in mixing efficiency. According to the manufacturer, V-type blenders should never be charged above the axis of the intensifier bar.

4. *Mixing:*   In the preliminary phase of these mixing studies, twenty-one individual blends were prepared using the three chemicals, and two parameters (mixing time and use of the intensifier bar) were studied for their effect on final blend homogeneity.

Table 5-6 gives details of the mixing conditions studied with rotenone in feed at a dose concentration of 0.05%. Table 5-7 shows the analytical results from these blends, and Figure 5-5 presents the same data in graphic form. From Figure 5-5 it is apparent that conditions used for blend 5 gave optimum homogeneity. Blend 6 demonstrated that mixing for more than 15 min did not improve homogeneity. A comparison of results obtained on blends 3, 4, and 5 indicated that continuous use of the intensifier bar had an adverse effect on homogeneity but that some use of the intensifier bar is desirable. The results for blend 7 show the necessity for charging the blender sandwich style.

Blends prepared with 4-hydroxyacetanilide in feed at the 2% level were directed at confirming several observations made on rotenone blends. Table 5-8 shows the various mixing conditions studied, Table 5-9 gives the analytical results obtained, and Figure 5-6 presents the results in graphic form. In these mixes, the value of sandwich-style loading was again demonstrated. Mixes 3, 4, and 5 are essentially repeat blends, which show reproducibility of the mixing method in the hands of more

Table 5-6.   Rotenone Feed Blend Mixing Conditions (0.05% Dose Level)

Blend	Mixing Time, Min	Special Conditions
1	5	Intensifier bar in operation
2	10	Intensifier bar in operation
3	15	Intensifier bar in operation
4	15	Intensifier bar OFF during mixing
5	15	Intensifier bar ON for first 5 min only
6	30	Intensifier bar ON for first 5 min only
7	15	Repeat of blend 5, with premix loaded in one end of blender
8	15	Repeat of blend 5, using chemical passing 200 mesh sieve
9	15	Intensifier bar operated for 30 sec at 5, 10, and 15 min intervals

Note: Premix size: 200 g.

Table 5-7. Analytical Results for Rotenone Feed Blends

Blend	Right Shell, %	Left Shell, %	Bottom Port, %	Max Δ% between Ports
1	0.0561 ± 0.0010	0.0480 ± 0.0005	0.0516 ± 0.0000	0.0081
2	0.0503 ± 0.0004	0.0469 ± 0.0002	0.0485 ± 0.0001	0.0034
3	0.0526 ± 0.0036	0.0460 ± 0.0005	0.0514 ± 0.0053	0.0066
4	0.0510 ± 0.0013	0.0490 ± 0.0005	0.0505 ± 0.0004	0.0020
5	0.0502 ± 0.0002	0.0502 ± 0.0002	0.0500 ± 0.0008	0.0002
6	0.0504 ± 0.0006	0.0508 ± 0.0010	0.0496 ± 0.0008	0.0012
7	0.0481 ± 0.0000	0.0519 ± 0.0035	0.0494 ± 0.0006	0.0038
8	0.0499 ± 0.0000	0.0497 ± 0.0000	0.0493 ± 0.0000	0.0006
9	0.0508 ± 0.0001	0.0495 ± 0.0003	0.0498 ± 0.0001	0.0013

Note: Pooled standard deviation: ± 0.0015%.

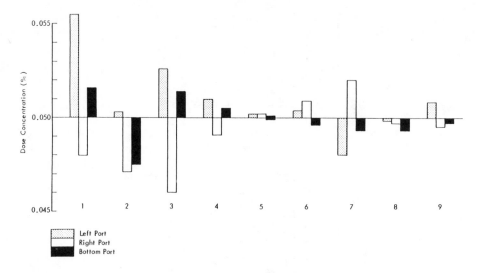

Figure 5-5. Homogeneity of rotenone—feed mixes (0.05% level).

than one operator. Blend 6 was an attempt to produce the most homogeneous blend possible with this equipment. Following the 15 min mixing, the blend was discharged and briefly hand mixed. The batch was then returned to the blender for an additional 5 min of blending. Table 5-9 shows that excellent homogeneity was obtained for blends 3 through 6; variation in dose concentrations for these blends was comparable to the variation of the analytical method.

Blends made with sodium aluminosilicate were produced at the highest dose concentration used in the preliminary mixing studies (5%). The fine, powdery character of this inorganic chemical made it a good candidate for testing various mixing

Table 5-8. 4-Hydroxyacetanilide Feed Blend Mixing Conditions (2% Dose Level)

Blend	Mixing Time, Min	Special Conditions
1	15	Intensifier bar OFF during mixing
2	15	Premix loaded in bottom of mixer, intensifier bar in operation first 5 min only
3	15	Premix loaded sandwich style, intensifier ON first 5 min only
4	15	Repeat of 3
5	15	Repeat of 3, different day and operator
6	15	Mixed 5 min with intensifier bar ON, then 5 min with bar OFF; blend discharged, hand mixed 1 min, then returned to blender and mixed 5 min more with intensifier bar OFF

Note: Premix size: 200 g.

Table 5-9. Analytical Results for 4-Hydroxyacetanilide Feed Blends

Blend	Right Shell, %	Left Shell, %	Bottom Port, %	Max Δ% between Ports
1	1.98 ± 0.04	2.00 ± 0.03	2.00 ± 0.04	0.02
2	2.01 ± 0.03	2.02 ± 0.04	2.05 ± 0.02	0.04
3	1.99 ± 0.00	2.00 ± 0.01	2.02 ± 0.00	0.03
4	2.00 ± 0.02	2.00 ± 0.01	2.02 ± 0.03	0.02
5	2.00 ± 0.02	2.00 ± 0.01	2.02 ± 0.03	0.02
6	1.99 ± 0.00	2.01 ± 0.02	2.00 ± 0.01	0.02

Note: Pooled standard deviation: ± 0.024%.

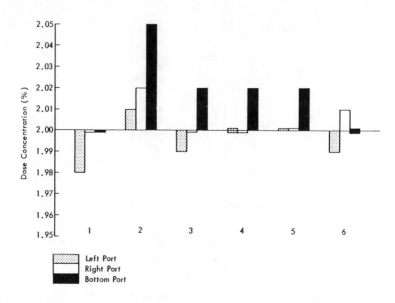

Figure 5-6. Homogeneity of 4-hydroxyacetanilide—feed mixes (2% level)

parameters by the tentative mixing method. The mixing parameters studied are described in Table 5-10. Analytical results on samples from these mixes are shown in Table 5-11; Figure 5-7 shows the homogeneity data in graphic form. Results from these studies confirmed even more dramatically the observation seen in the rotenone mixes—that prolonged operation of the intensifier bar causes increasing inhomogeneity with extended mixing time. The exact mechanism of this phenomenon is not clearly understood. It is theorized that in the early stages of mixing, the intensifier bar effectively disperses the chemical/feed premix throughout the blend. However, as the intense whipping action of the pins on the intensifier bar (rotating at ~3,300 rpm) continues to disperse the feed in the blender, a winnowing effect may result, thereby promoting in unmixing and the development of inhomogeneity (see results for mixes 3 and 4 in Figure 5-7).

Table 5-10. Sodium Aluminosilicate Feed Blend Mixing Conditions (5% Dose)

Blend	Mixing Time, Min	Special Conditions
1	10	Intensifier bar in operation during mixing
2	15	Intensifier bar in operation during mixing
3	20	Intensifier bar in operation during mixing
4	30	Intensifier bar in operation during mixing
5	10	Intensifier bar in operation first 5 min only
6	15	Intensifier bar in operation first 5 min only

Note: Premix size: 400 g for all blends.

Table 5-11. Analytical Results for Sodium Aluminosilicate Feed Blends

Blend	Right Shell, %	Left Shell, %	Bottom Port, %	Max Δ% between Ports
1	4.82 ± 0.05	4.48 ± 0.33	4.47 ± 0.26	0.35
2	4.69 ± 0.05	4.51 ± 0.13	4.41 ± 0.12	0.28
3	4.78 ± 0.05	4.84 ± 0.05	4.31 ± 0.10	0.53
4	4.59 ± 0.06	5.08 ± 0.16	4.13 ± 0.00	0.95
5	4.87 ± 0.10	5.10 ± 0.10	5.07 ± 0.02	0.23
6	4.85 ± 0.00	4.84 ± 0.02	4.83 ± 0.02	0.02

Note: Pooled standard deviation: ± 0.11%.

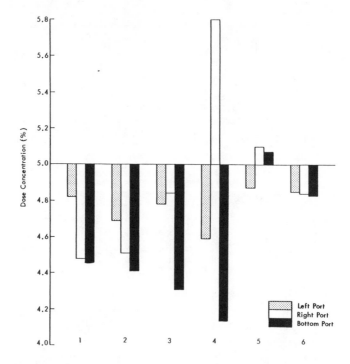

Figure 5-7.   Homogeneity of sodium aluminosilicate—feed mixes (5% level)

On the basis of observations made on the twenty-one blends from these preliminary mixing studies, conditions for producing homogeneous blends were tentatively defined as:

1.   Use chemical with particle size meeting the 99% rule (Table 5-3) for the desired dose concentration.
2.   Use chemical/feed premix constituting at least 10% of total blend weight.
3.   Charge premix into blender sandwich style (Figure 5-4).
4.   Operate intensifier bar for first 5 min of mixing only.
5.   Use total blending time of 15 min.

Subsequently these mixing conditions were applied to the preparation of blends involving thirty different chemicals.

HOMOGENEITY EVALUATION

Determination of the effectiveness of mixing in the preliminary phase of these studies was based on the measurement of homogeneity. Since it was not practical to analyze the total contents of each blend to obtain a complete distribution profile for each chemical, measurement of homogeneity had to be based on a relatively small number of samples drawn from selected locations in the blender. With this limitation in mind, the importance of understanding the effect of sampling and analysis variables on homogeneity results is obvious.

Sampling Methods

Feed blends produced in the preliminary mixing studies were sampled by two methods. Method 1 was used for the majority of mixes produced in both the preliminary phase and extended studies. Method 2 was performed to verify that results obtained by method 1 adequately represented the homogeneity of the blends.

- Method 1: After mixing, approximately 50 g of the blend was sampled by spatula from each of the three blender ports and sealed in individual 4 oz screw cap jars. Duplicate 10 g portions of sample from each port were weighed into 200 ml centrifuge bottles for the analysis. Homogeneity was determined by comparing mean analytical results determined for samples from each of the three ports.
- Method 2: After mixing, the batch was divided into thirds by discharging ~500 g of blend into three 1 liter beakers. The feed in each beaker was leveled, and three 10 g core samples were taken at one hundred and twenty degree intervals about 1 cm from the wall of each beaker (9 samples total) as shown in Figure 5-8. The samples were accurately weighed into 200 ml centrifuge bottles and

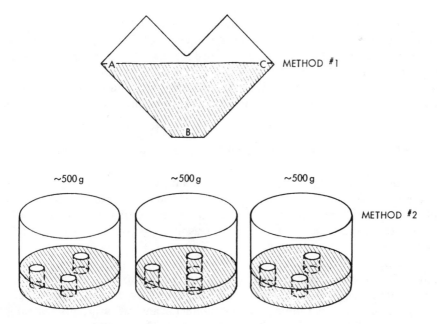

Figure 5-8. Sampling procedures.

analyzed. Mean values of analyses on these samples were used to assess homogeneity. Comparative homogeneity evaluations by methods 1 and 2 were performed with blends containing 4-hydroxyacetanilide at the 2% level.

Since homogeneity results obtained by method 2 were not significantly different from results obtained by method 1 and because method 2 was more time-consuming, all subsequent sampling of blends for homogeneity analysis was by method 1.

Analytical Methods

Rotenone samples (10 ± 0.01 g in 200 ml centrifuge bottles) were extracted by shaking for 1 hr with 100 ml of reagent grade acetonitrile. After clarifying the extracts by centrifuging for 5 min, 10 ml aliquots were diluted to 50 ml with acetonitrile. The absorbance of the solutions was measured spectrophotometrically versus acetonitrile at 294 nm. Sample absorbance readings were corrected for the mean feed blank absorbance prior to calculating concentrations of rotenone.

Dosed feed samples containing 4-hydroxyacetanilide were extracted with methanol, following the procedure described for rotenone. Aliquots of the extracts (2 ml) were diluted to 100 ml with methanol, and the absorbance of the diluted solutions was measured spectrophotometrically at 248 nm. Sample absorbance readings were corrected for the mean feed blank absorbance prior to calculating concentrations of chemical in the samples.

Samples (5 ± 0.01 g) of feed blend dosed with sodium aluminosilicate were ashed overnight at 575°C in previously ignited, cooled, and weighed (± 0.1 mg) porcelain crucibles. The ash weights obtained for the dosed feed samples were corrected for the mean ash content of the undosed feed. The amount of added sodium aluminosilicate in the blend was then determined from the difference in ash weights using a mean determined ash value for sodium aluminosilicate of $84.8 \pm 0.2\%$ ($n = 6$).

Estimation of Analytical Method Precision

The accurate assessment of homogeneity in feed blends requires a knowledge of the precision of the analytical method. To establish that a mix is inhomogeneous, one must show that the variations between sample concentrations measured at various points exceed the variation that can be reasonably attributed to the analytical method.

In the case of rotenone, the precision of the analytical method was established initially from results obtained on six solution-spiked 10 g portions of feed, a situation in which inhomogeneity is not a variable. This precision estimate was then compared with results obtained by running a similar number of analyses using different sample weights of a well-homogenized rotenone-feed blend. The objective of these comparisons was to confirm that valid analytical precision estimates could be obtained from replicate analyses on feed blends. The data shown in Table 5–12 indicate that valid precision estimates can be obtained if the sample size for replicates taken from the blends is greater than 5 g (1.4% versus 1.8% RSD for blends versus solution spikes). However, results of replicate 2 g feed blend samples, also shown in Table 5–12, indicate that this sample size cannot be used to obtain a valid precision estimate (1.4% RSD versus 7.4% for 2 g samples).

In view of the rotenone study, the precision of the analytical methods for the extended studies was estimated from the pooled standard deviation for replicate analyses on 10 g samples removed from a 50 g grab sample taken at each blender port. Thus, the precision of each method was obtained by pooling data from three sets of triplicates.

Precision estimates were then used to evaluate homogeneity of the blends from the extended mixing study, using standard statistical mean comparison techniques. To do this, the maximum variation between means (max $\Delta\%$) at the three sampling points was compared to the test variability limit (TVL), calculated at the 95% confidence level:

$$\text{TVL} = \pm\, t_{95\%}\, S_p \sqrt{\frac{N_1 + N_2}{N_1 N_2}}$$

where: $t_{95\%}$ = critical value for t at 95% confidence level for ($N_1 = N_2 - 2$) degrees of freedom

S_p = pooled standard deviation for the method obtained by pooling all S passing the F test

N_1 and N_2 = number of replicates used in calculating the means compared between sampling points (i.e., $N_1 = N_2 = 3$)

Using these data, homogeneity of the various blends was assessed by comparing max $\Delta\%$ to TVL. If the max $\Delta\%$ exceeded TVL, the variations between values at the two ports could not reasonably be attributed to analytical method variation, and

Table 5–12. Effect of Sample Size on Estimated Precision: Rotenone

Replicate Number	Wet Spiked Feed 10 g Samples	Feed Blend 2 g Samples	Feed Blend 5 g Samples	Feed Blend 10 g Samples
1	0.0558	0.0494	0.0491	0.0489
2	0.0570	0.0482	0.0494	0.0506
3	0.0557	0.0502	0.0503	0.0497
4	0.0570	0.0506	0.0505	0.0507
5	0.0552	0.0510	0.0487	0.0504
6	0.0578	0.0450	0.0493	0.0498
S	0.0010	0.0037	0.0007	0.0007
RSD	1.8%	7.4%	1.4%	1.4%

the blends could be judged inhomogeneous. For instance, using this criterion, the results for extended mixing studies with liquid chemicals (Table 5-13) indicate homogeneity (max $\Delta\% <$ TVL) for all chemicals except d-carvone, with only a barely significant difference for d-carvone.

EXTENDED MIXING STUDIES

The recommended mixing method was further tested in extended mixing studies on blends prepared with thirty additional chemicals—eight liquid and twenty-two solid chemicals—with dose concentrations ranging from 5 to 50,000 ppm. This evaluation used the mixing conditions developed in the preliminary phase of these studies and sampling method 1.

Homogeneity evaluations were made by comparing means of triplicate determinations on samples from each blender port. Results from blends made with liquid chemicals are shown in Table 5-13. Table 5-14 shows the analytical results for blends made with solid chemicals. These results confirmed the effectiveness and general applicability of the recommended mixing conditions.

DISCUSSION

Mixing studies conducted on twenty-one feed blends containing rotenone, 4-hydroxyacetanilide, and sodium aluminosilicate at dose concentrations ranging from 0.05% to 5% were used initially to evaluate the effect of various mixing parameters on homogeneity. On the basis of results from these experimental blends, mixing parameters for obtaining homogeneous blends in a minimum of time were defined tentatively. Of the various mixing parameters investigated, perhaps the most unique observation was seen in blends with solid chemicals where continuous operation of the intensifier bar during the mixing period actually contributed to the development of inhomogeneity. Although continuous use of the intensifier bar had an adverse effect, use of this accessory during the first 5 min of mixing was shown to be beneficial in rapidly dispersing the chemical in the blender.

By employing a model crystal, criteria based on particle size and weight relationships were formulated. These criteria served as guidelines for recommending the degree of fineness for chemicals being added to feed at various dose concentrations. The rationale behind these criteria was to provide feed blends at any dose concentration with at least 50 particles of chemical per g, using as the size basis the coarsest fraction allowable by the 99% rule shown in Table 5-3. Theoretically, chemicals meeting these criteria should permit the preparation of feed blends with no more than 1 to 2% variability in dose concentration.

To confirm the effectiveness of the tentatively established mixing parameters and particle size criteria, blends with thirty chemicals were prepared and analyzed for homogeneity. Homogeneity determinations on feed blends made with twenty-two

Table 5-13. Homogeneity Results: Extended Studies with Liquid Chemicals (Dose Concentrations as % Chemical, w/w ± S)

Chemical	Left Shell[a]	Right Shell[a]	Bottom Port[a]	Pooled S	Maximum Δ (%)	TVL (95% CL)
β-Cadinene	2.00 ± 0.010	1.99 ± 0.010	2.00 ± 0.015	0.012	0.01	0.024
d-Carvone	0.951 ± 0.009	0.964 ± 0.005	0.953 ± 0.003	0.006	0.013	0.012
Dichlorovos	0.0587 ± 0.0005	0.0594 ± 0.0012	0.0590 ± 0.0001	0.0008	0.0007	0.0016
Di-(2-ethylhexyl) phthalate	0.603 ± 0.008	0.605 ± 0.010	0.608 ± 0.002	0.007	0.005	0.014
Diethyl phthalate	4.71 ± 0.035	4.74 ± 0.023	4.78 ± 0.052	0.039	0.07	0.078
o-Nitroanisole	0.383 ± 0.003	0.386 ± 0.003	0.384 ± 0.002	0.003	0.003	0.006
Polysorbate 80	4.91 ± 0.028	4.90 ± 0.022	4.91 ± 0.048	0.035	0.01	0.070
2, 6-Xylidine	0.981 ± 0.008	0.973 ± 0.008	0.973 ± 0.005	0.007	0.008	0.014

[a]Triplicate samples.

Table 5-14. Homogeneity Results: Extended Studies with Solid Chemicals

Chemical	Dose Concentration as % Chemical, $w/w \pm S$			Pooled S (%)	Maximum Δ% between Ports	TVL (95% CL)
	Left Shell	Right Shell	Bottom Port			
1-amino-2,4-dibromoanthraquinone	0.200 ± 0.001(s)	0.200 ± 0.002(s)	0.204 ± 0.002	0.002	0.004	0.004
2-amino-5-nitrophenol	0.596 ± 0.000	0.594 ± 0.010	0.596 ± 0.012	0.010	0.002	0.020
DL-amphetamine sulfate	0.050 ± 0.001	0.050 ± 0	0.050 ± 0	0.0006	0.000	0.002
Boric acid	0.097 ± 0.001	0.098 ± 0.002	0.099 ± 0.001	0.001	0.002	0.002
Chlorpromazine-HCl	0.0988 ± 0.001	0.1002 ± 0.002	0.1003 ± 0	0.0001	0.0015	0.0002
Chlorendic acid	0.101 ± 0.001	0.098 ± 0.001	0.101 ± 0.002	0.001	0.003	0.002
C.I. Pigment Red No. 3	0.0979 ± 0.017	0.989 ± 0.005	0.991 ± 0.009	0.011	0.012	0.022
C.I. Pigment Red No. 23	1.00 ± 0	1.00 ± 0.01	1.00 ± 0	0.006	0.000	0.012
4,4'-diamino-2,2'-stilbenedisulfonic acid	1.003 ± 0.003	0.979 ± 0.029	0.978 ± 0.010	0.018	0.025	0.036
Diphenhydramine-HCl	0.100 ± 0.002	0.098 ± 0.001	0.101 ± 0.002	0.002	0.003	0.004
Methyldopa sesquihydrate	0.499 ± 0.016	0.500 ± 0.020	0.504 ± 0.010	0.016	0.005	0.032
Nitrofurazone	0.151 ± 0.002	0.152 ± 0.002	0.151 ± 0.001	0.002	0.001	0.004
Nitrofurantoin	0.197 ± 0.005	0.198 ± 0.006	0.196 ± 0.002	0.005	0.002	0.010
Oxytetracycline-HCl	0.989 ± 0.007	0.974 ± 0.010	0.968 ± 0.009	0.009	0.021	0.018
Pentaerythritol tetranitrate	0.0105 ± 0.0002	0.0103 ± 0.0004	0.0104 ± 0.0003	0.0003	0.0002	0.0006
Phenylbutazone	0.508 ± 0.010	0.510 ± 0.058	0.509 ± 0.014	0.035	0.002	0.070
Probenecid	0.988 ± 0.013	1.007 ± 0.005	1.014 ± 0.004	0.008	0.026	0.016
Quercetin	0.999 ± 0.004	0.997 ± 0.002	0.998 ± 0.005	0.004	0.002	0.008
Reserpine	4.98 ± 0.10[a]	5.11 ± 0.21[a]	5.1 ± 0.22[a]	0.18[a]	0.18[a]	0.36[a]
Rhodamine 6G	1.02 ± 0.000	1.03 ± 0.006	1.00 ± 0.017	0.010	0.030	0.020
Roxarsone	0.0298 ± 0.0005	0.0302 ± 0.0006	0.0302 ± 0.0010	0.0007	0.0004	0.0014
Sucrose	4.98 ± 0.081	4.91 ± 0.062	5.02 ± 0.115	0.089	0.11	0.178

[a] Results as parts per million.

solid chemicals bracketing dose concentrations of 5 to 50,000 ppm exhibited maximum deviations in concentration (max $\Delta\%$) ranging from 0.1% to 3.54%, with the highest deviation at the 5 ppm level. Blends made with eight liquid chemicals exhibited maximum deviations in concentration ranging from 0.05% to 1.48%. When these max $\Delta\%$ values between means at the various sampling points in the blends were compared with analytical method variability at the 95% confidence level, the blends produced by the recommended mixing procedure were judged homogeneous in the majority of cases.

CONCLUSION

Results from these studies suggest that if the recommended mixing procedure is used, homogeneous chemical-feed blends can be achieved, even at very low dose levels.

CHAPTER 6

Formulations of Insoluble and Immiscible Test Agents in Liquid Vehicles for Toxicity Testing

J.M. Fitzgerald and V.F. Boyd
Department of Chemistry, Litton Bionetics, Inc.,
5516 Nicholson Lane, Kensington, Maryland 20895

A.G. Manus
Department of Toxicology, Litton Bionetics, Inc.,
1330 Piccard Drive, Rockville, Maryland 20854

Administration of test articles to rodents by gavage is a preferred method of ensuring a precisely measured dose. Also, gavage is sometimes useful for administration of test articles that yield unsatisfactory formulations in feed vehicles (for example, if they are unstable or nonhomogeneous). In some studies, gavage administration is required for technical reasons not related to the difficulty in formulating in the vehicle chosen; for example, if results from bioassay of several closely related chemicals are to be compared, a common vehicle simplifies matters. Furthermore, liquid formulations may be necessitated by sensitivity of the test chemical to light, heat, moisture, or other factors even when it is not soluble in (or miscible with) the vehicle required for the study.

Verification that rodents are, in fact, dosed precisely when the test chemical is insoluble or immiscible in the vehicle requires the three following key steps:

1. *Chemical analysis for correctness of formulation at intended concentrations.* The sample taken for analysis must be representative of the entire batch of formulation. In our experience, the bulk formulation is often subaliquotted into smaller containers; the daily dosing aliquots are then resuspended by appropriate methods just prior to use for dosing animals. In such a case, the analytical sample we prefer is an additional aliquot taken after all daily dosing aliquots have been taken. In this way, the analytical sample represents a worst case of separation of chemical and vehicle after suspension.

2. *Resuspension of the analytical sample.* The analytical sample has usually separated by the time it arrives at the laboratory. If the sample was representative of

the bulk at the time taken, obviously some effort to resuspend the entire analytical sample must be made prior to taking accurately measured subsamples. The resuspension technique used on the analytical sample may approximate the method(s) used to suspend the original bulk formulations, but the volume of sample will be much smaller than that of the total preparation. We have found suspensions of an insoluble material of varying particle size to be particularly difficult to subsample.

    3. *Confirmation of the concentration at the time of dosing.*   Correctness of concentration of suspensions at the time of dosing must be confirmed by chemical analysis. The sampling strategy at this stage must consider whether continuous, intermittent, or no resuspension procedures are used during dosing. Samples are best taken directly from the syringes used for the administration to animals.

DISCUSSION

Formulation methods, analytical sampling procedures, and analytical results for three chemicals will be used to illustrate application of the three steps listed. Two of the chemicals discussed are from the National Toxicology Program/National Cancer Institute bioassay program. One is a liquid and one a solid. The vehicle for these chemicals (corn oil) was selected to permit comparison with other chemicals on study also administered in this vehicle. A third chemical, a photosensitive solid which is insoluble in water, is also discussed; this commercial product was administered to rats in a water vehicle to parallel an already completed mouse study using the same vehicle.

The Homogenizer

A commercially available homogenizer-blender turned out to be a key piece of equipment used for successful formulation and analysis of all three chemicals. This device combines ultrasonic vibrations with mechanical shearing action to homogenize, disperse, and emulsify insoluble material into the vehicle. A high-speed rotor, which also serves as the ultrasound transducer, pulls formulation materials between itself and an outer stator, which contains slots with knife edges. The blades shear and crush material at the same time that ultrasonically induced cavitation occurs. Very small quantities of heat are produced, yet good homogenization occurs within a minute or so, even with deciliter quantities of formulation. For larger volume formulations, a magnetic stirrer and stir bar are used to lift materials off the bottom of the beaker up to within range of the homogenizer probe. Placing the probe at a slant rather than vertically in the cylindrical container also facilitates good mixing. A second homogenizer was used for some formulations to resuspend the sample submitted for analysis prior to subsampling. Reblending is not always necessary, however; data show that vigorous shaking works as well as homogenization for some chemical/vehicle combinations.

A wide variety of rotor-stator probes is available, including probes for anaerobic or high-viscosity formulations. The homogenizing device was developed and patented by a scientific group in Switzerland [1]. Licenses of the patent rights to several commercial instrument organizations have resulted in two U.S. sources of homogenizer drives and probes, Tekmar Co. [1] and Brinkmann Instruments [2]. Brinkmann sells a device bearing the nameplate Polytron®; this is a name commonly used in laboratories to refer to any of these devices. The Tekmar device is called Tissumiser®.

Although a variety of probes, motors, and speed controllers is available, the devices are not inexpensive, and some thought before purchase as to size of formulations to be prepared and minimum number of units needed for all operations can result in substantial savings. The probes are precision machined and clean up easily by running briefly in organic solvents or water, so only one probe of a given size is needed for each work station. Probes range in cost from $500 to $1000. Packages of motor, speed control, and stand ranges between $1000 and $1700. Of course, costs of homogenizers are small when compared to total costs of running successful ninety-day or two-year chronic studies.

Liquid-Liquid Suspensions

The first test chemical used was DMMP (dimethylmethylphosphonate), a nerve gas simulator. This chemical is soluble in corn oil up to about 72 mg/ml; dose levels as high as 615 mg/ml (subchronic) and 308 mg/ml (chronic) were needed. Corn oil was used as vehicle because two other related chemicals, DMHP (dimethyl hydrogen phosphate) and DMMPA (dimethyl morpholinophosphoramidate) were also on study and were being dosed in corn oil; DMHP and DMMPA are both more soluble in corn oil than the dose levels required (50 and 180 mg/ml, respectively). See Table 6-1 for a comparison of the three compounds.

For the rat subchronic study, formulations of DMMP between 38.4 and 615 mg/ml were prepared using the homogenizer. Daily dosing aliquots were stored in 140 ml plastic, screw-cap cups and an analytical sample was taken last. Resuspension

Table 6-1. Corn Oil Solubilities and Formulation Concentrations Required for Three Related Organophosphorus Compounds in Chronic Studies

Compound	Solubility in Corn Oil	Highest Required Dosing Concentrations
DMMP	72 mg/ml	308 mg/ml[a]
DMHP	>> 50	50
DMMPA	>180	180

[a]Highest concentration for 90-day subchronic was 615 mg/ml.

of the analytical sample was found to be equally good using either the homogenizer or vigorous shaking by hand just prior to sampling. Positive displacement 100 to 500 μl pipets were used to measure gavage aliquots before extraction and GC determination of DMMP.

On each day of animal dosing, the contents of one 140 ml screw-cap cup per dose level were rehomogenized vigorously and transported to the animal room so that dosing began within 30 min of rehomogenization. In the animal room, the contents of a given cup were shaken vigorously by hand with a magnetic stirring bar in the cup; then the cup was placed immediately in a wooden jig, which located the cup precisely on top of a magnetic stirrer, already rotating. The cap was removed and the stirring rate increased until a vortex in the center was seen. (The animal room technicians had to be trained to use magnetic stirrers because of their lack of previous "hands on" experience.) Predosing and postdosing samples, taken directly from dosing syringes on days 1 and 7 following formulation, were all well within ±10% of target at all dose levels (see Table 6–2).

The data in Table 6–2 resulted from a combination of detailed written instructions for formulations and dosing personnel and close scientific supervision of the procedures. Both the principal investigator and the chemist in charge of the DMMP project were physically present for the critical operations of the start of the study. We believe that detailed written instructions and very close supervision are necessary for a study of this nature.

An overview of the strategy developed during the subchronic study, and used for the chronic studies of DMMP, may be outlined in the following way:

1. *Formulation steps*
    a. Combine required volumes of DMMP and corn oil.
    b. Use a magnetic stirrer to lift DMMP up within the range of the Polytron®.
    c. Homogenize for several minutes at a very high motor speed.
    d. Aliquot rapidly into 140 ml plastic, labeled cups. Pour off sample for chemical analysis last.
2. *Daily resuspension (may be omitted if analytical data show this step to be unnecessary)*
    a. Take each cup to be used that day and homogenize for at least 1 min at medium speed. Transport to animal room at once.
3. *Prior to dosing, in animal room:*
    a. Shake suspension vigorously.
    b. Use brisk magnetic stirring; look for vortex to indicate top-to-bottom mix.
    c. Take analytical samples directly from dosing syringe as scheduled (pre-, post-, or mid-dosing samples may be taken).

Data collected at the start of the chronic studies (308 mg/ml maximum DMMP concentration) showed that daily rehomogenization was not needed; vigorous shaking prior to and magnetic stirring during dosing resulted in correct concentrations even sixteen weeks after formulation. Table 6–3 presents the analytical

Table 6–2.   Analytical Results for DMMP Formulations Used in 90-Day Rat Subchronic Study

Target Concentration	Accuracy of Formulation		Animal Room Samples			
			First Day of Use		Last Day of Use	
	First Mix	Midstudy	Predosing	Postdosing	Predosing	Postdosing
38.4 mg/ml	40.2 mg/ml	38.5 mg/ml	39.6 mg/ml	39.0 mg/ml	37.9 mg/ml	37.5 mg/ml
77.0	77.9	74.8				
154	154	153	156	155	148	145
307	307	302			294	293
615	632	[a]	599	595	[a]	[a]

[a] All animals died in first few days. No further analyses of 615 mg/ml formulations needed.

Table 6-3. Stability and Resuspension Study: DMMP in Corn Oil, 308 mg/ml

Date	Formulation Treatment	% of Original Concentration
7/8/81	Formulation and subdividing of all dose level formulations	
7/14/81 (1 week)	Daily dosing aliquot rehomogenized and stirred. Animals dosed; samples taken.	101
7/23/81 (2 weeks)	Same aliquot (7/14/81) resuspended by shaking and stirring only. Samples taken.	103
10/29/81 (16 weeks)	Same aliquot, left in animal room since 7/23/81, resuspended by shaking and stirring only. Samples taken.	101

results that proved this point. On the other hand, continuous magnetic stirring was essential; the 308 mg/ml formulation was found to separate if it was not stirred for 50 min such that a syringe sample taken from the top of a daily aliquot was only 38.9% of target, while the original sample, taken at formulation, was 106% of target. The potential for misdosing, either high or low, if the formulation was not stirred was obvious.

Solid-Liquid Suspensions

The second NTP chemical studied was MDI (4,4'-diphenylmethanediisocyanate), which is very reactive, polymerizing in the presence of trace moisture. Although insoluble in corn oil to any large extent at room temperature, MDI was formulated in corn oil for comparison with TDI (toluene diisocyanate) for which chronic corn oil dosing studies had been completed. For the mouse subchronic study, formulation was accomplished by heating the MDI–corn oil mixtures until MDI dissolved; it reprecipitated within a few hours after cooling to room temperature, however. The water sensitivity of MDI was a major factor in the decision not to perform a chronic study; however, successful room temperature suspension was achieved in a special study (not used for dosing animals) using the commercial homogenizing apparatus. Stability at the 25 to 300 mg/ml range for seven days in sealed containers was found adequate for performance of a chronic study. No difference between rehomogenization and vigorous shaking was found when analytical samples were tested by either treatment prior to subsampling. No further data for MDI were available due to cancellation of chronic studies.

Solid-Water Suspensions

A third chemical that has been formulated and analyzed despite its insolubility in the water vehicle is a commercial solid, which is electrostatic and photosensitive to ultraviolet light; we refer to this chemical as KT-1013. Suspension of KT-1013 in water was done with the same commercial homogenization apparatus. Dose levels were 1, 3, 10, and 30 mg/ml. The water solubility is only 41 ppm. A thixotropic adjuvant (sodium carboxymethylcellulose, NaCMC) and a wetting agent (Tween 80®) were added to slow settling out of the test chemical. Problems in formulation were further complicated by difficulties in obtaining accurately measured analytical subsamples. Magnetic stirring and/or vigorous shaking were found not to be adequate; duplication of analytical results was variable and poor. It was found necessary to operate the homogenizer continuously during subsampling; 10 ml serological pipets, from which the tips had been cut, were used to measure about the required volume so that the larger particles of KT-1013 would not be trapped inside the pipet as formulation drained out. The subsamples were then weighed and the volume calculated from separately obtained density values. Accuracy of formulation was improved when longer (30 sec to 3 min) homogenizer treatment was used and when higher viscosity NaCMC was added. Surprisingly, the 10 and 30 mg/ml formulations proved easier to suspend near target than the 1 and 3 mg/ml levels.

When a second study with KT-1013 was started, a new lot of test material was used; this material was found to be less electrostatic, quite crystalline, and without the faint solvent odor of the first lot. Furthermore, suspensions could not be prepared by homogenizing. The test agent coagulated into large clumps when subjected to Polytron® treatment. Dose levels of 3, 10, and 30 mg/ml were used. Formulation was achieved by preparing a 50 mg/ml suspension in 0.5% NaCMC in a ball mill with ceramic balls; a 24-hr mix was used. The concentrated stock was then diluted to target concentrations.

Analytical samples were suspended by vigorous shaking only. Use of a homogenizer resulted in coagulation so no representative subsamples could be taken. Results showed formulation-suspension to be excellent; only three mixes out of thirty-five required a remix. Stability for five weeks was demonstrated to allow early formulation in the event a remix was needed.

CONCLUSION

We have found that detailed, written directions and periodic chemical analysis of check samples during dosing allow one to dose correctly over the time of a chronic study. A cooperative attitude between formulation, analytical, and dosing personnel is required. Close scientific supervision is also essential. We have seen here that homogenization may facilitate dosing with suspensions, but the technique is not a universal one. Also, chemical instability of the test chemical can overshadow successful suspension in a vehicle so that a viable study is still not feasible.

REFERENCES

1. Tekmar Company, P.O. Box 37202, Cincinnati, Ohio 45222, 1982 Catalog, p. 20.
2. Brinkmann Instruments, Inc., Cantiague Road, Westbury, New York 11590, Special Bulletin "Brinkmann Homogenizers—Applications."

CHAPTER 7

Analysis of Dosed Feed Samples

Evelyn A. Murrill, Gustav O. Kuhn, John J. Rollheiser, and Carlos A. Castro

Midwest Research Institute, 425 Volker Boulevard, Kansas City, Missouri 64110

C.W. Jameson

National Toxicology Program, P.O. Box 12233, Research Triangle Park, North Carolina 27709

Analysis of the dosed feeds used in a toxicity study is critical to the integrity of animal studies. The analysis is performed to prove that the chemical is mixed in a homogeneous manner throughout the feed, that it does not react significantly with components in the feed matrix, that it is stable as a mixture in the animal cage environment and while stored prior to use, and that the diet mix has been prepared at the specified dosage level.

For toxicity studies sponsored by the National Toxicology Program (NTP), analyses begin prior to the animal study and are continued on actual dose preparations during the study. Analytical methods are developed, and the homogeneity and stability analyses are performed prior to the animal study. Additional homogeneity testing and dosage analyses are performed at the laboratory on samples of the diet preparations used for the animal study. In addition, the NTP requires referee dosage analyses, which are performed at the analytical reference laboratory. The time frame and laboratory performing the dosed feed analyses are illustrated in Figure 7–1.

This chapter emphasizes the analytical aspects of dosage mixture testing. The feed matrix as it relates to the analysis and stability of the admixed chemical, the development of analytical methods for homogeneity, stability and dosage analysis, and the calculation and interpretation of analysis results will be discussed. The development of methods for obtaining homogeneous blends of chemicals in the feed matrix, the actual protocols used to judge the stability of the chemical in the feed blends, and the interpretation of these as they influence the total animal study are discussed in other chapters of this book.

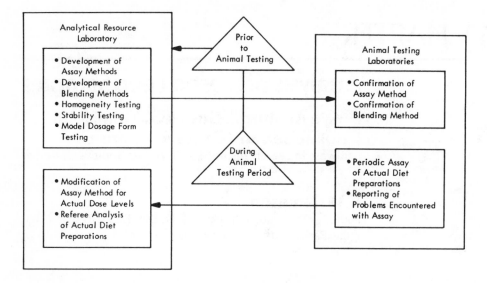

Figure 7-1. Time frame and laboratory performing the dosed feed analysis for NTP toxicity testing studies.

GENERAL COMMENTS CONCERNING THE CHEMICAL/FEED MIX

Oral dosing by means of the chemical/feed mix is often the method of choice for introducing the chemical into the animal system because it closely parallels the route of human exposure and is less labor intensive and thus more cost-effective than introduction by stomach intubation (gavage). It is important to remember, however, that the feed matrix is a complex mixture of chemicals sometimes capable of reacting chemically with the admixed compound. In other instances, no reactivity is indicated, but the variety of the matrix elements complicates chemical separation and analysis, especially when the chemical is added at low concentrations. Understanding the chemical and physical nature of both the chemical and the feed matrix is therefore primary to choosing feed as the diet vehicle and is the first step in the development of a rational plan for the analysis of dosed feed mixtures.

The composition of a typical feed matrix is shown in Table 7-1. Present in these components are exposed and reactive amines, aldehydes, acids, and so forth, as well as less reactive amides and esters. Also present is 5 to 10% water. Because of the reactive components in the animal feed, many chemicals are not stable when intimately mixed with the feed matrix; the concentration of recoverable chemical decreases with time of exposure to the feed vehicle. Typical examples of chemicals shown to be unstable in the presence of feed components are primary and secondary aromatic amines (eleven out of eleven tested indicated varying degrees of instability). On the other hand, the less reactive tertiary amines that were tested were found to be stable.

Table 7-1. NIH Open Formula Rat and Mouse Ration

Ingredient	Percentage by Weight
Dried skim milk	5.00
Fish meal (60% protein)	10.00
Soybean meal (49% protein)	12.00
Alfalfa meal (dehydrated 17% protein)	4.00
Corn gluten meal (60% protein)	3.00
Ground No. 2 yellow shelled corn	24.50
Ground hard winter wheat	23.00
Wheat middlings	10.00
Brewers dried yeast	2.00
Dry molasses	1.50
Soy oil	2.50
Salt	0.50
Dicalcium phosphate	1.25
Ground limestone	0.50
Premixes	0.25
	100.00

Note: Ingredients shall be ground to pass through a U.S. Standard Screen No. 16 prior to mixing.

Generally, oral dosing of amines, aldehydes, phenols, and other highly reactive compounds should be performed using a matrix other than animal feed because of their reactivity with feed components. When these or other chemical types are only moderately reactive, however, it is possible to decrease or eliminate reactivity with the feed components by minor procedural changes in the dose preparation and storage. For example, since the close contact between reactive groups of the chemical and the feed matrix promotes reactivity (for example, reactivity is increased if the chemical is a liquid or if it is added to the feed as a solution), surface contact and reactivity can be reduced by dry mixing all solid compounds with the feed. Reactivity also can be reduced by maintaining the mix at low temperatures during storage prior to introduction into the animal cage. The reactivity of amines can be reduced by administration of the amine salt rather than the base.

In addition to chemical reactivity, the physical characteristics of the chemical also affect its stability in the feed mix. Volatile chemicals may evaporate from the dosed feed. Even some relatively nonvolatile chemicals may vaporize in the open atmosphere of the feed hopper.

The experiments with 2,6-xylidine (Figures 7–2, 7–3, and 7–4) illustrate some of the problems of chemical/feed mixes. A 1% mix of 2,6-xylidine in rodent feed was exposed in an open rat cage environment to detect losses of chemical during the actual feeding period. Sealed bottle experiments were designed to determine the storage conditions necessary to prevent chemical loss during the period after diet preparation and before feeding. Both studies indicate losses of recoverable chemical with time. The sealed container experiments indicated apparent reactivity of the

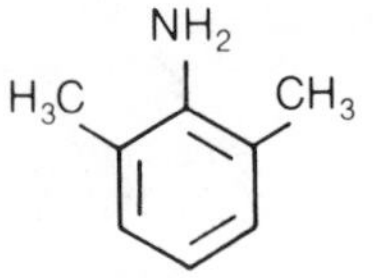

NH$_2$
H$_3$C   CH$_3$

2,6 = Xylidine
CONCENTRATION IN FEED: 1%

STORAGE OPEN IN A RAT CAGE AT AMBIENT TEMPERATURE

Days	2,6-Xylidine[a] Found (mg/g)	Chemical Found/ Theoretical (%)	Total Loss of Chemical (%)
1	8.96	90.1	9.9
	9.14	92.0	8.0
	9.02	90.8	9.2
	x̄ 9.04 ± 0.09 (s)	91.0 ± 1.0 (s)	9.0
3	7.77	78.1	21.9
	7.71	77.6	22.4
	7.58	76.2	23.8
	x̄ 7.69 ± 0.10 (s)	77.3 ± 1.0 (s)	22.7
5	7.11	71.5	28.5
	6.93	69.7	30.3
	7.03	70.7	29.3
	x̄ 7.02 ± 0.09 (s)	70.6 ± 0.9 (s)	29.4
7	5.77	58.0	42.0
	5.37	54.0	46.0
	5.58	56.4	43.6
	x̄ 5.57 ± 0.20 (s)	56.1 ± 2.0 (s)	43.9

Pooled standard deviation: ± 1.3%

a   Results were corrected for a mean recovery of 99.1 ± 0.3 (8)% (n = 9)

Figure 7-2.   Results of rat cage stability study of 1% 2,6-xylidine feed mixes.

chemical with feed components. The open environment studies indicated additional losses due to vaporization and possible reaction with light and air. In order to investigate the losses due to apparent reactivity with the feed, the compound was blended with isolated feed components. Water (10%) was added to simulate the moist atmosphere of the feed matrix. Large recovery losses were observed in the ingredient mixes containing high concentrations of carbohydrates. To identify specific chemical reactivity further, studies were conducted with selected sugars. The low reactivity obtained with the sucrose-amine mixture was expected because sucrose does not contain a "free" carbonyl group. However, the lack of reactivity with α-D-lactose, which does have a reactive carbonyl, was unexpected. The insolubility of the α versus the β anomer probably accounts for its low reactivity in this relatively dry mix.

STORAGE IN SEALED BOTTLES IN THE DARK

Days	2,6-Xylidine[a] Found (mg/g)	Chemical Found/ Theoretical (%)	Total Loss of Chemical (%)
7 Days (-20°C)	9.82	98.8	1.2
	9.84	99.0	1.0
	9.80	98.6	1.4
	x̄ 9.82 ± 0.02 (s)	98.8 ± 0.2 (s)	1.2
14 Days (-20°C)	9.75	98.1	1.9
	9.79	98.5	1.5
	9.88	99.4	0.6
	x̄ 9.81 ± 0.07 (s)	98.7 ± 0.7 (s)	1.2
7 Days (5°C)	9.56	96.2	3.8
	9.57	96.3	3.7
	9.59	96.5	3.5
	x̄ 9.57 ± 0.02 (s)	96.3 ± 0.2 (s)	3.7
14 Days (5°C)	9.59	96.5	3.5
	9.61	96.7	3.3
	9.67	97.3	2.7
	x̄ 9.62 ± 0.04 (s)	96.8 ± 0.4 (s)	3.2
4 Days (Room Temp.)	8.83	88.8	11.2
	8.88	89.3	10.7
	8.89	89.4	10.6
	x̄ 8.87 ± 0.03 (s)	89.2 ± 0.3 (s)	10.8
7 Days (Room Temp.)	8.81	88.6	11.4
	8.78	88.3	11.7
	8.76	88.1	11.9
	8.78 ± 0.03 (s)	88.3 ± 0.3 (s)	11.7
14 Days (Room Temp.)	8.45	85.0	15.0
	8.45	85.0	15.0
	8.56	86.1	13.9
	x̄ 8.49 ± 0.06 (s)	85.4 ± 0.6 (s)	14.6

Pooled standard deviation: ± 0.4%

a   Results were corrected for the mean recovery of 98.9 ± 0.4 (δ)% (n = 9)

Figure 7-3.   Results of sealed bottle stability study of 1% 2,6-xylidine feed mixes.

In addition to its reactivity with certain admixed compounds, the feed matrix places constraints on the analytical techniques used to test the mixture. Because of the highly polar nature of the feed matrix, the most effective primary solvents have been shown to be acetonitrile or methanol alone or with added acid (0.1 to 0.2 N). Experiments with solvents of varying polarity have indicated that even for relatively nonpolar chemicals, the recovery of the chemical is directly related to the polarity of the extracting solvent.

For NTP studies of dosed feed mixtures, a decision was made to limit the polarity of the extracting solvent to 0.2 N acid. This decision was not related to the recovery analysis of the chemical but rather to the animal portion of the toxicity study. Because the feed is just a vehicle for introduction of the chemical into the animal system, it is important that components in the feed do not bind or react with the

INTERACTION WITH FEED COMPONENTS

Analytical results for 2,6-xylidine in blends stored 12 days at room temperature are tabulated below.

Vehicle	Found/Theoretical (%)	$\bar{X}$ (%)
Corn Starch	95.2, 94.0	$94.6 \pm 0.8(s)\%$
Soy Protein Isolate	89.7, 92.9	$91.3 \pm 2.3(s)\%$
Whole Wheat Flour	81.0, 80.6	$80.8 \pm 0.2(s)\%$
Nonfat Dried Milk	62.4, 64.4	$63.4 \pm 1.4(s)\%$

INTERACTION WITH SPECIFIC CHEMICALS (12 Day Storage)

Vehicle	Storage Temperature	Found/Theoretical (%)	$\bar{X}$ (%, Normalized to $-20°$ C)
Sucrose	$-20°$ C	101.5, 99.5	$95.7 + 0.6(s)\%$
	R.T.	95.8, 96.6	
α-D-Lactose	$-20°$ C	100.1, 100.4	
	R.T.	100.1, 99.0	$99.2 + 0.8(s)\%$
β-D-Lactose	$-20°$ C	91.7, 92.7	
	R.T.	69.4, 74.0	$77.8 + 3.3(s)\%$
D-Glucose	$-20°$ C	101.4, 101.9	
	R.T.[a]	53.8, 56.4	$54.2 + 1.8(s)\%$

a Color of blend turned from white to brown during storage.

Figure 7-4.   Results of interaction study of 2,6-xylidine with rodent feed components.

chemical and modify its absorption characteristics. The extraction techniques therefore were limited to mild conditions to demonstrate that the chemical could be easily extracted intact from the feed matrix. This decision was intentionally a conservative choice; it could be argued that the animal system is more effective than the selected solvents and that more polar solvents or more strenuous conditions should be used. If conditions were made more severe, undoubtedly some compounds judged to be unstable on feed would be quantitatively extracted, even after extended storage, and thus judged to be stable. However, because the area between physical attraction and chemical reactivity is a continuum dependent on the individual bond strengths involved, stability criteria undoubtedly will remain subjective, dependent on perceptions of how the extraction efficiency is related to the chemistry of the animal system.

The heterogeneous nature of the feed matrix also affects the analysis of chemical/feed mixtures, particularly when the chemical is added in low concentrations to the feed. The feed matrix is a rather loosely defined mixture of natural components. The more closely regulated mixtures contain known amounts of nutrient and vitamins and are tested to ascertain that certain toxic compounds are not present at detectable levels. The precise chemical nature of many of the compounds present is not known and furthermore varies with the species of grain, harvest time, geographical location of the harvest, and other factors. For this reason it is sometimes difficult to translate published methods at the low ppm or ppb level into practice without at least some modification of the chromatography or extraction methods to avoid matrix elements not observed in the original analysis.

DEVELOPMENT OF THE ANALYTICAL METHOD

Methods developed for dosed feed samples must accurately quantitate the chemical mixed with the feed at dose concentrations of 5% to low ppm or ppb values. They must also be capable of distinguishing the parent chemical from products formed by reaction with the feed matrix elements or with environmental components such as air and light. Ideally the methods should be rapid and procedurally simple.

In order to achieve these goals, a two-tiered approach has been used for methods selection and development. Chromatographic methods, either gas chromatography (GC) or high performance liquid chromatography (HPLC), are developed first to test the stability of the compound in the mix. These methods are used because they are capable of resolving the test compound and structurally similar reaction products. Once the stability of the compound in the mix has been demonstrated, the method is simplified, if possible (for example, by substituting spectroscopy for HPLC or GC), for the homogeneity and multiple dosage analysis performed at the toxicity testing laboratory and for the referee dosage analysis performed at the reference laboratory.

For chemicals dosed into the feed at levels above 100 ppm, methods consisting of simple extraction, separation of the solid feed components by centrifugation, and direct analysis of the diluted supernatant extract by GC, HPLC, or ultraviolet (UV) spectroscopy are generally employed because they are applicable to a wide range of compound types and yield precise, accurate analytical data.

HPLC detection and quantitation techniques are chosen for nonvolatile and heat-sensitive compounds with chromophores whose ϵ values are greater than 5000. These methods are later adapted to UV spectroscopy for the multiple dosage analyses. GC techniques using flame ionization, electron capture, or nitrogen/phosphorus detection are chosen for the analysis of volatile compounds. Derivatization techniques are employed only in very selective cases to volatilize the compound or add a detectable functional group in order to simplify the cleanup or quantitation procedures.

Selection of Extraction Solvents

The solvent most often used to extract the compound from the feed is acetonitrile or methanol alone or in combination with 0.1–0.2 N acid. These solvents have good solution properties for a wide variety of chemicals. In addition, they reverse the attraction that some test chemicals have for the polar feed components. Because of these properties, the chemical is usually extracted quantitatively at zero time from the feed matrix, thereby enabling the analyst to interpret clearly the kinetic data obtained from the stability analysis.

In addition, these solvents have weak solvent properties for the chromophoric and fatty materials in the feed matrix that interfere with GC, HPLC, or UV analysis of the extract. Extracts using these solvents, after simple centrifugation to separate the solid portions of the feed matrix and dilution, can usually be injected directly without further cleanup onto the GC or HPLC for quantitation of the test compounds (Figures 7-5 through 7-8). When further cleanup is necessary, the extracts are evaporated to dryness and reextracted with other solvents or diluted and extracted with nonpolar solvents such as toluene and methylene chloride. The kepone analysis (Figures 7-9, 7-10, and 7-11) is an example of the cleanup of a primary acetonitrile extract by evaporation, hexane extraction of the residue, and removal of polar components into sulfuric acid.

When the test compound is not soluble in either acetonitrile or methanol, other primary solvents have to be employed (for example, cyclohexane with β-cadinene;

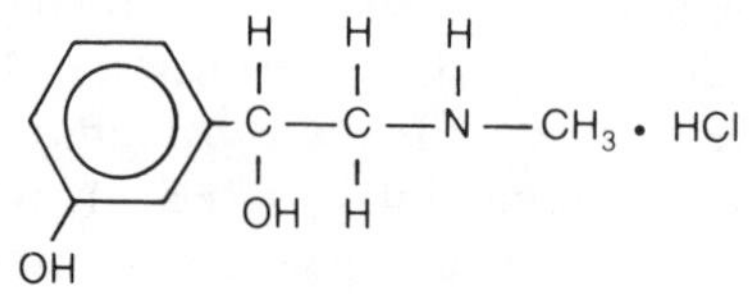

PHENYLEPHRINE HYDROCHLORIDE

CONCENTRATION ON FEED: 800 ppm

ANALYSIS PROCEDURE

Samples were extracted with 100 ml of a methanol:acetic acid (99:1) mixture by sonicating 30 sec and shaking 15 min on a New Brunswick gyrotory shaker set at 300 rpm. After clarifying the extract by centrifuging at 2,000 rpm for 5 min, a few milliliters of solution were filtered through a 0.5 μ Millipore syringe filter. The phenylephrine·HCl content of the filtrate was determined by the high pressure liquid chromatographic system described below:

Instrument: Waters associates ALC202 Liquid Chromatograph
Detector: Waters Model 440, 280 nm filter
Attenuation: 0.05 AU full scale
Column: μ Bondapak C$_{18}$; 300 mm x 4 mm ID stainless steel
Mobile phase: Pump A: 0.005 M sodium lauryl sulfate
                          in methanol:acetic acid (99:1)
                 Pump B: 0.005 M sodium lauryl sulfate in
                          water:acetic acid (99:1)
Mobile phase ratio: 40% A, 60% B
Flow rate: 1 ml/min
Volume injected: 16 μl
Retention time: Test chemical: 10.3 min

Figure 7-5. Analytical procedure for analysis of phenylephrine hydrochloride in rodent feed.

RESULTS

Storage Temperature	2 - Week Stability in Feed	
	Phenylephrine · HCl mg/g Found [a,b]	% Recovery (Found / Theoretical)
-20° C	808 813	101.2 ± 0.3 [c]
5° C	810 803	100.8 ± 0.5
25° C	775 775	96.8 ± 0
45° C	784 780	97.7 ± 0.3

a   No recovery correction was applied to the analysis values since the spiked recovery yield of 101.1 ± 0.5% was within the analytical error of the test.

b   Theoretical concentration of chemical on feed was 800.8 $\mu g/g$.

c   Error values are deviations from the mean.

Figure 7-6.   Results of two-week stability study of phenylephrine hydrochloride mixed in rodent feed.

dimethylformamide with theobromine). However, extractions using nonpolar solvents such as cyclohexane remove a larger quantity of fatty components from the feed and therefore usually require a cleanup step before quantitation. In addition, nonpolar solvents are useful only for hydrocarbons with no attraction to polar feed components; extraction efficiencies are reduced when the test compound possesses polarizable functional groups. Dimethylformamide, a relatively high polarity solvent, extracted theobromine efficiently, but like cyclohexane required a cleanup step to remove the high concentration of fatty components. Generally extractions with base have been avoided because of the emulsion problems encountered with the extracted feed components.

If a concentration step is necessary prior to analysis, any of the commonly used procedures are employed—drying with a stream of nitrogen, rotary evaporation, and so forth. Often a keeper such as ethylene glycol is added to the extract prior to evaporation. This technique has been found to be especially useful for heat-, light-, or oxygen-sensitive compounds. Drying agents such as sodium sulfate are used only rarely and are avoided with all amines because of the insolubility of many amine sulfates (for example, benzidine 0.098 g/l at 25° C) [1].

In the quantitation step, standards dissolved in the extract of undosed feed (matrix standards) are usually employed rather than, or in addition to, simple solution standards. The most obvious reason for the use of matrix standards is to account for the absorbance of the matrix elements in a UV spectroscopic analysis. However,

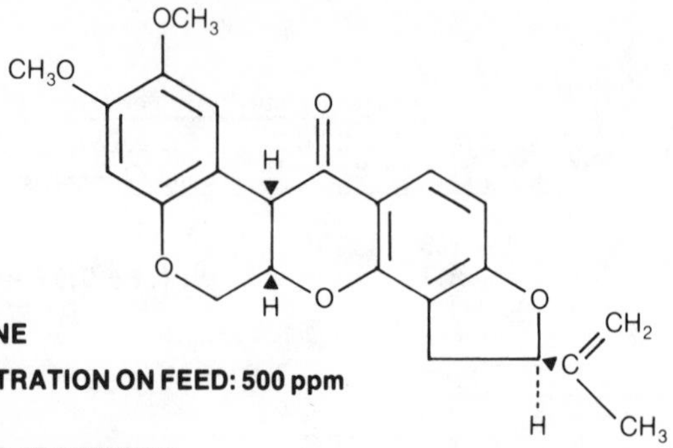

ROTENONE

CONCENTRATION ON FEED: 500 ppm

ANALYSIS PROCEDURE

Stored samples and freshly prepared spiked feeds for zero time recovery determinations were extracted with 100 ml of acetonitrile-acetic acid solution (99:1 v/v) by shaking 1 hr on a New Brunswick gyrotory shaker set at 300 rpm. Extracts were allowed to settle for 5 min, then a few milliliters of each solution was filtered through a 0.5 μ Millipore filter and analyzed directly by the high pressure liquid chromatography system described below:

Instrument: Waters Associates ALC202 Liquid Chromatograph
           equipped with programmable pumps
Column: μ Bondapak C_{18}; 300 mm x 4 mm ID
Detector: UV -280 nm
Attenuation: 0.2 AU/full scale
Flow rate: 1.0 ml/min
Injection volume: 15 μ l
Mobile phase composition: Acetonitrile:water (60:40 v/v)
Retention time: 6.1 min

Figure 7-7. Analytical procedure for analysis of rotenone in rodent feed.

Storage Temperature (°C)	ppm Chemical Found in Feed[a]	% Recovery Found/Theoretical[b]
−20	497.5 513.9	100.5 ± 1.6[c]
5	490.3 503.1	98.7 ± 1.3
25	490.9 503.7	98.9 ± 1.3
45	451.3 448.8	89.5 ± 0.3

a Results corrected for zero time spike recovery yield of 97.6 + 0.6%.
b Theoretical level of rotenone on feed was 503 ppm. The HPLC chromatogram of the 45° C samples exhibited a peak at 5.0 min which was not observed in the other samples.
c Error values are deviations from the mean.

Figure 7-8. Results of two-week stability study of rotenone mixed in rodent feed.

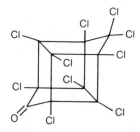

KEPONE

CONCENTRATION ON FEED: 0.2 ppm, 1 ppm, 6 ppm ı

ANALYSIS PROCEDURE

A. Feed samples (10.00 g weighed in triplicate into 200 ml centrifuge bottles) were extracted with 100 ml of reagent grade acetonitrile by shaking on a mechanical shaker for 30 min, followed by centrifuging for 5 min at 1,800 rpm to clarify the extracts.

B. Aliquots of the extracts (10 ml for the 0, 0.2, and 1 ppm samples, and 5 ml for the 6 ppm sample) were transferred to 30 ml septum vials and evaporated to dryness under a gentle stream of nitrogen while warming on a 60 °C hot plate.

C. The dry residues were dissolved in 20 ml of hexane by swirling the contents of the vials for several minutes. Concentrated sulfuric acid (5 ml) was then added, and the vials were sealed and shaken vigorously for 1 min.

D. The solutions were warmed to 60 °C in a water bath for 5 min to help eliminate the emulsions which formed, then they were centrifuged for 30 min at 1,800 rpm.

E. After cooling to room temperature, 15 ml aliquots of the clear hexane layers were evaporated to dryness in 30 ml septum vials as described in Step B.

F. The residues were dissolved in varying amounts of internal standard solution (chlordane, 0.018 μg/ml in methanol-toluene-hexane solution, 5:5:90, v/v/v).

Figure 7–9.   Analytical procedure for the analysis of kepone in rodent feed.

Instrument: Varian 3700 Gas Chromatograph
Column: 1.8 m x 2 mm ID glass, silanized, packed with
      10% SP-2100 on 80/100 mesh Supelcoport
Detection: Electron capture, [63]Ni
Temperatures: Inlet: 250 °C
          Oven: 235 °C, isothermal
          Detector: 300 °C
Carrier gas: Nitrogen
Flow rate: 30 ml/min
Injection volume: 4 μl
Attenuation: 64 x 10
Retention times: Kepone® — 7.9 min
          Chlordane (Internal Standard) — 4.5 min

Figure 7–10.   Gas chromatographic conditions for analysis of kepone doped feed extracts.

Labeled Kepone Concentration (ppm)	Kepone Found (ppm)	% of Label Claim
0.2	0.242	
	0.261	
	0.260	
	$\overline{X} = 0.254 \pm 0.1\,(s)$ [a]	127%
1	Lost	
	0.986	
	0.947	
	$\overline{X} = 0.967 \pm 0.03$ [b]	96.7%
6	6.46	
	6.39	
	6.66	
	$\overline{X} = 6.50 \pm 0.14\,(s)$ [c]	108.3%

---

a Results were corrected for 0.2 ppm spiked recovery yield of 73.6 + 0.6%.
b Results were corrected for 1 ppm spiked recovery yield of 69.2 + 1.6%.
c Results were corrected for 6 ppm spiked recovery yield of 71.7 + 8.7%.

Average recovery for the three sample levels was 71.5 + 2.2 (s)%.

Figure 7-11.   Results of analysis of kepone doped feed mixtures.

matrix elements also modify the characteristics of GC or HPLC columns and decrease or increase the detection of the compound of interest. This effect was noticed during the analysis of kepone by GC using electron capture detection. The GC response to kepone, dissolved in the extract of undosed feed, was enhanced as compared to the response obtained from a simple solution standard.

Internal standards are added to extracts prior to the quantitation step to monitor chromatographic conditions and injection volumes during the analysis. The necessity for structural similarity between the test compound and the internal standard is important in HPLC analysis using paired-ion or buffered systems; it is less important for GC or unbuffered HPLC systems.

STABILITY ANALYSIS

The stability analysis is performed prior to the toxicity study in order to prove that the compound is stable in the feed matrix and to determine the storage conditions necessary for maintaining the stability of the mix prior to placing it in the animal cage. Studies are also performed to ascertain the stability of the mix in the open environment of the animal cage.

The quantitation methods for stability analysis are usually chromatographic (GC or HPLC) techniques considered capable of resolving the test chemical from reaction or degradation products produced by feed components or environmental conditions. A significant change in concentration of test compound versus time or temperature is used to judge the stability or instability of the compound (see Figures 7-2, 7-3, 7-6, and 7-8). The percentage concentration change necessary for significance is calculated by comparing the means of the analyses by standard mean comparison techniques. Values outside the 95% confidence limit are considered different and therefore indicative of instability.

Quantitative recoveries and low method variabilities narrow the limits of the stability range and enable the analyst to accurately judge reactions between the chemical and the feed matrix.

DOSAGE ANALYSIS

Routine dosage analysis is performed to ensure that the actual diet preparation used for animal feeding contains the correct concentration of test compound. These analyses are performed at the toxicity testing laboratory at specified intervals during the study. Referee analyses are also performed at less frequent intervals by the reference laboratory as a second verification of the chemical dose in the feed.

The extraction, cleanup, and quantitation methods used for routine dosage analysis are the same as those developed for the stability analyses except that UV quantitation is substituted for HPLC or GC if the dosed feed extract has an absorbance at least 2× the absorbance of an undosed feed extract. However, spiked feed standards, carried through the entire extraction and cleanup methods employed for the test sample, are used rather than the solution or matrix standards employed for the stability analysis.

Comparison of the spiked standards to the dosed samples allows direct calculation of the test chemical concentration and eliminates the need for establishing the test chemical recovery and the matrix influences at each dose level used for the study. This short-cut is possible only because previously acquired stability data have shown that the test compound is stable in the feed matrix and that the method is valid for determination of test compound concentration.

The strength of the spiked standard method is illustrated by its use for referee analysis. The theoretical concentration of the dose mixture sent to the reference laboratory is intentionally not specified. However, a dosage range bracketing the theoretical concentration of the sample is provided by the NTP project officer. The analysis is performed by preparing a spiked feed concentration curve that spans the specified dosage range. Spiked standards and the test mixture are then extracted and analyzed simultaneously, and the concentration of the test compound in the unknown mixture is determined from the spiked standard data by linear regression analysis.

The data obtained for a typical referee analysis are shown in Figure 7-12. In this case, the nitrofurazone in the feed mixture was specified to be within the 100 to 500 ppm (0.01 to 0.05%) range. The analyzed value was 322 ppm. The standard deviation obtained on the triplicate analysis was 7 ppm or ± 2% of the analyzed value. The animal study specified a target concentration of 310 ± 31 ppm. The analysis therefore

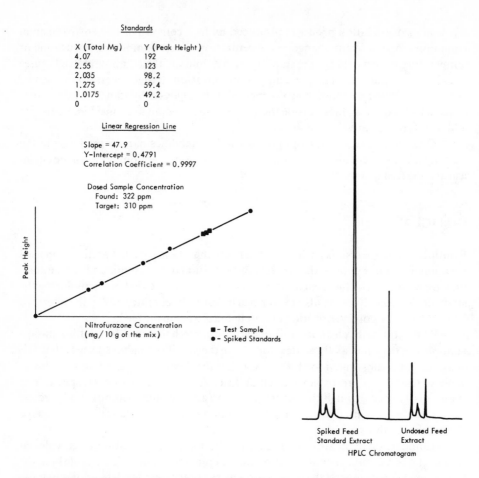

Figure 7-12.   Results of a referee analysis of nitrofurazone dosage mixture.

confirmed that the dose concentration was within specification of the target concentration.

Samples of pentaerythritol tetranitrate dosed feed analyzed simultaneously by both GC using electron capture detection and HPLC at 210 nm illustrate how the spiked standard curve can correct for severe matrix interference problems (Figure 7-13). The GC method is obviously not the method of choice for analysis of this dosage mixture; however, the results obtained from the GC analysis deviated only 1.5% from those obtained using the better HPLC analysis method.

CONCLUSION

Analyses of dosed feeds used in toxicity studies are performed to prove that the chemical feed mixes are homogeneous, to determine stability or compatibility of the chem-

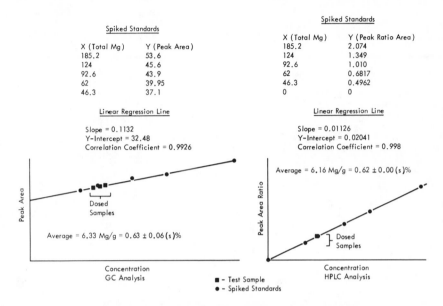

PENTAERYTHRITOL TETRANITRATE IN FEED TARGET CONCENTRATION: 0.62%

Figure 7-13. Comparison of GC and HPLC analysis of pentaerythritol tetranitrate feed mixtures.

ical with the feed matrix, and to confirm the dose level in the animal diet. Methods developed for these assays must accurately quantitate the chemical mixed with the feed and be capable of distinguishing the parent chemical from products formed by reaction with the feed matrix or with environmental components such as air or light. Ideally the methods should be rapid and procedurally simple. The two-tiered approach used by the NTP for methods selection and development has been developed from experience gained from analysis of approximately one hundred different mixes and has provided analytical procedures for a wide variety of chemicals tested by the NTP.

REFERENCE

1. Bissor, C.S., and A.W. Christie. "Note On the Solubility of Benzidine Sulfate in Water," *Ind. Eng. Chem.* 12:485 (1920).

CHAPTER 8

Stability Determinations for Chemical/Vehicle Mixtures

C.W. Jameson
National Toxicology Program, P.O. Box 12233,
Research Triangle Park, North Carolina 27709

John J. Rollheiser and Gustav O. Kuhn
Midwest Research Institute, 425 Volker Boulevard,
Kansas City, Missouri 64110

Toxicity testing programs have been established by the federal government, industry, and private organizations to evaluate the toxic potential of chemicals. These toxicity evaluations include long-term in vivo studies with the test chemical administered to the test species by various routes of administration, requiring the use of several different vehicles. Because of the requirement that the material being tested must be mixed with a vehicle for administration, the chemical stability of the chemical/vehicle mixture must be determined. This study should be run prior to any animal studies to ensure that the toxicity study is of the material in question and not a decomposition product caused by the interaction of the test chemical with the vehicle of administration. This chapter discusses how the National Toxicology Program (NTP) determines the stability of chemical/vehicle mixtures prior to initiation of studies in its carcinogenesis testing program.

ROUTES OF ADMINISTRATION

There are many reasons why a particular route of administration is selected. The most often cited rationale for selection of the route of administration is because it mimics human exposure. For example, if a chemical selected for test is a food additive or found in drinking water, then an oral route is the one of choice. If the test material is used in topical applications either as a drug or a cosmetic, skin paint would be used. A secondary reason for selecting a particular route of administration could be the cost of the toxicity study. If the test chemical has several uses leading to exposure by more than one route, then the toxicity study may be designed using the route that mimics a human exposure but is less costly to run. For example, if exposure is potentially by both an inhalation and oral route, an oral toxicity study may be run because it is less costly than an inhalation study.

Another important consideration in determining the route of administration is the stability of the test chemical when mixed with the vehicle of administration. If the test chemical is not compatible with the vehicle to be used, then an alternative vehicle or route of administration must be used to ensure a valid toxicity study. It is therefore necessary that the stability of the chemical/vehicle mixtures be determined prior to any toxicity studies to make sure the route of administration is adequate for determining the toxicity of the material being investigated.

The NTP uses several routes of administration for its toxicity testing programs, including feed, drinking water, gavage, injection, skin paint, and inhalation. Once the route of administration and the vehicle have been selected, it is necessary to determine the stability of the test material when mixed and stored in the selected vehicle. Stability studies of chemical/vehicle mixtures discussed in this chapter are limited to feed, drinking water, gavage, and skin paint because they all require preparation of a chemical/vehicle dosage preparation. Stability determination for chemicals used in inhalation studies are discussed in Chapters 12 and 13.

Feed Studies

Before a feeding toxicity study can be initiated, both the homogeneity and the stability of the chemical feed blend must be established. Chapter 5 discussed how feed mixing protocols are developed to ensure adequate mixing technique and demonstrate that a homogeneous blend can be achieved at an estimated dosing level. It is from these same homogeneity study blends that samples are taken for stability studies.

Table 8–1 outlines the protocol used by the NTP for the determination of chemical feed mixture stability. Chemical feed blends at an estimated dosing level are stored, sealed, in the dark at –20°, 5°, and 24° C to determine the optimum storage conditions for up to a twenty-one-day period. Samples are taken for analysis at day 7, 14, and 21, which allows for the determination of a trend in decomposition at the three storage temperatures. An additional sample is stored at room temperature open to air and light to mimic actual dosing conditions. Sampling times for this stability sample are 3 and 7 days, again to follow how an actual dosage feed mixture would be handled and to see if decomposition increases with time. The results of

Table 8–1.   Stability Protocol for Dosed Feed Studies

Storage Temperature (° C)	Storage Time (days)	Storage Conditions
−20	7,14,21	Sealed in the dark
5	7,14,21	Sealed in the dark
24	7,14,21	Sealed in the dark
24	3,7	Open to air and light

these stability studies are used to prepare storage and handling procedures for the testing laboratories. For example, if a dosed feed blend showed long-term instability at room temperature but appeared stable at 5° C, then storage at 5° C prior to use in the toxicity study would be required.

Analysis of the feed stability samples is conducted by isolating the test chemical by extraction with a suitable solvent followed by centrifugation to separate out the solid feed components. Determination of the test chemical concentration normally involves dilution of the supernatant and quantification by gas chromatography (GC), high-performance liquid chromatography (HPLC), or spectroscopy. These methods are generally employed because they are applicable to a wide range of compound types and yield precise accurate analytical data. A more detailed discussion of the feed matrix and how it relates to the analysis and stability of chemicals mixed in feed can be found in Chapter 7.

The NTP's Carcinogenesis Testing Program has studied 148 chemicals in the past three years. Of the 148 chemicals, feed was the original vehicle of choice for 50% of these studies. Of the 74 chemicals tested in feed, 37 were found not to be stable. Stability is defined as a recovery of $\geq 95\%$ of the original test material after 7 days at room temperature open to air and light in a rat cage or $\geq 98\%$ of the original test material after storage for 14 days at 5° C sealed and protected from light. These data demonstrate the importance of determining chemical vehicle stability prior to initiation of any animal studies.

Table 8–2 breaks down the chemicals tested for stability on feed by the NTP by functional group. These stability studies show that a majority ($> 50\%$) of the primary and secondary amines, organo halides, amides, hydroxyl, and nitrate/nitrile compounds tested were unstable when mixed with rodent feed. Of all the functional groups studied, the predominant one (59%) belongs to the benzene ring class, and of

Table 8–2.   Stability on Feed, by Functional Group

Functional Group	No. Unstable/No. Tested on Feed
Primary amine	13/17 (76%)
Halide	11/17 (65%)
Secondary amine	7/11 (64%)
Amide	6/10 (60%)
Benzene ring	25/44 (57%)
Hydroxyl	16/30 (53%)
NO $_N$	8/15 (53%)
Ether	4/8 (50%)
Acid	6/12 (50%)
Hetero ring	6/13 (46%)
SO $_N$	4/9 (44%)
HX salt	4/9 (44%)
Ketone	7/16 (44%)
Alkene	7/18 (39%)
Tertiary amine	5/14 (36%)
Nonaromatic fused ring	4/13 (31%)

Table 8-3. Stability on Feed, by Functional Groups on Benzene Rings

Second Functional Group	No. Unstable/No. Tested on Feed
Primary amine	8/8 (100%)
Secondary amine	3/3 (100%)
Hydroxyl	8/13 (62%)
NO N	7/12 (58%)
Halide	5/9 (56%)
Acid	1/2 (50%)
Ether	3/7 (43%)
Amide	1/3 (33%)
Tertiary amine	0/2 (0%)

Table 8-4. Incidence of Compound-Related Nasal Lesions in Fischer 344 Rats Fed 300, 1000 and 3000 ppm 2,6-Xylidine for 2 Years

	Control	Low Dose	Medium Dose	High Dose
Male rats				
Nasal Cavity (No. Examined)	(56)	(56)	(56)	(56)
Carcinoma, NOS				25
Adenocarcinoma, NOS				3
Papillary adenoma			1	10
Rhabdomyosarcoma				2
Mixed tumor, malignant				1
Inflammation, acute	12	21	32	42
Inflammation, acute/chronic		1	1	2
Inflammation, chronic			5	
Hyperplasia, epithelial			1	3
Metaplasia, squamous				5
Female rats				
Nasal Cavity (No. Examined)	(56)	(56)	(56)	(56)
Carcinoma, NOS			1	23
Papillary adenoma				6
Sarcoma, NOS				1
Rhabdomyosarcoma				1
Inflammation, acute	7	14	15	38
Inflammation, chronic	1			
Hyperplasia, epithelial			1	9
Metaplasia, squamous				4

Table 8–5. Stability of 2,6-Xylidine in Feed: Summary of Stability
Loss Data

Storage Condition	Mean Daily Loss (%)
Open/rat cage/room temperature	7.2 (n=12)
Sealed/dark/−20° C	0.13 (n=6)
Sealed/dark/5° C	0.38 (n=6)
Sealed/dark/room temperature	1.8 (n=9)

these, the majority (57%) were found to be unstable. This benzene ring class is further broken down by secondary functional group in Table 8–3. This table demonstrates that all primary and secondary aromatic amines tested were found to be unstable when mixed in rodent feed. Tertiary aromatic amines, however, were found to be stable, which is not surprising considering the relative reactivity of primary and secondary aromatic amines compared to tertiary aromatic amines. The results of these stability studies also show that the majority of the aromatic hydroxyl, nitrate/ nitrile, or halide compounds tested were also unstable when mixed in rodent feed.

An interesting example of how feed stability data could assist in interpreting results of animal studies would be the chronic feeding study of 2,6-xylidine:

$$H_3C \overset{NH_2}{\underset{}{\bigcirc}} CH_3$$

The compound-related nasal lesions found in the rats used for a feeding study of 2,6-xylidine are listed in Table 8–4. The most striking observation was that there was a very high incidence of nasal cavity carcinomas, which, for a feeding study, is very rare. In this particular example, the study was initiated before the NTP was involved, and a feed stability study was not conducted prior to initiation of this animal study. The NTP conducted a stability study for 2,6-xylidine feed mixtures after the completion of the animal studies; the results are presented in Table 8–5. These results show that 2,6-xylidine was lost at a rate of 7.2% per day and that 70 to 80% of the loss was due to evaporation of the test chemical from the feed. Therefore the test animals may have gotten a significant exposure by the inhalation route, which could help explain the high incidence of nasal lesions. (A discussion of the reactivity of 2,6-xylidine with individual feed components is contained in Chapter 7.)

Gavage

Gavage, or direct stomach intubation, is the second most frequently used route of administration used by the NTP. For this route, solutions or suspensions of the test

Table 8-6. Stability Protocol for Gavage/Injection Studies

Storage Temperature (°C)	Storage Time	Storage Conditions
5	7,14,18,21 days	Sealed in the dark
24	1,7,14,18,21 days	Sealed in the dark
24	3 hours	Open to air and light

material are made up in either water or corn oil for administration to the test animals. The stability protocol for these studies is outlined in Table 8-6. As in the feed stability protocol, the first two sets of conditions are used to determine optimum storage and handling conditions; the last set is used to mimic actual study conditions. Results of these studies are used to prepare storage and handling procedures for the testing laboratories.

Analysis procedures for gavage solutions and/or suspensions are similar to those used for dosed feed analysis. If water is used as the vehicle, the dose mixture is usually a solution since water is not a good suspending agent. Analysis of water solutions typically is carried out by dilution followed by analysis either by GC, HPLC, or spectroscopy. Corn oil solutions and/or suspensions usually require extraction using either methanol or acetonitrile followed by analysis by GC, HPLC, or spectroscopy. (A more detailed discussion of mixing and analysis procedures for insoluble and immiscible test agents in liquid vehicles was presented in Chapter 6.)

Of the 148 chemicals studied, 21 were tested by gavage using water as the vehicle. Only 1, glycidol, was found to be unstable. Stability for gavage dose mixtures is defined as a recovery of $\geq 95\%$ of the original concentration after 7 days at room temperature. Analysis of the glycidol/water solutions was accomplished by dissolving the mixture in acetonitrile followed by quantitation by GC using a glass column packed with 10% Carbowax 20M on 80/100 mesh Chromasorb W(AW):

$$\underset{H_2C-CH-CH_2OH}{\overset{O}{\frown}}$$

Glycidol

It was determined that when glycidol was dissolved in water at an estimated dose level of 20 mg/ml, it exhibited losses of 21.7% and 37.6% after 7 and 14 days, respectively, at room temperature in the dark. However, solutions stored in the dark at 5°C exhibited an acceptable 1.8% loss after 7 days but a significant 4.6% loss after 14 days. A sample exposed 3 hr to air and light, mimicking actual dosing conditions, showed no significant change from the zero-time sample. These results were used to establish storage and handling protocols requiring that glycidol water solutions should be refrigerated, protected from light, and kept no longer than 7 days.

Of the 62 chemicals tested for stability in corn oil, only 4 (6%) showed any instability. These results demonstrate that corn oil is a very useful vehicle for administration of test materials. This is due in part to its organic solvent properties and also its viscosity, which makes it useful as a suspending medium for insolubles.

An interesting example of a chemical found to be unstable in corn oil is that of p-chloroaniline:

$$Cl \text{—} \bigcirc \text{—} NH_2$$

Analysis for p-chloroaniline in corn oil gavage solutions was accomplished by dilution of the samples with hexane and analysis by GC using a glass column packed with 3% SP-2401 on 100–120 mesh Supelcoport. When mixed at the estimated dose level of 5 mg/ml, it was observed that freshly prepared solutions of p-chloroaniline in corn oil analyzed only ~96.5% of the theoretical concentration. The analytical results for the samples stored for up to a 14-day period indicated that p-chloroaniline did not suffer any significant additional loss within the limits of the ±1% test error after the initial zero-time loss. Additional studies demonstrated that the test material was reacting with something in corn oil in the amount of approximately 0.2 mg/g of oil. Since p-chloroaniline is known to be very vulnerable to oxidation, it was suspected that it was reacting with small amounts of peroxides in the corn oil. This suspicion was tentatively confirmed by performing an analysis for peroxide in the corn oil used for this study. The results showed a good correlation between the peroxide content of the oil and the amount of p-chloroaniline lost, and it was therefore concluded that the peroxide present in the corn oil caused the initial decomposition observed. After all the peroxide had been reacted, no further decomposition occurred in the gavage solution. Because of this initial decomposition in corn oil, a decision was made to administer p-chloroaniline in water as the hydrochloride salt.

Drinking Water Studies

Drinking water is another major route of administration used by the NTP. The stability protocol for drinking water test solutions is shown in Table 8–7. As in the previous stability studies, the protocol is set up to determine optimum storage and handling conditions. Analysis of these stability samples is similar to that described for water gavage studies, and stability here is similarly defined as a recovery of ⩾95% after storage for seven days at room temperature.

Table 8–7. Stability Protocol, Drinking Water Studies

Storage Temperature (°C)	Storage Time	Storage Conditions
5	7,14,18,21 days	Sealed in dark
24	1,7,14,18,21 days	Sealed in dark
24	3,6,24,18,48 hours	Open to air and light

Two of the twelve chemicals tested under this protocol were found to be unstable. In one case, the test material (chloramine) is used as a water treatment chemical, and therefore drinking water was continued as the route of administration for this toxicity study even though instability was demonstrated. The route of administration was changed to gavage for the second chemical.

Skin-Paint Studies

The last route of administration used by the NTP to be discussed here is skin paint. Table 8–8 shows that the stability protocol used for these studies is similar to that of the gavage stability studies and again is used to determine optimum storage and handling conditions. The solvents used by the NTP for skin-paint studies include acetone, 95% ethanol, and water. Analysis of these solutions is similar to those discussed for gavage studies. None of the ten chemicals studied in the skin-paint stability protocol were found to be unstable.

Table 8–8. Stability Protocol, Skin-Paint Study

Storage Temperature (° C)	Storage Time	Storage Conditions
5	7,14,18,21 days	Sealed in the dark
24	1,7,14,18,21 days	Sealed in the dark
24	3 hours	Open to air and light

CONCLUSION

This chapter has discussed the various routes of administration used by the NTP that require mixing the test material with a vehicle and determining the stability of these dosage mixtures. The original route of choice for a majority of the studies conducted by the NTP's Carcinogenesis Testing Program was dosed feed. The results of stability studies conducted on the dosed feed mixes demonstrated that in 50% of the cases, feed was not a suitable vehicle for administration of the test material. Results of studies to determine the compatability of the test chemical with other vehicles for dosage administration were much better than with feed, with only a minor percentage of the chemicals tested showing any instability.

Feed is selected as the route of choice when possible because it mimics human oral exposures and is the most economical (i.e., less labor intensive) toxicity study to run. Drinking water studies are also fairly economical but are limited by water solubility of the test material. The other alternative routes of administration, including gavage and skin paint, are more labor intensive and expensive to run and also require almost daily handling of the test animals, which could influence study results. Alternatives to direct blending of the test chemical into feed such as microencapsulation of the test chemical in a suitable material to improve its stability are currently being investigated by the NTP.

PART III

Chemical Inhalation Studies

CHAPTER 9

Inhalation Toxicology: An Overview

Trent R. Lewis
Division of Biomedical and
Behavioral Science, National Institute
for Occupational Safety and Health,
4676 Columbia Parkway,
Cincinnati, Ohio 45226

Inhalation toxicology, as does general toxicology, utilizes many disciplines ranging from the physical sciences (such as engineering, physics, and chemistry) to the biological sciences (such as physiology, biochemistry, and pathology). Through inhalation toxicology, chemicals present in industrial, mining, and agricultural atmospheres and in general ambient air pollution are studied. More specialized applications involve testing volatile or aerosolized drugs, and gases and smokes used by armed forces. The ubiquity of exposure by inhalation and the difficulty of abating such exposure make this branch of science essential for protecting the health and welfare of mankind.

In conducting inhalation toxicology, a number of special critical factors have to be considered: design and operation of exposure chambers in which experimental subjects are housed; generation, monitoring, and control of the atmospheric concentrations of the test materials; and an operational health and safety program to protect personnel directly involved in, or proximal to, the conduct of the study. The design of the experiment, animal maintenance during the study, assessment of biologic responses to the toxic challenge, and adherence to quality assurance are key elements.

CHAMBER DESIGN AND OPERATION

Most inhalation toxicology studies are conducted in chambers that expose the whole animal and that are operated dynamically. Early studies were conducted in a static mode; animals were placed in an enclosed chamber into which a known quantity of the material to be studied was released. The limitations of static exposure were readily apparent and included the short duration (usually up to one hour) possible be-

117

cause of changes in partial pressures of oxygen and carbon dioxide as the animals breathe, accumulation of moisture and volatile excretory products, and fall in atmospheric concentration of the test chemical as it became adsorbed on surfaces and adsorbed or absorbed by the animals.

Dynamic exposures are ones in which air mixed with a test material or agent flows continuously through the chamber at a rate sufficient to maintain temperature, humidity, carbon dioxide, and ammonia at controlled desirable levels and to ensure that animals are exposed to the desired concentration of the material under investigation. Such systems may range from simple chambers such as modified desiccators or aquariums, to glove boxes, to highly sophisticated and automated chambers constructed from polished stainless steel with large areas of glass. Systems of this nature permit large numbers of animals to be exposed simultaneously. Mixing of species is usually avoided because of transfer of disease from one species to another; however, inhalation studies are expensive, and the numbers of chambers available are limited, so species are sometimes mixed. In most instances, animals should not be group housed but should be housed in individual cages to preclude huddling together, which may cause filtering by the animal's fur or hairs of test atmosphere, cannibalism of dead or moribund animals by cage mates, or fighting, such as occurs among male mice establishing an order of dominance. Problems of uniform distribution of the material are minimal in a properly designed and operated chamber, and the objective of exposing many animals to essentially the same airborne concentration is readily attained.

The size of an exposure chamber is determined by the number and types of animals it is to house. The rule is that the volume of the animal population should not exceed 5% of the chamber volume; denser animal loading leads to marked losses in atmospheric concentrations of the test material.

The shape of exposure chambers must permit uniform airborne distribution of test material throughout the chamber. With stable gases and vapors, distribution is readily achieved whenever dead space within the chamber is minimal. If the material under study is an aerosol, liquid or solid, or an unstable vapor or gas, more attention must be directed to chamber design to ensure uniform distribution within the chamber.

In addition to the whole-body type of inhalation exposure, methods for other types of exposures can be employed. Such methods include apparatuses so that only the head or nose and mouth of each animal protrudes into the test atmosphere; face masks so that only the nose and mouth are in contact with the test atmosphere; and surgical techniques such as tracheostomies, which permit studying either the nasopharyngeal portion of the respiratory tract or conversely introducing the material directly into the tracheae and studying effects on the lung.

CHARACTERISTICS OF EXPERIMENTAL ATMOSPHERES

The complexity of test atmospheres may vary from simple ones that contain a single test material, to mixtures of several materials in simple combination, to complex mixtures generated by a process designed to simulate practical situations difficult to synthesize with individual components, such as emissions from internal combustion engines and military smoke obscurants. Materials to be tested exist in three physical states: gases, vapors, and aerosols (liquid or solid). All three states may be present simultaneously in a test atmosphere.

Gases or vapors of low-boiling liquids may be generated by admixture with air or an inert carrier gas if the material is supplied under pressure in a cylinder. The gas or vapor is passed through a reducing valve to bring the pressure to a constant value and then through a needle valve to control flow. The gas or vapor is then mixed with filtered, conditioned air and introduced into the exposure chamber.

Vapors may be generated using evaporation devices; their concentration will be limited by the vapor pressure of the substance at a particular temperature. Saturated vapor concentrations often are prepared by blowing air or an inert gas through a liquid, which may be heated. In the latter case, care must be taken to remove any condensed particles when the vapor cools to airstream temperatures. The vapors must be stable to aeration and heating in order to apply such methods. Vapors must be prepared from pure liquids; otherwise components with varying vapor pressures will result in atmospheres that change qualitatively and quantitatively during the duration of the experiment. Another means of generating vapors is to deliver the liquid from a syringe at a regulated rate into a vaporizing device.

The generation of liquid or solid-state aerosols is most demanding since the particle size distribution must also be determined. The latter is essential since the aerodynamic particle size will determine where the particles are deposited in the respiratory tract; and this in turn will affect toxicity.

Liquid aerosols may be produced from a variety of generators, which include atomizers, ultrasonic nebulizers, spinning disc generators, and vibrating rod or orifice generators. Solid aerosols may be produced by an array of devices such as the Wright Dust Feed generator, whereby a rotating blade scrapes presized and packed material into a high-velocity carrier airstream, or fluidized-bed generators in which an airstream circulates through the feedstock powder and picks up and carries particles through in-stream stages of impaction or settling forces. Fibers, solid particles with a length-to-width ratio of three to one or greater, often pose special difficulties in obtaining adequate quantities of a specified size to conduct a long-term inhalation study and in generating the desired concentrations. Problems of electric charge on the particle, though not limited to fibers, are often encountered.

Whatever the nature of the experimental atmospheres, it is imperative that the test material be generated at a constant and known concentration and that there be analytical control of the atmospheric concentrations.

HEALTH AND SAFETY OF EMPLOYEES

In the conduct of inhalation studies, the health and safety of the personnel directly involved in the day-to-day conduct of the study is of paramount importance. Minimal requirements range from standard work uniforms, safety shoes, and safety glasses to full sets of disposable clothing, gloves, air-supplied respirators, and other specialized items for personnel protection. The specific requirements will be dictated by the compound or mixture under study. A key feature of worker health protection is a periodic physical examination, which ideally includes an examination prior to exposure to toxic substances in order to provide baseline data. The interval between physicals will vary but is usually no more than a year. Other safety and health procedures include the provision for shower facilities so that employees will not contaminate their street clothes with toxic compounds. Eating, drinking, and smoking should be prohibited in the inhalation facility. Workers need to be provided with instruction in basic safety procedures: the use of respirators, safe pipetting techniques, safe handling of gas cylinders, and decontamination procedures in the event of spills or accidents. The inhalation facility should have limited access to prevent the accidental exposure of individuals not associated with the operation. Written operating procedures should be readily available which specifically describe all routine laboratory operations.

MAINTENANCE OF EXPERIMENTAL ANIMALS

Animals may be housed continuously in exposure chambers provided the chambers have been designed with this in mind. Under such conditions, food is removed during the daily exposure period; deprivation of water during this time is optional. It is highly desirable but not mandatory to place excreta pans under the animal caging. A major advantage of continuous housing is that materials under investigation are sequestered in the chamber and are less likely to contaminate the remainder of the facility and elsewhere.

Animals may be housed intermittently and removed to other accommodations during the nonexposure period. There are several advantages of intermittent housing: there is no need to feed and water the animals while they are in the chamber; at the end of the exposure period, there is an opportunity to evaluate the animals; and it is easier to clean the chamber. Disadvantages to this system include increased work associated with twice-daily handling of the animals, increased animal handling with resultant stresses, and greater likelihood of contaminating the general facility with the substances being investigated. Animals should be housed and serviced using procedures that maximize containment of the material under study, minimize circumstances that introduce unwanted confounding variables into the study, and minimize animal handling and servicing requirements.

EXPERIMENTAL DESIGN

Experiments to assess the likely effects on humans under accidental situations may range from a few minutes to several hours. To ascertain human risk from long-term, low-level exposures, chronic exposures of two or more years may be required, with interim testing or sacrifice to evaluate various routinely used toxicologic criteria and those selected according to the particular toxicologic character of the substance under test.

Multilevel exposure concentrations are standard operating procedure. A minimum of two exposure concentrations should be tested; three or more exposure levels are preferable. One concentration should be such as to elicit definite target organ effects so that the animal response can be precisely delineated. The second exposure concentration is one in which minimal effects occur in a small percentage of the animals exposed. A third and most important exposure concentration is one termed "no-effect" level. It is obvious that the term *no effect* is relative to the criteria employed for its determination.

In all inhalation studies, it is imperative to maintain a group of control animals under identical conditions but without addition of the test substance to the chamber air and which, at the end of the experiment, are subjected to the response criteria used for the animals exposed to the substance under investigation. This is particularly significant when the no-effect levels of chemicals are sought; otherwise minor changes in biologic criteria may be attributed to the test material, when they are, in reality, due to such nontreatment variables as unmeasured environmental factors, intercurrent disease, and/or natural biologic variance, including intrinsic disease or genetic predisposition.

The selection of the number and species of experimental animals in the study will depend on the purpose of the investigation. In experiments related to accidental occupational exposures, it is customary to study the effects of high concentrations on relatively small groups of animals in order to assess the likely acute effects on humans. To determine chronic health hazards, large-scale, long-term studies are performed with daily exposures of multiple species with numbers of animals judged to provide adequate statistical power.

ASSESSMENT OF BIOLOGIC EFFECTS

The prime objective of toxicity testing in animals is to derive data applicable to humans. Therefore, it is necessary to monitor subtle as well as gross effects following exposure. Comprehensive and sensitive testing procedures should be employed to evaluate response. Preferably these procedures should be well established and designed in a manner that permits the ultimate application of the results to the population at risk. Although classic criteria of toxic response have been morphologic and biochemical alterations, significant advances in assessing dysfunction in organ systems have been achieved, but more emphasis and application are needed in this area.

QUALITY CONTROL

In any long-term inhalation study, the maintenance of the desired exposure conditions (concentration, temperature, humidity, airflow, and so forth) over several months or years can be difficult. Prolonged periods of downtime when the chambers are not in operation must be avoided. Thus, the need exists for a thorough evaluation of every aspect of the inhalation system (air supply, filters, chambers, generation and monitoring devices) prior to the initiation of the animal exposures. It is equally important that preventive maintenance be performed at periodic intervals throughout the study. The presence of alarms or sensing devices, designed to detect deviations from the desired exposure conditions, are very useful in maintaining quality control. Periodic recalibration of analytical instrumentation is required to ensure that desired conditions are maintained throughout the study. It may even be desirable to check analytical results by contract with an outside group, which periodically would make unannounced samplings to be correlated with routine, internally obtained results.

SUMMARY

This overview has been directed to the methodological aspect of performing inhalation studies with particular emphasis on some of the unique and peculiar issues for chemists. The administration of an agent in an airborne form and the equating of biological responses to varying specific airborne concentrations is of marked concern whether it relates to community ambient air pollution or various occupational atmospheres. Inhalation toxicology is a specialized branch or arm of the broader science of toxicology and has evolved to answer those health questions relating to air quality.

CHAPTER 10

Methods for Generation of Test Atmospheres

Robert T. Drew

Medical Department, Brookhaven National
Laboratory, Upton, New York 11973

Accurate and reproducible generation of airborne toxic agents in both gaseous and particulate form is essential to the proper conduct of inhalation toxicity studies. Generation of vapors is usually straightforward using basic principles such as evaporation and diffusion, and combinations of the two. Generation of particles is more complicated because several forces, including momentum, gravity, and electrostatic forces, operate on particles, causing them to settle out and also to agglomerate. In addition, the aerosol can be in the form of liquid droplets, as well as solid particles, and the techniques for producing them differ. The intent of this chapter is to provide an introduction to the methods for producing stable, reproducible test atmospheres for assessing inhalation toxicity. After describing certain basic principles, techniques currently used to produce both vapors and aerosols will be reviewed with liberal reference to already published work. Neither space nor time permits a comprehensive review of all the techniques available. However, this chapter will provide an overview which should enable the reader to become generally familiar with the technology and should provide an entry into the specific literature of interest.

BASIC PRINCIPLES

Definitions

For this discussion, gases and vapors are synonymous, and both refer to molecules of a compound, in gaseous form, usually mixed in another gas or gas mixture (air). No distinction is made among materials that are solids, liquids, or gases at room temperature because once they are in gaseous form, they follow the same physical laws. Concentrations can be expressed as moles/liter, grams/liter, or ppm, where ppm refers to a volume-volume relationship. By definition, $1 \mu \ell$ of gas per liter of air is 1 ppm. In order to convert ppm to mg/m^3, the following equation must be used:

$$\text{ppm} = \frac{\mu \ell_x}{\ell \text{ air}} = \frac{m \ell_x}{m^{3 \text{ air}}} \cdot \frac{\text{mmole}_x}{22.4 \, m \ell_x} \cdot \frac{mg_x}{\text{mmole}_x} \cdot \frac{273}{T} \cdot \frac{P}{760} = \frac{mg_x}{m^{3 \text{ air}}}$$

where the subscript x refers to the specific compound in question.

To convert mg/m^3 to ppm, the following equation should be used:

$$\frac{mg_x}{m^{3\,air}} \cdot \frac{mmole_x}{mg_x} \cdot \frac{22.4\,m\ell_x}{mmole_x} \cdot \frac{T}{273} \cdot \frac{760}{P} = \frac{m\ell_x}{m^{3\,air}} = ppm.$$

It is important to note that ppm has no meaning if used to describe aerosol concentrations. They must be described in units of mass/unit volume.

Aerosols

An aerosol can be defined as a suspension of particles in air. The particles can be solid or liquid and can be described by a number of parameters, including shape, surface area, chemical composition, and electrical charge. Most often they are characterized by size, with particles of a similar size said to be monodisperse and particles of a wide variety of sizes said to be heterodisperse. Both particle size and mass concentration are necessary to characterize an aerosol adequately. A particle can be described by a number of different diameters, however, and it is important to define which diameter is being described and to understand the relationships between the different diameters.

If a particle is being measured microscopically, its size can be measured in two dimensions. Liquid droplets dry and appear as circles of the original droplet [1]. Solid, irregularly shaped particles provide a variety of ways to measure the diameter. Figure 10–1 depicts three different ways of describing the diameter of the particle. Feret's diameter is the length of a horizontal projection of the particle and changes with the orientation. Martin's diameter is the length of a horizontal line bisecting the

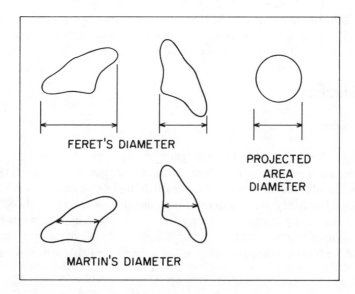

Figure 10–1.   Ways of measuring particle size.

particle into two equal areas. A third way of measuring the diameter is to compare it to a circle with equal area. This is known as the projected area diameter [2].

The size of a particle can also be defined in terms of its aerodynamic characteristics. The most widely used aerodynamic measure is the aerodynamic diameter, defined as the diameter of a sphere of unit density having the same settling velocity as the specific particle in question [2]. Thus, irregularly shaped particles pose less of a problem when the aerodynamic diameter is used. The aerodynamic diameter is preferred over any two-dimensional diameter in inhalation toxicity studies because it is primarily the aerodynamic characteristics of the particles that determine the site and extent of deposition in the respiratory tract.

Most aerosols have size distributions best characterized by a log-normal function. This distribution of sizes allows for simple mathematical transformations. The characteristic parameters of a log-normal distribution are the median (the geometric mean) and the geometric standard deviation (σ_g). The median of a distribution of diameters is called the count median diameter; the median of the mass or volume distribution is called the mass median diameter (MMD) and the volume median diameter (VMD), respectively. An example [3] of a log-normal distribution function with a count median diameter of 1.0 and a σ_g of 2.0 is shown in Figure 10–2. Aero-

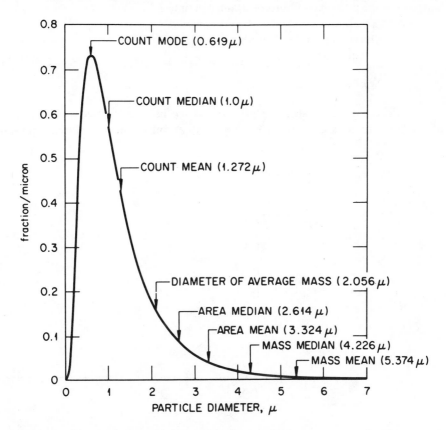

Figure 10–2.   A normalized log normal distribution function.

sols with σ_g less than about 1.2 are generally considered to be monodisperse, while those with $\sigma_g > 1.2$ are considered to be heterodisperse [3]. In addition to particle size, an aerosol must also be described in terms of mass concentration. The techniques for measuring both aerosols and vapors are the subject of other papers in this book and will not be discussed further here.

Inhalation Chamber Dynamics

The buildup and removal of materials in inhalation chambers were first described by Silver [4], who confirmed his theoretical calculations with experimental data. The equilibrium concentration of any material in a chamber is related to the amount of material entering the chamber and the quantity of air passing through the chamber. The buildup and removal of material (Figure 10–3) is a logarithmic function of the air turnover rate having the general form:

$$T_x = K a/b \qquad (10-1)$$

where x = the percent equilibrium attained in time T
K = a constant
a = the volume of the chamber
b = the flow rate

For T_{99}, $K = 4.6$; for T_{95}, $K = 3$.

Unfortunately, a misleading term, *air change,* has been carried over to the field of inhalation toxicology from the heating, ventilation, and air-conditioning termin-

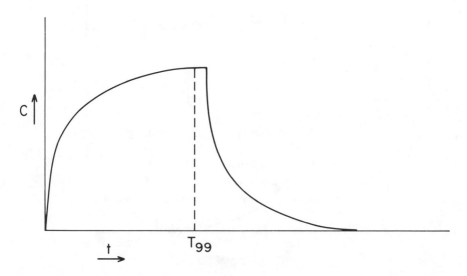

Figure 10–3. Buildup and removal of pollutants in a chamber.

ology. One air change is defined as the addition and withdrawal of a volume of air equal to the volume of the room or chamber being considered. However, because the incoming air mixes with the air already in the chamber, a complete change of the air has not occurred. This will happen only if the chamber has laminar or plug flow instead of turbulent flow. In his original paper, Silver stated that the term air change was confusing and misleading, and we are still arguing about it thirty-five years later [5].

For purposes of this discussion, one air change is defined as the replacement of a quantity of air equal to the volume of the chamber. Referring back to equation 10-1, if a chamber is operating at 15 air changes per hour:

$$b = 15a/\text{hr} = 15a/\text{hr} \times \text{hr}/60 \text{ min} = a/4 \text{ min}$$

$$T_x = Ka/b = Kab^{-1} = Ka \times 4 \text{ min}/a = 4K \text{ min}$$

Therefore, $T_{99} = (4.6) \, 4 \text{ min} = 18.4 \text{ min}$ and $T_{95} = (3) \, 4 \text{ min} = 12 \text{ min}$. Various constants for T_{99} and T_{95} are summarized in Table 10-1.

Table 10-1.   Various Constants for T_{99} and T_{95}

Air Changes/Hr	a/b Min/Air Change	T_{99} (min)	T_{95} (min)
60	1	4.6	3
30	2	9.2	6
15	4	18.4	12
10	6	27.6	18

The concentration during a typical exposure is shown in Figure 10-4, with the generator being turned on at t_a and off at t_b. The duration of the exposure, T, is usually the time defined by $t_b - t_a$, assuming the concentration is relatively stable between T_{99} and t_b, and the logarithmic buildup and decay occur at the same rate. Notice that T is long compared to T_{99}. The exposure after t_b is small and equal in area to that missing (shaded area between t_a and T_{99}) during the buildup of the material in the chamber. If exposures of short duration are contemplated, the time required for buildup and decay is important. McFarland [6] has described techniques for increasing flows to shorten T_{99}. This can also be accomplished by programming pollutant flows, and concentration-time curves approaching square waves have been produced [7]. Another way to minimize buildup and decay effects is to construct drawer units, which can be inserted into the chamber after equilibrium has been attained [8].

Although Silver's original studies were developed for gases, they are equally applicable to particles. The atmospheric concentration of both gases and particles will fall rapidly to very low values after cessation of pollutant flow. Two precautions should be mentioned. With vapors, it is possible that unreacted materials stored inside the animal will be exhaled when the chamber concentration is reduced. Thus, when handling animals, the investigator must consider the potential exposure result-

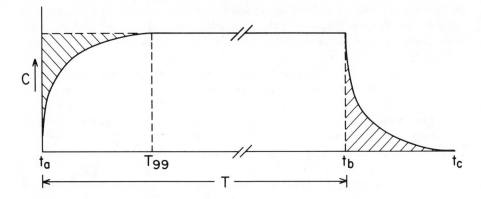

Figure 10–4.   Chamber concentration versus time.

ing from exhaled, unreacted test gases. The problems with particles are even more complicated. While the chamber atmosphere may be devoid of particles, they remain deposited on every surface inside the chamber. When animals are being serviced subsequent to exposure to particles, animals and cages must be handled with gloves since contact with surface-deposited material is unavoidable. In addition the possibility of reentrainment into the air must be considered.

TECHNIQUES FOR GENERATION OF VAPORS

Techniques for producing known concentrations of gases and vapors have been reviewed by several authors [9–14], with a discussion of some of the lesser used methods found in a review by Hersch [15]. Since inhalation chambers are operated mainly as dynamic (constant flow) systems, procedures for generating vapors in static systems will not be discussed. These were reviewed by Drew and Lippmann [13].

   The simplest method of generating gases is to meter them directly from cylinders into the inlet of the inhalation chamber. Cylinders can contain the pure test gas or a mixture of the test gas in air or nitrogen. Techniques for filling cylinders are discussed by Cotabish [11] and by Roccanova [16].

   Pressure regulators and low flow rate rotometers are available for accurate control of the test agent flow. Saltzman [17, 18] has described other ways of accurately metering low quantities of gas. If pressurized cylinders are used, it is important that a normally closed solenoid valve be included in the system to prevent buildup of the test agent in the event of a power failure. It is useful if the solenoid valve has a manual reset to avoid inadvertent start-up when the electric power is reestablished.

   Many agents such as SO_2, N_2O_4, fluorocarbons, and vinyl chloride are available as liquids in pressurized cylinders. The pressure in the cylinder remains constant until no more liquid is present. These systems are particularly amenable to simple metering techniques since the internal pressure is constant. However, care must be taken to avoid undesirable compounds in the head space gas. This can sometimes be accomplished by inverting the cylinder or by having a tube inside the cylinder extend to the bottom and drawing the liquid out and then having it vaporize.

With materials that are liquid at room temperature, a volatilization step is necessary. In some instances, such as with benzene, the vapor pressure is sufficient to keep enough vapor in the atmosphere above the liquid to allow a metered airstream to carry the agent to the chamber. If more material is needed, the airstream can be passed through the liquid using a fritted bubbler. If bubblers are used, a filter should be in the system to prevent droplets from entering the chamber and then evaporating. Two or more bubblers in series with the first bubbler maintained at a higher temperature will provide higher and more consistent outputs (Figure 10–5).

As liquids with higher boiling points are used, it becomes necessary to heat the system to provide vapor for the chamber. One technique is to meter the volatile liquid onto a heated surface and then sweep the resultant vapor into the chamber with a carrier gas (Figure 10–6). Syringe pumps, peristaltic pumps, and pressure systems can be used to meter the liquid onto the heated surface. In some cases, to avoid condensation, it is necessary to heat the line carrying the volatilized material from the point of vaporization to the chamber. Heating tapes are often used for this purpose. Nelson [19] described a system such as this for producing mercury vapors. A new system, recently described by Decker et al. [20], allows for a heated wick to be mounted directly in the chamber intake, thus avoiding any condensation.

Other principles could be applied to the generation of gases for inhalation studies. Theoretically, permeation tubes [21] could be used to generate some gases, but it is not known if this technique is being applied to inhalation chambers. If low concentrations are required, diffusion cells [22] could be used. Recently a device based on countercurrent volatilization was described; it uses a multiplate high-efficiency distillation column [23]. This system minimizes the chances of thermal decomposition. Finally, in some cases such as with ozone, it is necessary to produce the agent when needed since the compounds are unstable and cannot be stored.

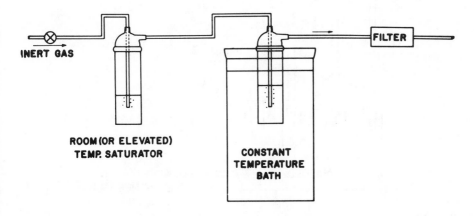

Figure 10–5.   Two bubblers in series.

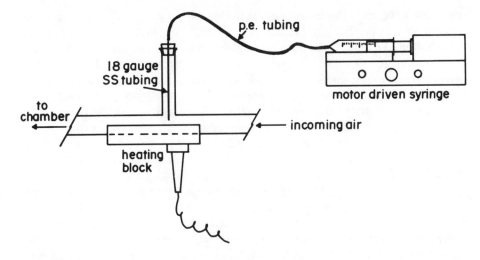

Figure 10-6. A syringe drive mechanism metering liquid onto a heated surface for evaporation.

When performing dose-response studies, if condensation is not a problem, it is convenient to construct a distribution manifold near the chambers and meter the gas from the manifold to each chamber. One such system for use with these exposure chambers is shown schematically in Figure 10-7. The manifold contains an inlet port and four outlet ports (one more than the number of chambers). Each port has a rotometer to measure the flow to the chambers. The extra port is vented through an air-cleaning device and then to the exhaust system. It provides more flexibility in the system, allowing proportionate adjustment of the other three rotometers if necessary. Such a system is very useful when metering dilute test agent mixtures from cylinders.

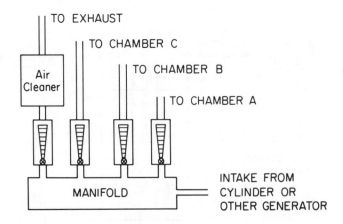

Figure 10-7. A manifold gas distribution system.

TECHNIQUES FOR GENERATION OF AEROSOLS

Large numbers of devices for production of respirable aerosols are described in the literature. More thorough discussions are provided in several reviews [3,24–29]. Aerosol generators use either liquids or solids as their source material. The aerosol resulting from a liquid source can be either wet or dry, depending on how the generator operates. Wet-dispersion generators break up bulk liquid into droplets, and if the liquid is nonvolatile, the resulting aerosol will consist of liquid droplets. When volatile liquids are aerosolized, the resulting particles will consist of the nonvolatile residues and will be much smaller than the droplets originating from the generator. Dry generators usually disperse a previously ground material by mechanical means, usually with the aid of an air jet. The aerosols produced are composed of solid irregular particles having a broad size range. The rate of generation depends on hardness of the bulk compound, packing density, uniformity of the feed drive mechanism, and the air jet pressure.

Nebulizers

Raabe [28] described nine different types of compressed air nebulizers, many of them commercially available. He also compared the operating characteristics of most of those devices providing information on the operating pressure, output characteristics, volumetric flow rate, and droplet size distribution. More recently, Drew et al. [30] described the construction and operation of the Laskin nebulizer. Miller et al. [31] also compared the outputs of three commercial nebulizers. One problem with nebulizers is that the concentration of the solute increases over the course of operation, thereby causing particle size to increase. This growth of particles can be reduced by saturating the incoming air with solvent [32], by adjusting temperature and pressure [33], by continuously supplying fresh solution [34], or by modifying the reservoirs from which the solutions are nebulized [35]. Compressed air nebulizers are still very popular, with papers appearing recently using this principle to provide coal liquid aerosols for inhalation studies [36], aerosols of carcinogenic amines [37], and aerosols of sulfates for human studies [38]. Ultrasonic nebulizers are also available [3,28,39], but these have not been used for inhalation studies nearly as much as compressed air nebulizers.

Dry Dispersion Devices

Of the numerous dry dispersion devices described for use in inhalation studies, the one most frequently used in the past was the Wright Dust Feed [41]. In this system (Figure 10–8), a gear drives the surface of a packed plug of finely ground powder against a scraping mechanism. A high-velocity airstream disperses the powder. Chamber concentrations resulting from the Wright Dust Feed depend on the pack-

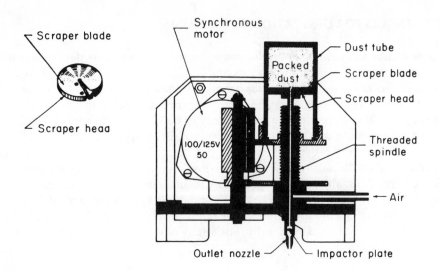

Figure 10–8.   The Wright Dust Feed.

ing density of the powder, the use of very dry air, and the rate at which the plug moves against the scraper blade. Many other mechanical devices for producing aerosols have been described [25,41–47]. Most of these devices have a mechanism such as a chain, conveyer belt, or screw to carry the powder to a point where it is suspended by an air jet. In most cases the material is preground. However, at least two generators have been described [48] where the dust was ground as needed and directed through an ellutriator and into the chamber. These systems were reviewed by Tillery et al. [27], Raabe [29], and more recently Hinds [49]. Two newer devices operating on the same general principles were described by Leong et al. [50] and by Milliman et al. [51] who used rotating brushes to move the powder. Techniques for dispersing fibers have also been described by several authors [52–55].

Drew and Laskin [56] created a fluidizing bed with the use of a high-speed four-blade fan and then aspirated a preground dust from this fluidizing bed through a baffling chamber and into an inhalation chamber. Air-activated fluidizing beds (Figure 10–9) have recently been described by several authors [47,57–59] with at least two versions being commercially available [59]. Fluidizing bed generators have also been used to generate aerosols of fiber glass for inhalation studies [60,61].

Solid insoluble aerosols can be produced by nebulization of chelated metal ions [62] or metal carbonates, acetates, or oxalates [63], followed by oxidation to the metal oxide in a tube furnace and then cooling the aerosol. The resulting metal oxide spheres can be plumbed directly to the chamber. Other less common principles of aerosol generation include exploding wires [64,65], vaporization and condensation [66], creation of metal fumes [67], and the use of packaged aerosol products to produce test aerosols [68,69]. Finally, nebulization of suspended particles has been used to produce aerosols [70].

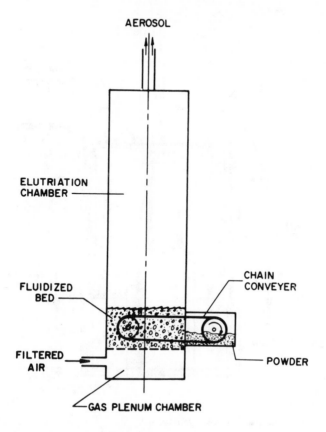

Figure 10-9.   An air-activated fluidized bed.

Monodisperse Aerosols

Occasionally, it is necessary to produce monodisperse aerosols for inhalation studies. The device most often used for such studies is the spinning disc generator (Figure 10-10); several authors have described [71-74] or reviewed [2,13,28] generators of this type. In these systems, a liquid is metered onto the center of a spinning disc, and the centrifugal force accelerates the liquid toward the edge of the disc. The liquid leaves the disc as droplets or as filaments that break up into droplets. Secondary droplets are separated from the primaries aerodynamically. For a description of other systems to produce monodisperse aerosols from solutions, see Drew and Lippmann [13]. Monodisperse condensation aerosols were first described by LaMer and Sinclair [75], and several modifications of this design have been described [66,76-78]. Finally, as reviewed by Raabe [28], monodisperse aerosols can be produced by generating an aerosol of heterodisperse particles, separating the particles into monodisperse size groups using a spiral dust aerosol centrifuge, and resuspending the monodisperse particles.

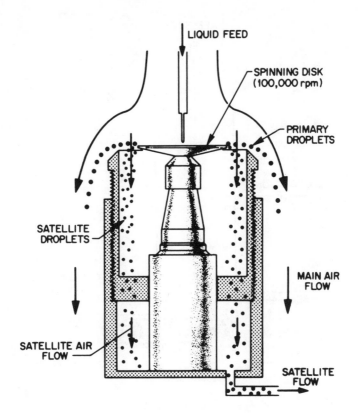

Figure 10-10. A spinning disk aerosol generator.

SUMMARY

This chapter has introduced the subject of gas and particle generation for inhalation studies and has given some of the basic principles involved in producing replicable test atmospheres for toxicological research.

REFERENCES

1. Whitby, K.T. and R.A. Vomela. "Response of Single Particle Optical Counters to Non-ideal Particles," *Environ. Sci. Technol.* 1:801–814 (1967).
2. Marple, V.A. and K.L. Rubow. "Aerosol Generation Concepts and Parameters," in *Generation of Aerosols and Facilities for Exposure Experiments,* K. Willeke, Ed. (Ann Arbor, Mich.: Ann Arbor Science Publishers, 1980), p. 3–29.
3. Raabe, O.G. "Generation and Characterization of Aerosols," in *Inhalation Carcinogenesis,* M.G. Hanna, Jr., P. Nettesheim, and J.R. Gilbert, Eds., U.S. Atomic Energy Commission, CONF-691001, U.S. Department of Commerce, Springfield, Va. (1970), pp. 123–172.

4. Silver, S.D. "Constant Flow Gassing Chambers: Principles Influencing Design and Operation," *J. Lab. Clin. Med.* 31:1153–1161 (1946).

5. Moss, O.R., Y. Alarie, R.T. Drew, H.N. MacFarland, and B.K.J. Leong. "Post-symposium Correspondence," in *Inhalation Toxicology and Technology,* B.K.J. Leong, Ed. (Ann Arbor, Mich.: Ann Arbor Science Publishers, 1981), pp. 299–307.

6. MacFarland, H.N. "Respiratory Toxicology," in *Essays in Toxicology,* Vol. 7. (New York: Academic Press, 1976).

7. Van Stee, E.W. and Moorman, M.P. "Monitoring for Temperature, Humidity, and Concentration," in *Proceedings Workshop on Inhalation Chamber Technology,* R.T. Drew, Ed., BNL Formal Report 51318 (1978), pp. 81–87.

8. Drew, R.T. "Exposure of Rodents to Particulate Carcinogens," in *Proceedings Workshop on Inhalation Chamber Technology,* R.T. Drew, Ed., BNL Formal Report 51318 (1978).

9. Bryan, R.J. "Generation and Monitoring of Gases for Inhalation Studies," in *Inhalation Carcinogenesis,* M.G. Hanna, Jr., P. Nettesheim, and J.R. Gilbert, Eds., U.S. Atomic Energy Commission, CONF-691001, U.S. Department of Commerce, Springfield, Va. (1970), pp. 193–205.

10. Lodge, J.P. "Production of Controlled Test Atmospheres," in *Air Pollution,* 2nd ed., Vol. II, A.C. Stern, Ed. (New York: Academic Press, 1968).

11. Cotabish, H.N., P.W. McConnaghey, and H.C. Messer. "Making Known Concentrations for Instrument Calibration," *Am. Ind. Hyg. Assoc. J.* 22: 392–402 (1961).

12. Nelson, G.O. *Controlled Test Atmospheres—Principles and Techniques* (Ann Arbor, Mich.: Ann Arbor Science Publishers, 1971).

13. Drew, R.T. and M. Lippmann. "Calibration of Air Sampling Instruments," in *Air Sampling Instruments for Evaluation of Atmospheric Contaminants.* 5th ed. (American Conference of Governmental Industrial Hygienists, 1978), pp. I-1–I-38.

14. Silverman, L. "Experimental Test Methods," in *Air Pollution Handbook,* P.L. Magill, F.R. Holden, and C. Ackley, Eds. (New York: McGraw-Hill, 1956), pp. 12:1–12:48.

15. Hersch, P.A. "Controlled Addition of Experimental Pollutants to Air," *J. Air. Pollut. Contr. Assoc.* 19:164–172 (1969).

16. Roccanova, G. "The Present State of the Art of the Preparation of Gaseous Standards." Presented at the Pittsburgh Conference on Analytical Chemistry and Spectroscopy (available from Scientific Gas Product, 1968).

17. Saltzman, B.E. "Preparation and Analysis of Calibrated Low Concentrations of Sixteen Toxic Gases," *Anal. Chem.* 33:1100–1112 (1961).

18. Saltzman, B.E. and A.F. Wartburg, Jr. "Precision Flow Dilution System for Standard Low Concentrations of Nitrogen Dioxide," *Anal. Chem.* 37:1261–1264 (1965).

19. Nelson, G.O. "Simplified Method for Generating Known Concentrations of Mercury Vapor in Air," *Rev. Sci. Inst.* 41:776–777 (1960).

20. Decker, J.R., O.R. Moss, and B.L. Kay. "Controlled Delivery Vapor Generator for Animal Exposures," *Am. Ind. Hyg. Assoc. J.* 43:400–402 (1982).

21. O'Keefe, A.E., and G.O. Ortman. "Primary Standards for Trace Gas Analysis," *Anal. Chem.* 38:760–763 (1966).

22. Altshuller, A.P. and L.R. Cohen. "Application of Diffusion Cells to the Production of Known Concentrations of Gaseous Hydrocarbons," *Anal. Chem.* 32:802–810 (1960).

23. Potts, W.J. and E.C. Steiner. "An Apparatus for Generation of Vapors from Liquids of Low Volatility for Use in Inhalation Toxicity Studies," *Am. Ind. Hyg. Assoc. J.* 41:141–145 (1980).

24. Kerker, M. "Laboratory Generation of Aerosols," *Adv. in Colloid and Interface Sci.* 5:105–172 (1975).

25. Grassel, E.E. "Aerosol Generation for Industrial Research and Product Testing," in *Fine Particles,* B.Y.H. Liu, Ed. (New York: Academic Press, 1976) pp. 145–172.

26. Mercer, T.T. *Aerosol Technology in Hazard Evaluation* (New York and London: Academic Press, 1973).

27. Tillery, M.I., G.O. Wood, and H.J. Ettinger. "Generation and Characterization of Aerosols and Vapors for Inhalation Experiments," *Env. Hlth Perspect.* 16:25–40 (1976).

28. Raabe, O.G. "The Generation of Aerosols of Fine Particles," in *Fine Particles,* B.Y.H. Liu, Ed. (New York: Academic Press, 1976) pp. 57–110.

29. Corn, M., and N.A. Esmen. "Aerosol Generation," in *Handbook on Aerosols,* R. Dennis, Ed. (TID-26608, Technical Information Center, 1976).

30. Drew, R.T., D.M. Bernstein, and S. Laskin. "The Laskin Aerosol Generator," *J. Toxicol. Environ. Health* 4:661–670 (1978).

31. Miller, J.L., B.O. Stuart, H.S. Deford, and O.R. Moss. "Liquid Aerosol Generation for Inhalation Toxicology Studies," in *Inhalation Toxicology and Technology,* B.K.J. Leong, Ed. (Ann Arbor, Mich.: Ann Arbor Science Publishers, 1981), pp. 121–138.

32. Lauterback, K.E., A.D. Hayes, and M.A. Coelho. "An Improved Aerosol Generator," *AMA Arch. Ind. Health* 13:156–160 (1956).

33. Burke, H.L. and T.E. Hull. "An Improved Aerosol Generator," *Am. Ind. Hyg. Assoc. J.* 36:43–48 (1975).

34. Liu, B.Y.H. and K.W. Lee. "An Aerosol Generator of High Stability," *Am. Ind. Hyg. Assoc. J.* 36:861–865 (1975).

35. DeFord, H.S., M.L. Clark, and O.R. Moss. "A Stabilized Aerosol Generator," *Am. Ind. Hyg. Assoc. J.* 42:602–604 (1981).

36. Springer, D.L., M.L. Clark, D.H. Willard, and D.D. Mahlum. "Generation and Delivery of Coal Liquid Aerosols for Inhalation Studies," *Am. Ind. Hyg. Assoc. J.* 43:486–491 (1982).

37. Avol, E.L., R.M. Bailey, and K.A. Bell. "Sulfate Aerosol Generation and Characterization for Controlled Human Exposures," *Am. Ind. Hyg. Assoc. J.* 40:619–625 (1979).

38. Rappaport, S.M., and D.J. Gettemy. "The Generation of Aerosols of Carcinogenic Aromatic Amines," *Am. Ind. Hyg. Assoc. J.* 39:287–294 (1978).

39. Fulwyler, M.J. and O.G. Raabe. "The Ultrasonic Generation of Monodisperse Aerosols." Presented at the American Industrial Hygiene Conference, Detroit, May 11–15, 1970.

40. Wright, B.M. "A New Dust-Feed Mechanism," *J. Sci. Instrum.* 27:12–15 (1950).

41. Deichmann, W.B. "An Apparatus Designed for the Production of Controlled Dust Concentrations in the Air Breathed by Experimental Animals," *J. Ind. Hyg. Toxicol.* 26:334–335 (1974).

42. Crider, W.L., N.P. Barkley, and A.A. Strong. "Dry Powder Aerosol Dispensing Device with Long-time Output Stability," *Rev. Sci. Instrum.* 39:152–155 (1968).

43. Ebens, R. and M. Vos. "A Device for the Continuous Metering of Small Dust Quantities," *Staub-Reinhalt Luft in English* 28:24–25 (1968).

44. Stead, F.M., C.U. Dernehl, and C.A. Nau. "A Dust Feed Apparatus Useful for Exposure of Small Animals to Small and Fixed Concentrations of Dusts," *J. Ind. Hyg. Toxicol.* 26:90–93 (1944).

45. Fuchs, N.A. and F.I. Murashkevich. "Laboratory Powder Dispenser (Dust Generator)," *Staub-Reinhalt Luft in English* 30:1–3 (1970).

46. Dimmick, R.L. "Jet Disperser for Compacted Powders in the one-to-ten Micron Range," *A.M.A. Arch. Ind. Health* 20:8–14 (1959).

47. Marple, V.A., B.Y.H. Liu, and K.L. Rubow. "A Dust Generator for Laboratory Use," *Am. Ind. Hyg. Assoc. J.* 39:26–32 (1978).

48. Laskin, S., R.T. Drew, V.P. Cappiello, and M. Kuschner. "Inhalation Studies with Freshly Generated Polyurethane Foam Dust," in *Assessment of Airborne Particles,* T.T. Mercer, P.E. Morrow, and W. Stober, Eds. (Springfield, Ill.: Charles C. Thomas Publishers, 1972) pp. 382–402.

49. Hinds, W.C. "Dry-Dispersion Aerosol Generators," in *Generation of Aerosols and Facilities for Exposure Experiments,* K. Willeke, Ed. (Ann Arbor, Mich.: Ann Arbor Science Publishers, 1980), pp. 171–187.

50. Leong, B.K.J., D.J. Powell, and G.L. Pochyla. "A New Dust Generator for Inhalation Toxicological Studies," in *Inhalation Toxicology and Technology,* B.K.J. Leong, Ed. (Ann Arbor, Mich.: Ann Arbor Science Publishers, 1981), pp. 157–168.

51. Milliman, E.M., D.P.Y. Chang, and O.R. Moss. "A Dual Flexible-Brush Dust-Feed Mechanism," *Am. Ind. Hyg. Assoc. J.* 42:747–751 (1981).

52. Timbrell, V., A.W. Hyett, and J.W. Skidmore. "A Simple Dispenser for Generating Dust Clouds from Standard Reference Samples of Asbestos," *Ann. Occup. Hyg.* 11:273–281 (1968).

53. Holt, P.F. and D.K. Young. "A Dust-Feed Mechanism Suitable for Fibrous Dust," *Ann. Occup. Hyg.* 2:249–256 (1960).

54. Smith, D.M., L.W. Ortiz, R.F. Archuleta, J.F. Spalding, M.I. Tillery, H.J. Ettinger, and R.G. Thomas. "A Method for Chronic Nose Only Exposures of Laboratory Animals to Inhaled Fibrous Aerosols," in *Inhalation Toxicology and Technology,* B.K.J. Leong, Ed. (Ann Arbor, Mich.: Ann Arbor Science Publishers, 1981) pp. 89–105.

55. Spurny, K.R. "Fiber Generation and Length Classification," in *Generation of Aerosols and Facilities for Exposure Experiments,* K. Willeke, Ed. (Ann Arbor, Mich.: Ann Arbor Science Publishers, 1980), pp. 257–298.

56. Drew, R.T. and S. Laskin. "A New Dust Generating System for Inhalation Studies," *Am. Ind. Hyg. Assoc. J.* 32:327–330 (1971).

57. Guichard, J.C. "Aerosol Generation Using Fluidized Beds," in *Fine Particles,* B.Y.H. Liu, Ed. (New York: Academic Press, 1976), pp. 174–193.

58. Willeke, K., C.S.K. Lo, and K.T. Whitby. "Dispersion Characteristics of a Fluidized Bed," *Aerosol Sci.* 5:449–455 (1974).

59. Agarwal, J.K. and P.A. Nelson. "A Large Flow Rate Fluidized Bed Aerosol Generator," in *Inhalation Toxicology and Technology,* B.K.J. Leong, Ed. (Ann Arbor, Mich.: Ann Arbor Science Publishers, 1981), pp. 157–168.

60. Carpenter, R.L., J.A. Pickrell, B.V. Mokler, H.S. Yeh, and P.B. DeNee. "Generation of Respirable Glass Fiber Aerosols Using a Fluidized Bed Aerosol Generator," *Am. Ind. Hyg. Assoc. J.* 42:777–784 (1981).

61. Bernstein, D.M., R.T. Drew, and M. Kuschner. "Experimental Approaches for Exposure to Sized Glass Fibers," *Env. Health Perspect.* 34:47–57 (1980).

62. Kanapilly, G.M., O.G. Raabe, and G.J. Newton. "A New Method for the Generation of Aerosols of Spherical Insoluble Particles," *Aerosol Sci.* 1:313 (1970).

63. Friedman, J.M. and S.W. Horstman. "A Simple Method for the Generation of Metallic Oxide Aerosols," *Am. Ind. Hyg. Assoc. J.* 35:825–831 (1974).

64. Phalen, R.F. "Evaluation of an Exploded Wire Aerosol Generator for Use in Inhalation Studies," *Aerosol Sci.* 3:395–406 (1972).

65. Wegrzyn, J.E. "An Investigation of an Exploding Wire Aerosol," in *Fine Particles,* B.Y.H. Liu, Ed. (New York: Academic Press, 1976) pp. 253–273.

66. Liu, B.Y.H. and J. Levi. "Generation of Submicron Sulfuric Acid Aerosol by Vaporization and Condensation," in *Generation of Aerosols and Facilities for Exposure Experiments,* K. Willeke, Ed. (Ann Arbor, Mich.: Ann Arbor Science Publishers, 1980), pp. 317–336.

67. Homma, K., K. Kawai, and K. Nozaki. "Metal-Fume Generation and its Application to Inhalation Experiments," in *Generation of Aerosols and Facilities for Exposure Experiments,* K. Willeke, Ed. (Ann Arbor, Mich.: Ann Arbor Science Publishers, 1980), pp. 361–377.

68. Mokler, B.V., E.G. Damon, T.R. Henderson, and R.K. Jones. "Consumer Product Aerosols: Generation, Characterization and Exposure Problems," in *Generation of Aerosols and Facilities for Exposure Experiments,* K. Willeke, Ed. (Ann Arbor, Mich.: Ann Arbor Science Publishers, 1980), pp. 379–398.

69. Drew, R.T., B.N. Gupta, and M.T. Riley. "Inhalation Studies with Aerosol Oven Cleaners." Presented at the Annual Meeting of the American Industrial Hygiene Association (1975).

70. Reist, P.C. and W.A. Burgess. "Atomization of Aqueous Suspensions of Polystyrene Latex Particles," *J. Colloid Interface Sci.* 24:271–273 (1967).

71. Walton, W.H. and W.C. Prewitt. "The Production of Sprays and Mists of Uniform Drop Size by Means of Spinning Disc Type Sprayers," *Proc. Phys. Soc.* (London) 62:341–350 (1949).

72. Lippmann, M. and R.E. Albert. "A Compact Electric Motor Driven Spinning Disc Aerosol Generator," *Am. Ind. Hyg. Assoc. J.* 28:501–506 (1967).

73. Albert, R.E., H.G. Petrow, A.S. Salam, and J.R. Spiegelman. "Fabrication of Monodisperse Lucite and Iron Oxide Particles with a Spinning Disk Generator," *Health Phys.* 10:933–940 (1964).

74. Sehmel, G.A. "The Density of Uranine Particles Produced by a Spinning Disk Aerosol Generator," *Am. Ind. Hyg. Assoc. J.* 28:491–492 (1967).

75. LaMer, V.K. and D. Sinclair. "An Improved Homogeneous Aerosol Generator," OSRD Report No. 1668 (U.S. Department of Commerce, Washington, D.C., 1943).

76. Muir, D.C.F. "The Production of Monodisperse Aerosols by a LaMer-Sinclair Generator," *Ann. Occup. Hyg.* 8:233–238 (1965).

77. Huang, C.M., M. Kerker, E. Matijevic, and D.D. Cooke. "Aerosol Studies by Light Scattering. VII. Preparation and Particle-Size Distribution of Lindenic Acid Aerosols," *J. Colloid Interface Sci.* 33:244–254 (1970).

78. Rapaport, E. and S.G. Weinstock. "A Generator for Homogeneous Aerosols," *Experimentia* 11:363 (1955).

CHAPTER 11

Monitoring Vapor Concentrations in Test Atmospheres

Bruce A. Burgess and David P. Kelly
E.I. du Pont de Nemours & Company, Inc. Haskell Laboratory for Toxicology and Industrial Medicine, Elkton Road, P.O. Box 50, Newark, Delaware 19711

Inhalation toxicity studies vary widely in duration, from very brief exposure (minutes) to periods spanning the test animal's lifetime. The difficulty of the analytical task may vary from analysis of a single nonreactive gas to analysis of a complex mixture of reactive gases. Although analytical problems posed by each situation differ markedly, all analytical monitoring systems must accomplish the same basic tasks: collection of a representative sample and subsequent analysis.

Atmospheric samples may be collected directly or by extraction of the test substance from the air. Direct techniques are highly efficient, rapid, easily automated, and less prone to error. Extractive techniques can be labor intensive, less efficient, and time-consuming, but they can be advantageous when used to concentrate atmospheric samples and increase analytical sensitivity or to solve tricky sampling problems such as are encountered with reactive or low vapor pressure materials.

Sample analysis may be achieved by numerous techniques. The most commonly used methods are gas chromatography and infrared spectroscopy. Aside from the normal analytical criteria of specificity, accuracy, and precision, speed of analysis is very important since analytical data are generally the basis for control of test atmosphere concentrations.

SAMPLE COLLECTION

Collection of a representative sample is critical [1,2]. A representative sample quantitatively reflects the chemical state of the test material as it exists in the animal

139

breathing zone. Problems such as sample loss can occur in the chamber or sampling system due to sample reactivity, adsorption, or condensation. The presence of animals and excreta makes hydrolysis and absorption frequent problems with reactive chemicals. It is a good idea to sample the chamber atmosphere with and without the presence of animals and to analyze for any breakdown products. Finally, a chamber concentration profile should be established to ensure that each animal is receiving a similar dose and that the sample collection point reflects true breathing zone concentrations.

Direct Samples

Direct or nonextractive samples may be instantaneous (a grab sample) or continuous in nature. Since grab samples represent only a brief interval of the overall test, they should be taken with sufficient frequency to reflect fluctuations in chamber concentration. Grab samples may be collected in evacuated glass or metal containers, inflatable polymer bags or, most commonly, by gas-tight syringe (Figure 11-1). Grab samples also may be taken remotely by piping test atmosphere through sample lines and injecting aliquots of the sample stream into the analytical instrument by sample valve [3]. Continuous samples can be taken by pumping a constant stream of gas directly through a detector.

Extracted Samples

Extractive sampling involves removal of the test material from air by scrubbing through a solvent or reagent, adsorption to a collection surface, or condensation on a cold surface. Such sample collection requires use of a sample collection apparatus, which may include sample lines, a scrubbing device, an airflow rate or volume meter, a suction pump, and other specialty pieces.

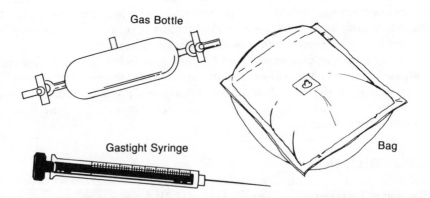

Figure 11-1. Preparation of standards or collection of samples from gas or vapor atmospheres frequently may be accomplished by use of gas-tight syringe, gas bottle, or gas bag.

Some useful scrubbing devices are impingers, simple gas washing bottles, spiral or helical bubblers, and packed bead columns (Figure 11–2). In our experience, the most useful devices are the standard and fritted midget impingers. These devices offer high-efficiency collection over a wide range of atmospheric concentrations.

Other methods of collection such as solid adsorbents (for example, charcoal or porous polymers) or cold traps are less frequently used for inhalation toxicology atmospheric monitoring. These methods are usually more time-consuming and require that adsorption and desorption efficiencies be evaluated.

For a rough, rapid approximation of chamber concentration, commercially available detector tubes may be useful, especially when the time required by the primary analytical method is too lengthy to allow adequate concentration control.

Remote Monitoring

Frequently it is necessary to remotely monitor exposure chambers from a control room or other nearby facility. Depending on the analytical method, individual detectors may be used for each chamber, or several atmospheres may be analyzed by a single detector. Sample lines may be connected to an instrument through a stream selection valve or by individual line solenoid valves. If the instrument used is a gas

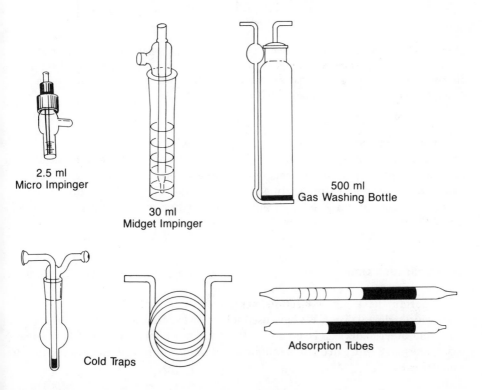

2.5 ml
Micro Impinger

30 ml
Midget Impinger

500 ml
Gas Washing Bottle

Cold Traps

Adsorption Tubes

Figure 11–2.   Some common extractive sampling devices.

Exposure Chambers

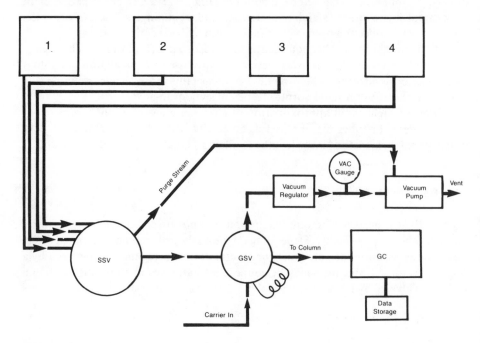

Figure 11-3. Schematic diagram demonstrates how four inhalation chambers may be remotely analyzed. Chamber air is purged through sample lines; a stream selection valve (SSV) diverts the line of interest to a gas sample valve (GSV), which injects a plug of sample atmosphere into the gas chromatograph (GC).

instrument used is a gas chromatograph, a gas sampling valve is required to inject a small aliquot of the selected stream (Figures 11–3 and 11–4). Microprocessor-controlled instruments with internal clocks allow automatic monitoring, as well as data manipulation and storage. In addition, systems may be designed to control chamber concentrations through a feedback loop to the atmospheric generation system [4,5].

Collection Lines

It is important that sample collection lines be inert to the analyzed compound so that sample losses do not occur. We have used collection lines of stainless steel, glass, Teflon®, and other materials. Glass and Teflon® are most universally useful. In some cases, lines may be treated (for example, glass silanization) or heated to minimize sample losses.

Figure 11–4. Actual test setup described in Figure 11–3. The chambers in the adjacent room are continually sampled through Teflon lines and analyzed by gas chromatography. A Teflon® gas bag, containing a standard atmosphere, is to the right of the GC.

SAMPLE ANALYSIS

In our experience, a small number of methods can handle the vast majority of routine analytical problems involving gases and vapors. In order of general utility, these include gas chromatography, infrared spectroscopy, ultraviolet-visible spectroscopy, ion selective electrode analysis, and a handful of other methods.

Gas Chromatography

Gas chromatography (GC) is the most versatile and frequently used analytical technique for monitoring gases and vapors [3,6]. GC offers chemical separation of components for specific analysis, low detection limits, rapid turnover of data for feedback to concentration control, capability to analyze direct or extracted samples, and ease of automation. Furthermore, GC analysis has an added advantage in that multiple components can be analyzed, and it is frequently possible to spot contaminants in the test atmosphere resulting from sample degradation or extraneous air pollution.

Most inhalation test atmospheres are well defined and simple in composition. In our experience, more than 90% of typical GC separations can be accomplished with commercially available column materials [7]. The following are frequently used:

1.   Dimethyl silicone (SE-30, SP-2100, OV-101).
2.   50% Phenyl methylsilicone (OV-17, SP-2250).
3.   Polyethylene glycol (Carbowax® 20M).
4.   Porous polymers (Poropak® Q).

The wide variety of selective detectors [8] greatly expands the concentration range of analyzable materials by GC. The flame ionization detector (FID) responds to virtually all organic materials, is dependable, and has a broad linear response range. These characteristics make it the detector most commonly used for atmospheric monitoring.

Thermal conductivity detectors (TCD) are less frequently used due to the relative insensitivity of the detector. During direct air sampling, normal atmospheric components (N_2, O_2, and H_2O) appear as major interfering peaks in the chromatogram. However, TCD is convenient for analyzing concentrations above the linear range of the flame ionization detector. When nitrogen is used as a carrier gas, TCD sensitivity is diminished, but the interference of atmospheric nitrogen is eliminated from the chromatogram.

Commonly used specific detectors [8] such as electron capture (ECD), thermionic (TID), flame photometric (FPD), and others such as the Hall electrolytic detector and photoionization detector can greatly simplify the general chromatographic problem. The major advantages they offer are selectivity and sensitivity.

Electron capture detectors (ECD) are especially useful with halogenated organics, aromatics, and other electronegative species. The major drawback in direct air monitoring with ECDs is poor stability predominantly due to the effects of water vapor and O_2 on detector response.

Thermionic detectors (TID or N/P) are highly specific to nitrogen and phosphorus compounds, with relatively little response to general hydrocarbons. The recent generation of TID detectors is highly reliable.

Flame photometric detectors (FPD or P/S) selectively respond to sulfur- and phosphorus-containing compounds with little response to hydrocarbons. The linear response range of FPD detectors, however, is relatively narrow.

For identification problems, combined GC/mass spectrometry or GC/infrared analysis can be quite useful, but for routine monitoring these instruments are comparatively elaborate and expensive.

Infrared Spectroscopy

Infrared (IR) spectroscopy is a useful technique for chamber concentration monitoring [1,2]. Most gases and vapors give reasonably intense and unique IR spectra. Thus, IR Is sensitive as well as specific. Furthermore, IR spectrometers are available in gas or solution models and can be used to analyze both direct and extracted samples.

By use of variable wavelength gas analyzers, many gases may be rapidly determined in part per million ($\mu L/L$) or lower concentrations. The Miran Portable Gas Analyzer (Figure 11-5) offers variable wavelength selection from 2.5 to 14.5 microns, as well as variable path lengths from 0.75 to 20 meters. This instrument features continuous analysis and a wide linear response range and is available in microprocessor controlled models for automated multi-wavelength analysis.

Other Analytical Methods

A number of other instruments are available for monitoring test atmospheres. We have frequently used ion-selective electrodes (Cl^-, F^-, CN^-) as well as UV-visible spectrophotometers for analyzing extracted air samples. Some examples of commercially available instruments for use in continuous monitoring are: dedicated IR detectors (CO, CO_2, CH_4), UV detectors (Hg, O_3, SO_2), scrubbing colorimeters (HCHO, SO_2, NO_2), and impregnated paper tape monitors (H_2S, toluene diisocyanate, NO_2). Finally, it is frequently possible to have an analyzer specially prepared for a nonstandard test material. Instrument cost versus benefit must be assessed in such cases.

INSTRUMENT CALIBRATION

Frequent calibration of analytical instruments is essential. Standard curves should be prepared frequently and verified throughout each monitoring day. Standards should be prepared that are of the same composition and physical state as samples to be analyzed. Standards and unknowns should be introduced into the analytical instrument in the same manner.

To prepare gas standards, a known amount of test gas or vapors of a volatile liquid can be injected into an inert vessel of known volume. Glass gas bottles may be used when small sample volumes are necessary (such as with syringe grab samples). Inflatable polymer gas bags are useful when large sample volumes are necessary (such as with continuous analysis). In all cases the investigator should be watchful for problems of sample reactivity or adsorption to vessel walls.

For extended studies or with some reactive materials, it may be desirable to prepare a dynamic calibration manifold, which provides a steady-state calibration stream [2,9,10,11]. This requires a constant temperature cell housing and a constant vapor source (for example, a permeation tube, diffusion tube, or other evaporative device) containing the test material. These are commercially available.

SUMMARY

In summary, monitoring test concentrations entails two basic tasks: collection of a representative sample and subsequent analysis. Direct analysis of test substances in air is more desirable because of ease and speed of analysis. When this is not possible,

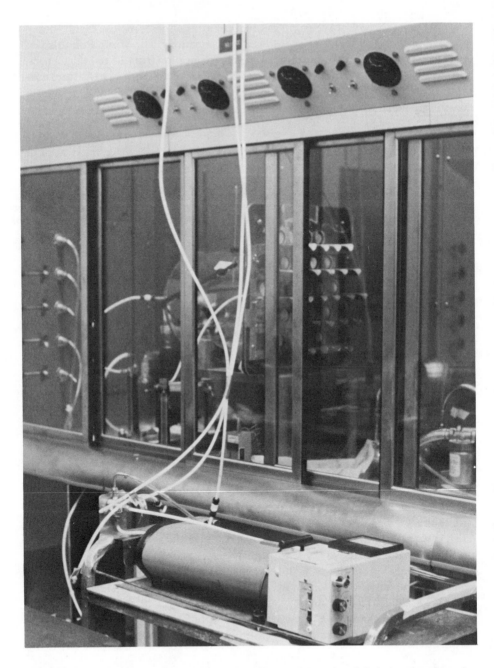

Figure 11-5. A Miran portable gas analyzer set up to monitor three inhalation chambers. A 40 L glass chamber is visible in fume hood.

test substances are extracted from air and subsequently analyzed. The most desirable analytical techniques are gas chromatography and infrared spectroscopy because of their speed, sensitivity, and specificity. Both techniques are easily automated, can be used for direct and extractive samples, and can be used to analyze numerous components in the same atmospheres simultaneously. Specific sampling and analysis techniques vary widely depending on test duration and the physical-chemical state of the test atmosphere.

REFERENCES

1. Keenan, R.G. "Direct Reading Instruments for Determining Concentrations of Aerosols, Gases, and Vapors," in *Air Sampling Instruments,* 5th ed. (Cincinnati: American Conference of Government Industrial Hygienists, 1978).
2. Katz, M. *Methods of Air Sampling and Analysis* (Springfield, Va.: Byrd Pre-Press, 1977), pp. 3–205.
3. McNair, H.M. and E.J. Bonelli. *Basic Gas Chromatography* (Berkeley, Calif.: Consolidated Printers, 1968), pp. 247–258.
4. McLaughlin, S.B., V.J. Schom, and H.C. Jones. "A Programmable Exposure System for Kinetic Dose-Response Studies With Air Pollutants," *Journal of the Air Pollution Control Association* 26(2):131–135 (1976).
5. Koizumi, A. and M. Ikeda. "A Servomechanism for Vapor Concentration Control in Experimental Exposure Chambers," *AIHA Journal* 42:417–425 (1981).
6. Grob, R.L., Ed. *Modern Practice of Gas Chromatography* (New York: John Wiley and Sons, 1977).
7. Hawkes, S., D. Grossman, A. Hartkropf, et al. "Preferred Stationary Liquids for Gas Chromatography," *J. Chrom. Sci.* 13:115–117 (1975).
8. Farwell, S.O., D.R. Gage, and R.A. Kagel. "Current Status of Prominent Selective Gas Chromatographic Detection: A Critical Assessment," *J. Chrom. Sci.* 19:358–376 (1981).
9. Nelson, G.O. *Controlled Test Atmospheres* (Ann Arbor, Mich.: Ann Arbor Science Publishers, 1972).
10. Freeland, L.T. "An Industrial Hygiene Calibration Manifold," *Am. Ind. Hyg. Assoc.* 38:712–720 (1977).
11. Tsang, W. and J.A. Walter. "Instrument for the Generation of Reactive Gases," *Anal. Chem.* 40(1):13–17 (1977).

CHAPTER 12

Chemical Monitoring of Aerosols in Inhalation Chambers

Owen R. Moss and John R. Decker

Battelle, Pacific Northwest Laboratories,
Richland, Washington 99352

To monitor aerosols (airborne suspensions of solid or liquid particles) in inhalation chambers, the chemist must measure the mass concentration of the chemical, the chemical composition as a function of particle size, and the particle size distribution of the aerosol. Ideally, in a toxicology testing program this could be accomplished at a minimum of expense by real-time chemical analysis with continuously sampling instruments. The information could be reported in a manner that would allow the test atmosphere to be duplicated by other investigators.

Unfortunately, in inhalation toxicology testing programs there are very few cases where the concentration of a specific chemical in an aerosol can be measured continuously. Although flame ionization detectors, atomic emission and absorption spectrometers, and atomic mass spectrometers have been used for this purpose, all have problems with obtaining representative samples of the airborne particles. In practice, the detectors that are used are designed to sample and detect the presence of particles irrespective of chemical composition and physical state (solid or liquid). Wet chemistry is then used to calibrate the instrument's response to the chemical composition of the airborne particles.

Instruments that can continuously measure the presence of aerosols in inhalation toxicology testing must be relatively durable because they are used in a busy exposure laboratory. They should also be able to detect aerosols in a concentration range from 0.01 mg/m^3 to 5,000 mg/m^3. At Battelle, we have considered units that detect the presence of aerosols by their electrical charge, mass, light attenuation, and light scatter. For our program, we chose three light–scatter devices that appeared to be durable and can cover this range of concentrations: two forward–scatter units, the RAM-1 light–scatter dust monitor (GCA Corporation, Bedford, MA 01730) and the TDA-2DN Particle Detection Apparatus (Air Techniques, Inc., Baltimore, MD 21207); and a back-scatter detector, the P-5A Particulate Monitor (ESC, Environmental Systems Corporation, Knoxville, TN 37091). We will report our experience in applying these units as primary aerosol detectors in support of chemical monitoring of exposure atmospheres.

For particle-size measuring devices, we have chosen the basic cascade impactor and the 10-mm nylon cyclone. The impactor (ACI Andersen 2000 Inc., Atlanta, GA 30320) separates particles into a number of size fractions according to their aerodynamic diameter [1,2]. The 10-mm nylon cyclone operates similarly to separate particles into two size fractions: the respirable fraction [1,2,3], which contains particles that deposit in the deep lung, and the remaining large particles.

No continuously sampling instruments are commercially available that measure both particle size and chemical concentration. These measurements must be made at least once during a study, if only to demonstrate that the inhalable portion of the aerosol (respirable fraction) is composed mainly of the chemical of interest. Instruments that continuously sample for particle size by detecting the intensity of scattered light or measuring individual particle mass in general require low concentrations of particles (less than 10^{+4} particles/cc) and reproducibly measure particle size if care is taken in their operation [1,2].

FORWARD SCATTER DETECTORS

TDA-2DN

The TDA-2DN particle detection apparatus (Figure 12–1) was the simplest light scatter unit we used. As delivered, the system could not be used to obtain a representative sample of the aerosol because of the tortuous path through solenoids, valves, and excess tubing that the aerosol was required to traverse before reaching the detection cell. When these excess valves were removed and the path to the detection chamber simplified, the instrument responded fairly well to liquid droplet aerosols during testing and during short-term animal exposures. This unit could not be used with solid aerosols such as talcum powder because the optics and the walls of the detecting cell became coated with the aerosol, resulting in a high, continuously changing background signal. For the liquid droplet aerosol, the calibration curve was not completely linear for the concentration range 10 mg/m³ to 1000 mg/m³ (Figure 12–2). The dashed line was based on early calibration at target concentrations

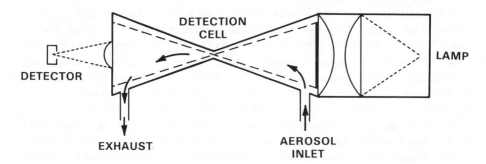

Figure 12–1.   Schematic of TDA-2DN aerosol detection cell showing airflow path. Light is focused from right to left along inner surface of cones.

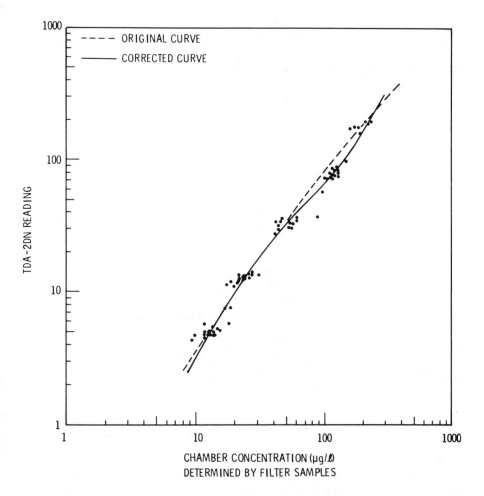

Figure 12–2. TDA-2DN calibration for an aerosol of liquid droplets, aerodynamic mass median diameters below 5 µm. (TDA-reading versus total mass concentration µg/l.)

around 10, 50, and 200 µg/l. This calibration curve was corrected (solid line), with further measurements of target concentrations at 25 and 200 µg/l. For use, the detector was placed on a cart and wheeled between chambers so that the concentration in each chamber could be checked every 20 to 30 minutes.

RAM-1

The second forward-scatter unit, the RAM-1, proved to be useful even though its detection range was only from 0.01 to 200 mg/m³. This unit was designed for robust use, with all walls and optics in its detection cell protected from aerosol particles by a continuous sheath of clean air (Figure 12–3). The unit can be used to measure total or respirable mass. When sampling for respirable mass [1,2,3], the aerosol passes

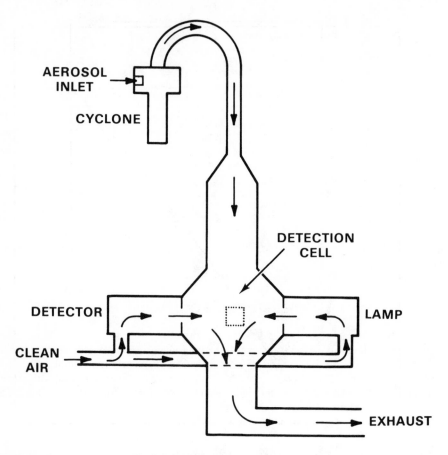

Figure 12–3. Schematic of the GCA, RAM-1 aerosol detection cell. Aerosol passes through a 10-mm nylon cyclone, for respirable concentration measurements, and travels down detection cell to exhaust line. Clean air is pumped past optics, enters detection cell, and is removed with aerosol. Light moves from right to left in schematic. Detection cell on left is offset from light source on right by 25°.

through a 10-mm nylon cyclone before traversing down the detection cell. The electronics in the unit were stable, and the output was easy to calibrate or check for stability.

The RAM-1, however, had what appeared to be an anomalous shift in calibration when the same unit was used to detect aerosols in several different chambers, although calibration remained constant for any one chamber. Figure 12–4 shows that when the filtered sheath air was drawn from the room while the aerosol was sampled from the chamber, the instrument calibration was slightly different for each of five chambers run at different target concentrations. This shift was due to different vacuums in the various chambers and the way that we were obtaining samples.

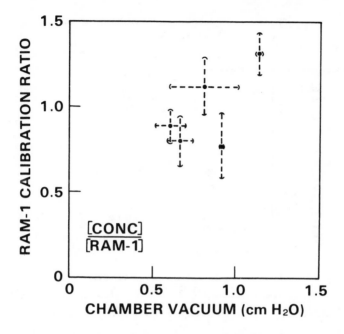

Figure 12–4. Plot of GCA, RAM-1 (sheath air from room) calibration ratio versus chamber vacuum. Calibration ratio is (concentration from chemically analyzed grab sample)/(RAM-1 reading). Data from a 2-week study: solid o-chlorobenzalmalononitrile aerosol with target concentrations, listed according to increasing chamber vacuum, of 6.0, 0.75, 3.0, 0.4 and 1.5 μg/l.

Because the unit was designed to monitor dust conditions in the workroom or mine environment, the operating instruments "assume" that the air to be cleaned for the sheath air and the dust-laden air sample come from the same area. In our tests, samples were drawn from inside the chamber, while sheath air was drawn from the room. The sample air inlet was at chamber vacuum with respect to the sheath air inlet. Changes in chamber vacuum caused changes in the sample and sheath air flow, resulting in shifts of as much as 30% in the calibration of the instrument. When the sample air and sheath air were drawn from the chamber (Figure 12–5), the calibration of the unit remained more consistent between chambers.

The examples in Figures 12–4 and 12–5 were obtained from two separate toxicity studies. The aerosols were different, but the target mass concentrations were approximately the same. The first aerosol (Figure 12–4) was composed of solid particles of o-chlorobenzalmalononitrile; the second (Figure 12–5) was composed of liquid drops of epinephrine HCl. The difference in the physical state of the particles would not explain the change in the spread of the calibration factors after sheath air was drawn from the chamber.

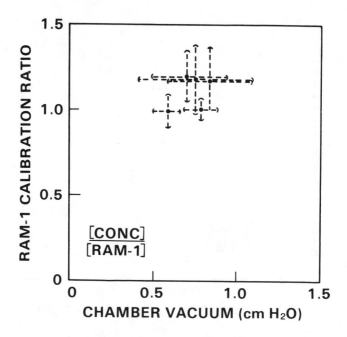

Figure 12–5.   Plot of GCA, RAM-1 (sheath air from exposure chamber) calibration ratio versus chamber vacuum. Calibration ratio is (concentration from chemically analyzed grab sample)/(RAM-1 reading). Data from a 13-week study; liquid epinephrine HCl aerosol with target concentrations, listed according to increasing chamber vacuum, of 40, 10, 2.5, 20 and 5.0 μg/l.

BACK SCATTER DETECTOR

P-5A

The back-scatter detector we used allows noninvasive determination of airborne particle concentration over a range of less than 5 mg/m^3 to 10,000 mg/m^3. An infrared light beam is projected through a 1.5-mm-thick lucite window into the chamber. The light back-scattered from a sensing volume of about 12 cm^3 is detected, in the same unit, containing the light beam by the outer edges of the light-focusing optics (Figure 12–6).

This unit proved very stable for high concentrations of sodium aerosols[4]. We used the same system, which consisted of only the optics head and control box. Additional temperature control systems that normally come with the unit to allow field sampling were not necessary in the controlled atmosphere of our toxicology laboratories.

The output of the P-5A is relatively independent of particle size for particles with physical size between 0.2 and 5 μm. The signal drops by several orders of magnitude for particles outside this size range. This response limitation can be important if the same P-5A optics head is being used to monitor aerosol concentration in several exposure chambers or aerosols of the same material but different size distributions.

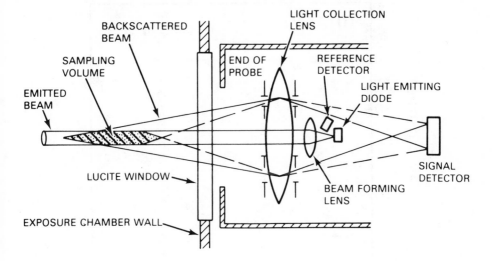

Figure 12-6. Schematic of ESC, P-5A instrument for optically monitoring aerosol mass concentration in inhalation exposure chamber. Optically defined sampling volume of P-5A is shown.

A liquid aerosol was generated, and the P-5A response was monitored over a wide range. The linearity of the P-5A response to the total mass concentration fell off at the highest level tested (Figure 12-7). The P-5A was used to record the stability of the aerosol continuously. Concentration was measured with grab samples collected on filters, which were then analyzed chemically. Whenever total mass and respirable mass samples were taken, the P-5A output was recorded for comparison. The respirable mass was obtained by pulling the sample through a 10-mm nylon cyclone [1,2,3]. In this experiment, the aerosols for the lower four concentrations were all approximately the same size: mass median aerodynamic diameter (MMAD) of about 2.0 μm with geometric standard deviation (GSD) of about 2.2 measured with an Andersen cascade impactor [1,2] versus an MMAD of about 2.9 with a GSD of 2.0 for the highest concentration. The respirable fraction of the aerosol in the highest concentration chamber was less than the respirable fraction for the aerosol in the other chambers. An increased portion of the particles in this last aerosol were larger than 5 μm and fell into the region of low P-5A response. When the respirable mass, instead of total mass concentration, was plotted, a linear relation was obtained (Figure 12-8).

For monitoring the relative stability of highly toxic dusts, this unit has the advantage of monitoring without extracting a sample from the test chamber.

CASCADE IMPACTOR OPERATION

For cascade impactors and cyclones [1,2] we found that the units must be placed inside the chamber to obtain the most representative sample of the aerosol size distribution. The air drawn from the chamber must be returned to the sampling line after

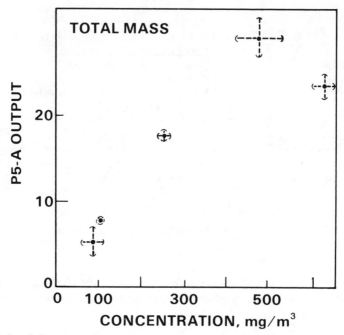

Figure 12-7. P-5A output versus total aerosol mass concentration (liquid particles of epinephrine HCl).

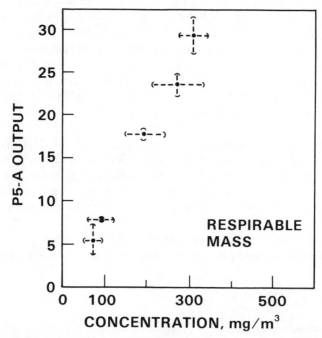

Figure 12-8. P-5A output versus respirable aerosol mass concentration (liquid particles of epinephrine HCl).

passing the sampler. Sampling lines of any length may bias the sample by removing the bigger particles before they can be sampled. To sample dry aerosol particles with an Andersen impactor, mass loading of about 60 mg total was found to be optimal. Larger quantities caused excessive buildup on the collection stages.

SUMMARY

We have attempted to use simple light-scatter devices as primary monitors for aerosol concentrations in exposure chambers. Our goal was to select durable, stable detection units to be used for real-time monitoring of an aerosol, thus reducing the need for time-consuming chemical monitoring techniques. Each of the three light-scatter units we tested fulfilled this need to some extent. The particle size analysis and chemical analysis of the variously sized aerosol particles within an exposure chamber must be performed with the same care as sampling for respirable particle concentration in the industrial workplace [3].

REFERENCES

1. Mercer, T.T. *Aerosol Technology in Hazard Evaluation* (New York: Academic Press, 1971).
2. Hinds, W.C. *Aerosol Technology, Properties, Behavior, and Measurement of Airborne Particles.* (New York: Wiley, 1982).
3. Lippmann, M. "Respirable Dust Sampling," in *Air Sampling Instruments for Evaluation of Atmospheric Contaminants,* 5th ed. (Cincinnati: ACGIH, 1978).
4. Briant, J.K. "Monitoring aerosols of sodium metal combustion," in *Pacific Northwest Laboratory Annual Report for 1980 to DOE Assistant Secretary for Environment, Part 1 Biomedical Sciences.* PNL-3700 PT1 (National Technical Information Service, 1981: Springfield, VA), pp. 127–129.

CHAPTER 13

Detection of Degradation Products in Inhalation Test Atmospheres and Analysis in Combustion Products Toxicology

David H. Steele, James M. Cholakis, Evelyn A. Murrill, and Jack H. Hagensen
Midwest Research Institute, 425 Volker Boulevard,
Kansas City, Missouri 04110

Protocols established by the National Toxicology Program (NTP) require complete physical and chemical characterization of inhalation test atmospheres. While it is necessary that test chemical concentrations in the atmospheres be accurately determined and that atmosphere homogeneity throughout the chamber be assured, it is equally important to ensure that the atmospheres contain the test chemical in the desired physical form. In addition, degradation products, which in some cases may be more toxic or carcinogenic than the test chemical, must be proved absent or, if present, determined to be below established acceptable levels.

The purpose of this chapter is to discuss some general considerations concerning the analysis of degradation products in inhalation test atmospheres, using as examples analyses performed on atmospheres generated from vinyl toluene and tetranitromethane. Related work, describing a system developed for the analysis of combustion products of some synthetic construction materials, is also presented.

DEGRADATION IN INHALATION TEST ATMOSPHERES

A typical inhalation test system consists of a generation system, a dilution system whereby the concentrated sample stream from the generation system is diluted to the desired chamber atmosphere concentration, the inhalation chamber itself (containing cages, racks, trays, and test animals), and postchamber apparatus, which includes the sampling and analytical systems.

159

Physical or chemical changes of the test chemical that occur in the prechamber apparatus (the generation or dilution systems) are likely to persist in the chamber atmosphere. In the case of polymerization or aerosol formation, this problem often can be corrected by filtering the unwanted species out of the stream before it enters the inhalation chamber. Other changes occurring in the prechamber apparatus (such as thermal decompositions that produce volatile products) are not so easily corrected.

Physical or chemical changes indicated by postchamber instrumentation should be carefully evaluated. For example, gas chromatographic detection of components other than the test chemical in the chamber atmosphere sample may actually result from thermal decomposition of the material in the heated inlet of the gas chromatograph rather than from chamber degradation.

Several general areas of concern with respect to degradation in the inhalation system can be identified.

Physical Form

Inhalation studies typically are designed to simulate human exposure to a given test chemical. It is therefore necessary to determine that the inhalation atmosphere contains the test chemical in the proper physical form because different forms of the same chemical may exhibit different toxicological properties.

If the test chemical is to be administered as smoke or dust, analyses should be conducted to ensure that the atmosphere contains an acceptable particle size profile. If a liquid aerosol is desired, determination of the amount of vapor in the atmosphere may be required.

The determination of aerosols in inhalation atmospheres designed to be tested as true vapors is especially important. In a typical heated generation system, warm air containing the test chemical as a concentrated vapor is diluted with cooler air to produce the desired inhalation chamber concentration. This process can cause the test chemical to condense as a liquid aerosol, which will be carried into the chamber, resulting in exposure of animals to a mixed-phase rather than to a pure vapor.

Decomposition

Decomposition, catalyzed by heat or light, can occur in the generation system or in the inhalation chamber itself. The walls of the inhalation chamber, as well as internal hardware (for example, racks, cages, and trays), can facilitate the decomposition of labile test chemicals.

In addition, if the test chemical is relatively nonvolatile and high chamber atmosphere concentrations are required, it may be necessary to heat the generation system to obtain sufficient vapor pressure of the test chemical. In such cases it is especially important to predict likely decomposition products and to design analyses to identify and quantitate them or to confirm their absence.

Chamber Atmosphere Matrix Reactions

A typical inhalation chamber atmosphere contains species that may react with the test chemical. Since a test chemical in the vapor phase is in intimate contact with the chamber atmosphere matrix, special attention should be paid to possible reactions of this type. Some components of the chamber atmosphere matrix will be present in far greater concentrations than the test chemical. These include atmospheric oxygen (21%) and water vapor, which will be present at a level of about 15,000 ppm if the chamber is kept at 50% relative humidity. Special consideration should be given to the possibility of reactions of the test chemical with these species.

In addition, test animal metabolism can produce low levels of carbon dioxide and ammonia in the inhalation chamber atmosphere. If reaction of the chemical with these species is suspected, analyses to detect the presence or to confirm the absence of the expected reaction products should be performed.

Experimental

The various considerations are illustrated by the analysis of vinyl toluene and tetranitromethane test atmospheres for degradation products.

Vinyl Toluene

Vinyl toluene is a highly reactive monomer used in the manufacture of plastics. In the characterization of vinyl toluene test atmospheres, aerosol formation, oxidation, and polymerization were major concerns.

Aerosol Formation.   Because of the relatively low vapor pressure of vinyl toluene, it was necessary to heat the generation system to 60° C to obtain the desired inhalation chamber concentrations. For this reason, analysis for aerosols in the test chamber atmosphere was performed.

Inertial impaction, an established procedure for the analysis of relatively nonvolatile aerosols, was chosen for the determination of aerosols in the test atmosphere. This analysis is performed by drawing an accurately measured sample through the impactor and measuring the aerosols deposited on each slip using an appropriate chemical or physical method. This procedure provides an aerodynamic size distribution profile, as well as a quantitation of the mass of the total aerosols present.

A seven-stage multijet cascade impactor (In-Tox Products, 1712 Virginia, N.E., Albuquerque, New Mexico, 87110) with individual stage cutoff values of 10.0, 6.1, 3.7, 2.2, 1.4, 0.8, and 0.5 μ was used for these measurements. Uncoated glass slips were used as collection plates. In addition, a 0.8 μ membrane filter (Gelman Instrument Company, Ann Arbor, Michigan) was installed at the exit of the impactor to capture reentrained material.

Sampling and analysis of the collected material was performed as follows. A 300 ppm vinyl toluene atmosphere was generated and its concentration confirmed by gas chromatography (GC). The atmosphere was then drawn through the impactor for 30 min at a rate of 5 l/min. At the end of the sampling period, the collection slips from each stage and the final filter were rinsed into 10 ml volumetric flasks with small portions of chloroform. The flasks were diluted to volume with chloroform and analyzed for the presence of vinyl toluene by GC. Using standard solutions of vinyl toluene in chloroform, each stage was found to contain less than 0.04% of the vinyl toluene that had passed through it, providing a limit of detection of 0.3% for the total system. From these data it was determined that < 0.3% of the vinyl toluene in the test atmosphere was present in the form of aerosols.

Oxidation.   Oxidation of vinyl toluene in the test atmosphere was expected to produce the oxide or the aldehyde as shown in Figure 13–1.

A standard of the aldehyde was found to be commercially available and was obtained for the analyses. The oxide was synthesized by reacting vinyl toluene with chloroperbenzoic acid. The identity of the product as the oxide was confirmed by gas chromatography/mass spectrometry (GC/MS).

A 400 ppm vinyl toluene atmosphere was generated and its concentration confirmed by GC. This atmosphere was then drawn through an impinger-type cold trap in a dry ice/acetone bath. The atmosphere was sampled for 30 min at a rate of 12 l/min. The condensate was thawed, extracted with chloroform, and the chloroform extract analyzed by flame ionization GC using the following system:

- Instrument: Varian Model 3700 gas chromatograph.
- Detector: Flame ionization.
- Column: 3% SP-2250 on 100/120 Supelcoport; 1.8 m × 2 mm I.D., glass.
- Carrier gas: Nitrogen.
- Carrier gas flow rate: 30 cc/min.
- Inlet temperature: 200° C.
- Detector temperature: 250° C.
- Column oven temperature program: 50° C for 5 min, then 50–200° C at 10° C/min.

The GC profile obtained from the chloroform extract was found to be identical with that obtained from a chloroform solution of the vinyl toluene used to generate the chamber atmosphere (see Figure 13–2 for GC profiles). This indicated that the test chemical composition in the chamber atmosphere was the same as that for the liquid vinyl toluene used for generation with respect to volatile components.

Analyses for the expected degradation products (aldehyde and oxide) were then performed using the GC system. Injection of standard solutions of the aldehyde and the oxide showed retention times of 10.5 and 12.0 min, respectively, on this system. Detection limits of 0.05% relative to the vinyl toluene concentration in the chamber atmosphere were established for both the aldehyde and the oxide. No peaks were seen at retention times characteristic of the oxide and aldehyde. Therefore, it was concluded that the oxide and aldehyde were not present in the vinyl toluene atmosphere at levels > 0.05% relative to the vinyl toluene concentration.

Polymerization.   In order to inhibit polymerization, commercially available vinyl toluene contains a free radical scavenger (t-butylcatechol) at low ppm levels. This inhibitor is relatively nonvolatile and tends to remain in the generation system when vinyl toluene atmospheres are generated. Because the generation system must be

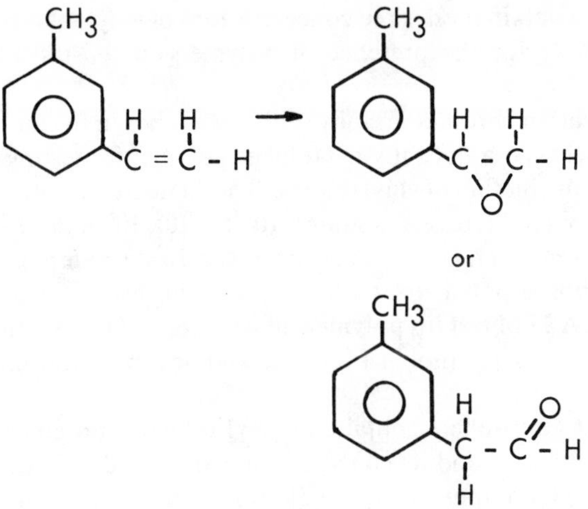

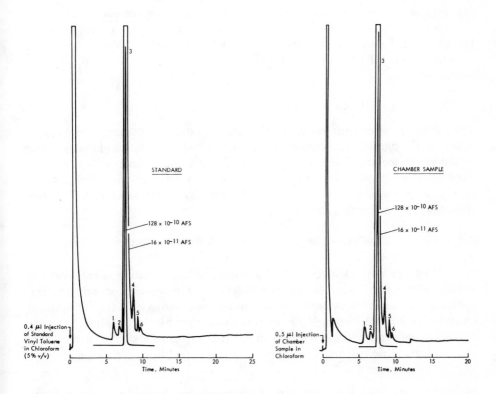

Figure 13-1.   Oxidation of vinyl toluene.

Figure 13-2.   Vinyl toluene oxidation study.

heated to 60° C to obtain the desired concentrations of vinyl toluene in the inhalation chambers, analyses for the presence of polymers in the test atmospheres were performed.

Gel permeation chromatography (GPC) was chosen for the detection of polymeric vinyl toluene. A sample of vinyl toluene polymer for testing the GPC method was obtained by distillation of vinyl toluene. The distillate was then analyzed by GPC using a bank of four μ-Styrogel® columns (10^2, 5×10^2, 10^3, and 10^4Å). The GPC data indicated the presence of high molecular weight ($> 10^4$Å) material.

The presence of polymers at a level $> 0.1\%$ in this distillate was further confirmed using the ASTM test for polymers in styrene[1]. (This method involved mixing the distillate with methanol in a 1:1 ratio and observing the amount of turbidity produced.)

A chamber atmosphere containing vinyl toluene at a concentration of 1000 ppm was then generated and its concentration confirmed by GC. This atmosphere was drawn through an impinger-type cold trap in a dry ice/acetone bath for 1 hr. When the condensate had thawed, the two layers present were separated and individually analyzed. The organic layer was confirmed to be vinyl toluene by comparison of its infrared spectrum with that of a vinyl toluene standard. Analysis of both the organic and the aqueous layers by GPC indicated that high molecular weight material was not present in either phase. Both layers also tested negative using the ASTM polymer test[1]. Based on these test results, it was concluded that polymers were not present at levels $> 0.1\%$ of the vinyl toluene concentration in the inhalation chamber atmosphere.

Tetranitromethane

The highest chamber atmosphere concentration produced in the tetranitromethane study was 10 ppm. Since this was readily accomplished by operation of the generator at ambient temperature, aerosol formation was not a major concern. Furthermore, due to the chemical nature of tetranitromethane, polymerization was not expected to occur. The major concern in this case was light-mediated decomposition of tetranitromethane in the chamber atmosphere:

$$C(NO_2)_4 \rightarrow 2.25\ NO_2 + CO_2 + 0.25\ N_2O + 1.25\ NO_2{}^2.$$

The decomposition of tetranitromethane by this mechanism was monitored by analyzing for the presence of nitrogen dioxide because it was the most abundant degradation product and because no natural atmospheric nitrogen dioxide background exists to produce interferences. In addition to nitrogen dioxide, analyses for nitric acid were conducted because of the possibility that nitrogen dioxide might react with water to form nitric acid under chamber atmosphere conditions ($\sim$15,000 ppm water vapor in the chamber).

Nitrogen Dioxide. A 10 ppm tetranitromethane test atmosphere was generated and its concentration confirmed by infrared spectroscopy. Analysis for nitrogen dioxide was performed using nitrogen dioxide 0.5/c Draeger® tubes (BGI, Inc., 58 Guinan Street, Waltham, Massachusetts 02154; Part No. CH30001). Draeger® tubes produce a color change on reaction with a specific analyte. The tubes are calibrated such that the length of the color change indicates the concentration of analyte in the test sample, provided that the requisite volume of sample is drawn through the tube.

The required volume (0.5 l) of the 10 ppm tetranitromethane test chamber atmosphere gave stain lengths of 4 and 5 mm in duplicate trials. This stain length was below the calibrated range of the tube (500 ppb). Atmosphere from a control chamber containing a full complement of racks, cages, and trays was tested in the same manner as the 10 ppm chamber atmosphere. No response to nitrogen dioxide was seen in the Draeger tubes. A 10 ppm tetranitromethane standard was prepared in a gas sampling bag by adding tetranitromethane to control chamber atmosphere. This standard also tested negative for nitrogen dioxide using the Draeger tubes.

These experiments indicated that nitrogen dioxide was produced in the test chambers but at levels below 500 ppb. They also indicated that neither chamber atmosphere matrix nor unreacted test compound was responsible for the positive reaction of the test chamber.

Nitric Acid. A 10 ppm tetranitromethane test atmosphere was generated and its concentration confirmed by infrared spectroscopy. Analysis for nitric acid was performed using 1/A Draeger tubes (BGI, Inc., 58 Guinan Street, Waltham, Massachusetts 02154; Part No. 6728311). To increase the sensitivity of the tube, recalibration was performed. It was found that the sensitivity was limited by the capacity of the prelayer to absorb water. A volume of 22.5 l of test atmosphere at 50% relative humidity could be sampled before water interfered; therefore, 22.5 l was used as the standard sampling volume. One hundred and 200 ppb standards of nitric acid prepared with control chamber atmosphere gave stain lengths of 3 and 6 mm, respectively, while the calibrated volume of atmosphere drawn from the 10 ppm tetranitromethane chamber gave no measurable response with the tube. The ability to determine 100 ppb of nitric acid in the 10 ppm tetranitromethane atmosphere was confirmed by spiking the tetranitromethane atmosphere with nitric acid at the 100 ppb level and drawing the requisite sample volume through the tube. A stain length of 3 mm was obtained, which was consistent with the results obtained for the nitric acid standards prepared with control chamber atmosphere. Based on these results, it was determined that nitric acid was not present in the 10 ppm tetranitromethane atmosphere at a level > 100 ppb.

COMBUSTION PRODUCTS TOXICOLOGY

Discussion

The increased use of synthetic materials in building construction and consumer products has led to a growing concern over the potential hazards of combustion products of these materials. The toxicity of the test material when combusted may be due to a combination of several combustion products. In most cases, the combustion products specifically responsible for the toxicity of the material must be determined.

Product concentrations in a combustion chamber operated in the static mode change drastically over the course of an exposure. Therefore a time-based profile, based on continuous or at least frequent determinations of combustion product concentrations, is highly desirable.

Continuous measurements are the most desirable and can be readily obtained using the flow-through instrumentation. In cases where this type of instrumentation is not available or the concentration or nature of the analyte does not lend itself to these types of measurements, analyses must be performed as frequently as available methods allow. This may range from every few minutes, as in the case of GC, to once an hour if collection of large volumes of atmosphere is required for subsequent wet chemical analysis.

In addition to the analysis of combustion products, the oxygen level in the chamber must be monitored closely and supplemented if necessary to ensure that the combustion process does not deplete the oxygen in the atmosphere to the point where test animals begin to suffer from oxygen starvation. Adequate oxygen is required to ensure that symptoms exhibited by test animals are due to the combusted material alone and not to oxygen deprivation.

LC_{50} and LC_{100} toxicities of Douglas fir, red oak, polyurethane, polystyrene, polyvinyl chloride, and five synthetic building materials provided by a major manufacturer were experimentally determined by dropping preweighed portions of each test material into a heated combustion furnace. The resultant combustion products were then statically administered by "nose-only" inhalation to male Fischer 344 rats. Toxicities were evaluated at furnace temperatures 25° C below and 25° C above the experimentally determined autoignition temperature of each test material. These temperatures represented two major modes of combustion: smouldering and flaming.

Experimental

A train-type sampling system that allowed determination of carbon dioxide, carbon monoxide, and oxygen on a continuous or frequent basis was developed for these studies (Figure 13–3).

Instrumentation incorporated into this system included a nondispersive infrared carbon monoxide analyzer, a polarographic oxygen monitor, and a gas chromatograph for measurement of carbon dioxide.

Chamber atmosphere was pulled with a vacuum pump through a filter to remove soot and smoke particles prior to entering the analytical system. The sample stream then passed through a needle valve. On the downstream side of the pump, the sample stream was measured using a rotameter. Due to accumulation of particulates on the filter as the duration of exposure increased, frequent adjustment of the needle valve was necessary to maintain a constant flow.

The sample stream was then passed through a calcium sulfate filter to remove water. To avoid interference in the determination of carbon monoxide, carbon dioxide was quantitatively removed by passing the sample stream through an ascarite filter prior to entering the nondispersive infrared analyzer. Volume corrections were

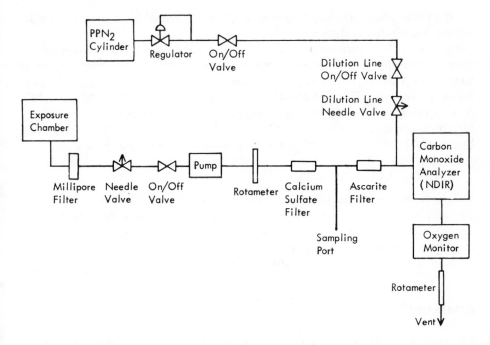

Figure 13-3.   Analysis train for combustion products.

applied to the measured carbon monoxide levels when the amount of carbon dioxide removed from the sample stream became significant ($> 10\%$). The sample stream was then passed through a polarographic oxygen monitor and vented. A dilution line was installed between the ascarite filter and the carbon monoxide analyzer to allow dilution of the sample stream with nitrogen when carbon monoxide levels exceeded the range of the instrument. The oxygen monitor served a dual purpose in the experimental system. It was used prior to the combustion experiment to measure the magnitude of the dilution sample stream. During the experiment, dilution was held constant and the monitor was used to measure the oxygen level in the exposure atmosphere.

A sampling port with a septum was installed between the calcium sulfate and ascarite filters so that samples could be removed with a gas-tight syringe and analyzed for carbon dioxide content by thermal conductivity GC.

The analysis train provided a means of monitoring species that would be present as combustion products of all of the test materials. Additional monitoring techniques were used to detect hydrogen chloride and hydrogen cyanide which are combustion products unique to certain test materials.

Hydrogen Chloride

In the combustion of polyvinylchloride, hydrogen chloride, an expected combustion product, was suspected to be largely responsible for the observed toxicity. Therefore accurate determination of hydrogen chloride was essential for polyvinylchloride combustion toxicology studies.

Analysis for hydrogen chloride was performed by sampling the combustion chamber atmosphere by vacuum pumping through mini-impingers containing about 50 ml of 0.1 N sodium hydroxide. The atmosphere was sampled at a rate of 1.5 l/min for a period of 3 min. The contents of the impingers were then acidified, diluted to 100 ml with distilled water, and the chloride ion content determined by titration with coulometrically generated silver ion. This procedure allowed the determination of hydrogen chloride at levels of ~5 ppm in combustion chamber atmospheres.

Hydrogen Cyanide

The combustion of polyurethane foam was expected to produce hydrogen cyanide as a combustion product. Cyanide 2/a Draeger® tubes were used to measure this species to low ppm levels on a real-time basis. The tubes are factory calibrated but can be made more sensitive by sampling a larger volume of atmosphere, provided that recalibration using known standards is performed.

SUMMARY

Vinyl toluene and tetranitromethane inhalation test atmospheres were characterized with respect to degradation products using a variety of analytical techniques, including GC, GPC, inertial impaction, and Draeger® tubes. In addition, a train-type analytical system was developed to monitor oxygen, carbon monoxide, and carbon dioxide levels in a combustion chamber on a real-time basis. Hydrogen chloride and hydrogen cyanide levels in combustion chamber atmospheres were monitored using analytical techniques specific for these compounds.

REFERENCES

1. American Society for Testing and Materials. *Annual Book of ASTM Standards.* Designation D2121-70, Method B, 1970.
2. Marshal, H.P., F.G. Borgarth, and P. Noble, Jr. "Thermal Decomposition of Some Polynitroalkanes," *J. Phys. Chem.* 72(5):1513-1516 (1968).

CHAPTER 14

Analytical Monitoring for Both Intentional and Unintentional Test Chemical Release during the Conduct of Inhalation Toxicity Studies

George W. Klein and Daniel L. Geary
Bushy Run Research Center, R.D. 4, Mellon Road, Export, Pennsylvania 15632

This chapter reviews an automated gas chromatograph (GC) sampling analysis system used at Bushy Run Research Center (BRRC) during the past six years. The system was developed to monitor airborne vapor concentrations in whole body animal inhalation exposure chambers used for acute, subchronic, and chronic toxicity studies. The system was also used to monitor for the presence of airborne test chemical vapor unintentionally released during study operations. Only ten equipment or operation malfunctions occurred over the six-year period, and each was rapidly detected and corrected. Laboratory personnel were not exposed to excessive test chemical vapor as a result of such malfunctions.

EQUIPMENT AND METHODS

During the past six years, chemical analysis services were provided for approximately twenty inhalation toxicity studies ranging in duration from 4 hr acute studies to repeated dose studies of up to two exposure years. The exposure regimen for each repeated-dose study was usually 6 hr per day, five days per week. Four whole body exposure chambers, each approximately 4000 l in volume, were used for most studies. Three of the chambers were assigned to the high, middle, and low concentration levels selected for the study, and the remaining chamber was used for the control level. The room ventilation system supplied conditioned air to the room, and an exhaust fan drew air from the room through each of the chambers and an exhaust duct manifold. From the manifold, air was exhausted to the outside of the building.

169

All components of the exhaust system located within the room (chambers, ducts, and duct manifold) were at a negative pressure compared to room air. The room ventilation system was separate from, and operated independently of, the main building ventilation system.

Vapor generation devices were mounted at each chamber inlet. For test chemicals with high vapor pressure (100 mm Hg or more), a cylinder containing the liquid chemical was placed in an insulated and thermostat-controlled bath located outside the building. Stainless-steel tubing connected the cylinder to a low pressure regulator (set at 3 psig), which was connected to a manifold. Additional tubing conveyed the test chemical from the manifold to the inlet of each chamber. For test chemicals with vapor pressures of 100 mm Hg or less, a vapor generation device was mounted on each chamber. Each vapor-generating device was hooded and vented to the outside of the building. The chemicals subjected to these inhalation toxicity tests over the past six years have included gases and liquids. The boiling points of these chemicals ranged from 10° to 140° C, and a few of the test chemicals were mixtures of two to ten isomers. Vapor pressures (at 25° C) ranged from 0.1 to 350 mm Hg. Exposure chamber concentrations ranged from a low of 0.06 ppm on one study to a high of 2000 ppm for another study.

The concentration of test chemical within each exposure chamber was monitored by equipment located in a separate room (see Figure 14–1). Vacuum pumps continuously drew chamber air through 50 to 80 ft lengths of (nylon, Teflon® or polypropylene) tubing to an automated sampling port selector valve. A microcomputer was programmed to control the selector valve as it sequentially sampled chamber air from each of the sampling lines. The air sample selected entered a sampling loop in the GC and was automatically injected into the carrier gas stream. Both hard-copy and magnetic tape recordings of the analytical sampling conditions and results were automatically recorded. Magnetic tape data were later entered into a computer for further collation and analysis of data.

In addition to monitoring air samples taken from each chamber (including the control chamber), room air was monitored for the presence of test chemical vapor as an early indication of equipment or operation malfunction.

Depending on the sampling and analytical conditions for the test chemical under investigation, chamber air was sampled every 3 to 10 min, and room air was sampled every 15 to 45 min. Therefore, for each study, at least five samples taken from each chamber and the room were analyzed every day. Generally, a lower limit of analytical sensitivity of approximately 0.05 ppm or less was attained for each study.

Personnel followed standard laboratory safety procedures, including the use of laboratory hoods and proper protective clothing and equipment. However, in part to reduce further the possibility of exposure of laboratory personnel to test chemicals under study, the following precautions were taken:

1.   An emergency generator was installed that could automatically supply electrical power in case of a building power failure. The generator was sized to maintain operation of all study equipment, including vapor generation, ventilation, and analytical systems.

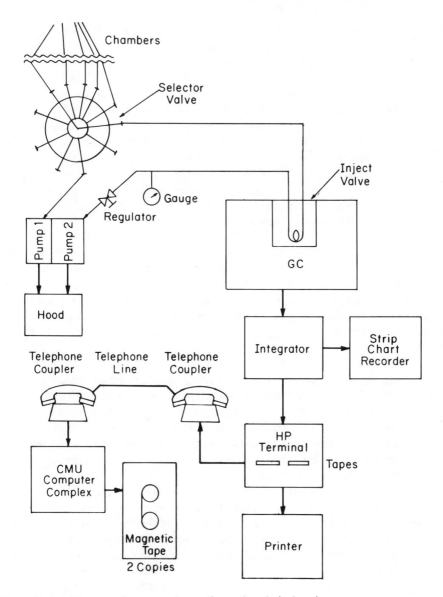

Figure 14-1. Diagram of automated sampling and analytical equipment.

2. The test chemical delivery system for gases was pressure tested for leaks prior to each day of use. The system was tested with nitrogen at 40 psig.

3. Prior to beginning each toxicity study, all systems were tested under simulated conditions using propane (for gaseous test chemicals) and toluene or pentane (for test chemicals of lower vapor pressure) to ensure proper operation.

4. An emergency exhaust fan capable of rapidly exhausting room air to the outside of the building was available and tested daily.

5.   Supplied-air respirators were available in the hallway just outside the room, and technicians were trained in their use.
6.   After the vapor delivery system was shut off at the end of each exposure day, the automated sampling system was programmed either to repetitively sample a single exposure chamber or sequentially monitor only the exposure chambers containing the high, middle, and low concentrations of the test chemical vapor. Technicians were not permitted to open the chambers until the concentration of test chemical had decayed to a safe level (an airborne concentration level of test chemical below which no adverse human health effects were expected). For the chemicals investigated at BRRC over the past six years, the safe level was considered to be 10% of the lowest exposure concentration level set for each study. By study design, no toxicologically significant animal health effects were expected at the lowest exposure level assigned in the study.

A typical day in the conduct of an inhalation toxicity study can be divided into three parts: the morning startup procedures, the period of animal exposure to the test chemical, and the afternoon shutdown procedures.

The morning startup procedure included starting the chamber exhaust fan, adjusting chamber airflow exhaust rates, loading animals into the exposure chambers, and charging and starting the test chemical vapor-generation and delivery system.

During the period of animal exposure to the test chemical (usually 6 hr), technicians periodically entered the room to make and record observations (chamber temperature and humidity and signs of toxic effect in the study animals) and to check chamber airflows and vapor generation system operations. Typically the technician was in the room for only 5 to 10 min, six times per day during the exposure period.

The afternoon shutdown procedures at the end of the exposure day included turning off the generation-delivery system, following which the exhaust fan continued to draw room air through the chamber. This resulted in a gradual decay of the test chemical concentration within the chamber. After the concentration sufficiently decayed, animals were removed from the chambers. If a slower decrease in concentration than expected was observed, the flow rate of the chamber-exhaust air was increased by a factor of two to decrease the time period for decay. The vapor generator was subsequently emptied and cleaned, and any remaining test chemical was removed and stored for later disposal.

RESULTS

Only a few building electrical system and study generation-delivery system failures occurred during the six-year period. None of these short-term failures had a serious impact on the toxicity studies in progress, nor did the malfunctions result in exposure of laboratory personnel to unsafe levels of the test chemicals under study.

The emergency generator was quickly activated following building power failures so that no interruptions in study operations were experienced. Partly as a result of the automatic activation of the emergency generator, no unintentional test chemical releases occurred during power outages.

Pressure tests of the vapor delivery system manifold and simulated tests of all study systems using propane, toluene, or pentane prior to beginning each study disclosed several problems that were corrected before any work was begun with the test chemical. Detection of trace amounts of propane, toluene, or pentane in the room air led to the repair of loose connections in the manifold and vapor-generation systems.

The supplied-air respirators were not needed for correction of malfunctions during the study due to the detection of test chemical releases at very low concentration levels soon after the malfunctions occurred. Nine malfunctions in the generation-delivery systems during the six-year period resulted in release of test chemical vapor to room air. In each case, the concentration measured in the room was below the designated safe level (10% of the lowest exposure concentration level). Three of the malfunctions were traced to leaking joints in the delivery manifold used for gaseous test chemicals, and six were the result of leaks from the liquid vapor generation systems. In each case, the chemical releases were found to be the result of leaks in generation-delivery system connections and occurred during the 6 hr animal exposure period.

One instance of improper shutdown of the vapor generation-delivery system because of technician error was disclosed by the monitoring system. At that time, monitoring results indicated that no decay of test chemical concentration was occurring in the exposure chamber. The problem was quickly corrected, and the decay in vapor concentration was monitored. After the safe level was attained, technicians opened the chamber to remove the study animals. Monitoring decay of concentration levels in the chambers indicated that for several test chemicals, actual concentration decay time was longer by a factor of two or more than the calculated time based on theoretical considerations. These differences were primarily attributed to slow desorption of the chemicals from internal chamber surfaces, caging, animal fur, and animal excrement.

CONCLUSION

Over a six-year period, serious operational problems were avoided because of thorough testing of the ventilation, vapor generation-delivery, and sampling-analytical systems prior to the start and throughout the duration of each study. However, a few malfunctions resulted in the release of test chemical to the room air. Analytical monitoring of the room air disclosed the presence of test chemical vapor before concentrations were reached that might have been hazardous to laboratory personnel.

The time necessary for decay of some test chemical concentrations in the exposure chamber differed by a factor of two or more from theoretical calculations. On the basis of very limited data, increases in the time necessary for vapor concentration decay were observed primarily in studies of unsaturated, high-boiling test chemicals.

PART IV

Chemistry Data Evaluation

CHAPTER 15

Data Evaluation and Management

Stephen S. Olin
Tracor Jitco, Inc., 1776 East Jefferson
Street, Rockville, Maryland 20852 4081

The title "Data Evaluation and Management" could mean data evaluation and (data) management or data evaluation and (laboratory or upper) management. This chapter deals with selected facets of each of these topics. The two are related in an important sense in that the management and evaluation of data in the analytical and toxicology laboratory must be monitored by laboratory and upper management to ensure that proper attention is being given to quality control and quality assurance. More than a few toxicology studies have been rejected because of inadequacies in the chemistry or the documentation of the chemistry, and the avoidance of that sort of a problem is clearly of interest to upper management.

This chapter focuses on practical management concerns at the interface between toxicology and chemistry in the testing laboratory. Techniques for monitoring and improving the quality of analytical chemistry in the toxicology laboratory are discussed, with emphasis on the application of control chart methodologies to dose analyses.

MANAGEMENT CONCERNS

Before we investigate the interactions between the toxicologist and chemist in a standard toxicity study, it may be helpful to review the primary functions of the analytical chemist working in support of a toxicology testing laboratory. The analytical chemist:

1. *Analyzes dose mixtures.* The analysis of dose formulations to ensure that the animals are getting the proper doses represents the majority of the analytical

Analytical data were generated by Battelle Pacific Northwest Laboratories, Litton Bionetics, and Southern Research Institute under subcontract to Tracor Jitco, the prime contractor for the National Toxicology Program's Carcinogenesis Testing Program (N01-ES43350). Methods were developed and modified either by these laboratories or by Midwest Research Institute.

chemist's work load. Depending on the protocol and the sponsor, dose formulations in a particular study may be analyzed as frequently as every day or as infrequently as every three or four months.

2.   *May analyze the test chemicals.* It is often necessary to reanalyze the test chemical itself at intervals to document the fact that it is not changing with time. The initial characterization of the chemical is usually done by the sponsor or another laboratory.

3.   *May develop or troubleshoot procedures.* The chemist in the toxicology lab may be called on to assist in the development of the procedures for preparing the dose mixtures, for storing and handling these mixtures or the test chemical itself, and for administering the doses to the animals. In the latter case, it is particularly important that the chemist be involved in setting up the generation and monitoring systems for inhalation studies because of the critical reliance of these studies on analytical, organic or inorganic, and physical chemistry. The most successful laboratories provide for full participation of the chemist in each of these activities. Not to do so invites problems later.

4.   *Perform metabolism studies.* Finally, the chemist must be involved in any uptake, tissue distribution, excretion, or metabolism studies that are performed.

Interrelationships

Because a toxicology study usually requires the participation of several disciplines including chemistry and a carefully scheduled scenario, interrelationships within the lab and between the lab and sponsor are important. In our experience, the chances of success are greatest when interactions work as shown in Figure 15-1. The sponsor's study monitor communicates the study requirements to the principal investigator (PI) at the laboratory, being certain that all aspects are well defined and clearly understood. The PI notifies project staff, in this case the analytical chemist, of the requirements and arranges a fail-safe system for supplying scheduled samples to the chemist. The chemist performs the required analyses on schedule and supplies the PI with the data and an evaluation or interpretation as necessary. The PI reports the results on a regular basis to the study monitor who, in turn, reviews them or (preferably) has a chemist review them. If there are problems, the sponsor's chemist recommends actions to the monitor. The critical feature here is that official communications on the overall performance of the work are between study monitor and PI, and any technical problem solving is accomplished by direct interaction between the specialists in the appropriate discipline, chemists talking to chemists, pathologists to pathologists, statisticians to statisticians, and so on. While this would appear to be a very obvious and logical approach, in our experience it is often neglected, to the detriment of the quality of the study.

Another key point is that management must ensure that the system is functioning. Chemistry and toxicology at the laboratory are frequently in different operating divisions, and management's responsibility is to ensure that the PI has the committed resources in chemistry when they are needed to meet schedules.

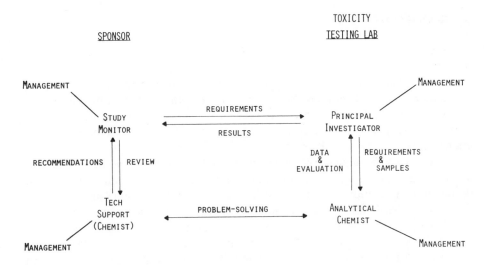

Figure 15-1. Interrelationships in toxicity testing and analytical chemistry.

Potential Problems

Problems can arise at the toxicology-chemistry interface in toxicology testing:

1. When responsibilities for notification of key personnel of actions that must be taken are not well defined, when the responsibilities for the actions themselves (for example, initiating the investigation of a peculiar analytical result) are not well defined, and when lack of assigned responsibility for follow-up results in a lot of finger pointing and shoulder shrugging when the work is not done.
2. When programs cross divisional lines in an organization but channels for communication and resource allocation are unclear.
3. When data being collected or submitted are not carefully reviewed. Do the analytical results show the test chemical to be within specifications? Are there slight changes compared to the last analysis that may be a hint of trouble in the future? Are the precision and accuracy slipping? Why? In many toxicology labs, the analytical chemistry group simply analyzes samples and sends the results to the PI but is not really involved in the conduct of the study. We have found that this "service lab" approach to toxicity testing eventually results in inadequate attention being given to the chemical aspects of these studies and have recommended as a result that a team approach be followed, including regular weekly meetings of the key scientific personnel and supervisors to review results and schedules.
4. When systems are not established for cross-checking to be sure errors of omission or commission are picked up and corrected promptly (and not on just a 10% random sample).
5. When management does not set priorities and provide a framework for conduct of studies that will ensure the quality of the product.

DECISION FLOWCHARTS

In this era of Good Laboratory Practices (GLPs), we all understand the importance of written protocols and standard operating procedures (SOPs) as quality assurance tools in both the toxicology and the analytical lab. It is sometimes convenient to summarize an SOP or show how several SOPs fit together by the use of a flowchart. As an example, Figure 15–2 depicts a typical decision tree for integrating a referee lab into the dosage analysis program, as has been done in the National Toxicology Program (NTP).

Following the sequence of events in Figure 15–2, doses are prepared and analyzed to determine if they are within the specified tolerance limits, normally ±10% of the target concentration. Dose preparation may involve, for example, mixing the test chemical in feed, dissolving or suspending it in corn oil for gavage administration, or dissolving it in a volatile solvent such as ethanol or acetone for skin application.

If the analytical results are "OK" (that is, within tolerance limits), the animals are dosed, and no further action is indicated. If the analytical results are not within tolerance limits, new doses must be prepared. If problems have been encountered with previous dose preparations of this chemical, it is normally advisable to have a referee laboratory analyze these same samples for comparison. If there have not been any problems with these dose preparations in the past, it may be sufficient just to prepare new doses and analyze them to be certain they fall within tolerance limits. If the new dose preparations are not within specifications, a referee analysis is clearly necessary.

If the referee analysis shows the suspect samples in fact to be within tolerance limits, the problem may be in the analytical procedures or performance at the toxicology laboratory. If, on the other hand, the referee analysis confirms the findings of the toxicology lab, attention is directed toward the mixing, sampling, and handling procedures for dose preparation. When a diagnosis of the problem has been arrived at, the required corrective actions are taken, and the next set of doses is analyzed by both the toxicology lab and the referee lab. If the results are still out of tolerance, we look for other possible causes. If the results are OK, we proceed on the assumption that the problem has been solved, still keeping a close eye on the next few sets of analyses for any sign of trouble.

Flowcharts, like Figure 15–2, are effective training aids and provide a common basis for understanding how a system is intended to function. Because the process is displayed in very simple and graphic terms, it is also frequently easier to identify weaknesses or flaws in the system from a flowchart as compared to reading an SOP or a protocol.

CONTROL CHARTS

Quality control must be an integral part of any toxicology study, in the biological operations as well as the chemical. An effective quality control tool that has not been used extensively in the toxicology laboratory but has in many other laboratory settings is the control chart. Control charts have been used for at least fifty years to monitor the quality of all manner of manufactured goods and technical services. In analytical and clinical chemistry, the most common use of control charts involves the periodic measurement of homogeneous and stable control samples (such as Standard Reference Materials) to determine if an analytical system is in a state of statistical control [1]. The criteria for statistical control depend to some extent on the measurement and the needs of the experimenter. This approach can also be used in the analytical lab participating in toxicology studies if appropriate control samples (homogeneous, stable, and representative of actual samples) can be obtained. Unfortunately, such control samples are seldom available for the wide variety of chemicals tested in toxicology laboratories.

Thus, in the analytical laboratory participating in toxicity testing, it is usually more practical to plot the data from actual samples prepared repetitively over an extended time period to monitor the accuracy and precision of both the sample preparation procedures and the analytical procedures. Deviations may reflect problems at any stage from sample preparation, storage, and handling through analysis. The remainder of this chapter presents several examples of how control charts for dose preparations can be constructed and how they are used.

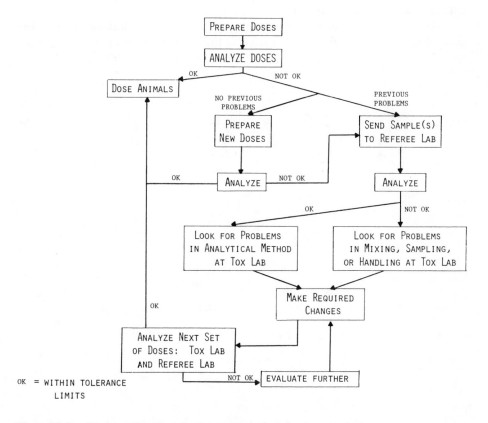

Figure 15–2. Decision flowchart for dosage analysis and referee analysis.

Amino Resin Monomer in Feed

Figure 15–3 is a control chart for the dosed feed formulations of an amino resin monomer over the course of a two-year chronic feeding study in rodents. The x-axis is time, with each data point representing a bimonthly analysis of dosed feed samples. The y-axis is split, with the upper graph plotting the concentration of monomer in the feed based on the average of duplicate analyses and the lower graph plotting the difference between the duplicates in each case. The target concentration for this dose level was 4500 ppm. For control limits on the concentration, this graph shows the + and –10% tolerance limits arbitrarily established for these studies.

While tolerance limits also could be established for the difference between replicates, an alternate approach is to establish 50% and 95% control lines. A system under statistical control should produce replicate differences, half of which are above the 50% line and half below the line. Only one in twenty differences should fall above the 95% line statistically. If a series of points consistently falls above the 50% line, the analyst should look for problems with homogeneity of the dose mixtures, improper sampling procedures, or reproducibility problems in the analytical method. Values for the control lines are established by multiplying the average difference $\bar{d}$ by appropriate statistical factors [2].

In this example, fairly good control was maintained throughout the two-year study. One of the mixes was outside the ±10% tolerance limits, but most were acceptable. When the one mix was found to be out of tolerance, the laboratory became

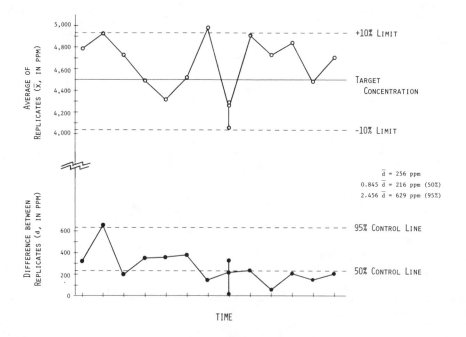

Figure 15–3.   Control chart: amino resin monomer in feed.

concerned they might be having homogeneity problems and so ran three sets of repli-cates the next time doses were analyzed on samples taken from different sections of the blender. In fact, if the laboratory personnel had been following the replicate dif-ferences in a control chart, they would have seen that homogeneity was probably not the problem since replicate agreement was acceptable for this sample and had been for the previous four samples. The fact that the homogeneity was satisfactory was confirmed in their follow-up study where neither the averages nor the replicates of the three sets of samples differed by more than 325 ppm. The out-of-tolerance mix was more likely a simple formulation error. Another interesting observation is that there appears to be systematic bias in the averages since they are mostly above the target concentration, perhaps arising from a basic calculation error throughout the study or a bias in the analytical method. Also note that performance improved as the study progressed, as evidenced by the progressively smaller differences between replicates. The one replicate difference above the 95% control line early in the study would have triggered a limited investigation, particularly with the average being right at the +10% limit, but it does not in itself mean that there was a lack of statistical control (does not require that there be an assignable cause for this event) since one in twenty results are expected to fall above this line in any case.

Fusarium Mold Metabolite in Feed

Figure 15–4 is another example of a two-year dosed feed study, this time of a mold metabolite. The target concentration is only 50 ppm, 1/100th of that for the amino

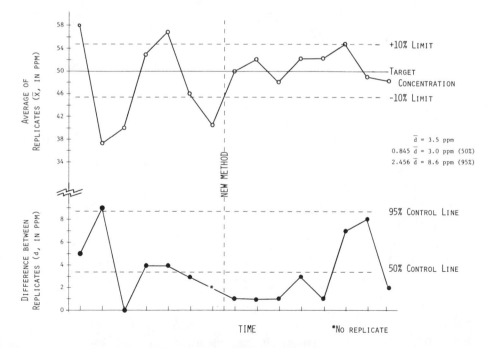

Figure 15–4.   Control chart: Fusarium mold metabolite in feed.

resin monomer. This in itself presents new formulation and analytical problems. Early in the study it is quite apparent that the system is out of control and unable to produce results reliably within the ±10% tolerance limits. Midway through the study, a new analytical procedure was introduced, with an improved column chromatography procedure and a change from gas chromatography to high-performance liquid chromatography, which removed the requirement for a derivatization step. The result is a dramatic improvement in the average concentrations. Interestingly, while there may be a slight initial improvement in the replicate differences, the last three points suggest a possible recurring problem with lack of microhomogeneity of the samples. Again, the control chart allows a rapid inspection of the total system and identification of problems and a graphic presentation of trends and presumed cause-and-effect relationships.

Organometallic in Feed

Figure 15–5 is the control chart for a real problem chemical, an organometallic fungicide, again administered in feed. The first five samples show a strong bias toward lower concentrations, well below the –10% limit. The first sample may have accidentally fallen within the tolerance limits because of an analytical problem (suggested by the extremely large difference between replicates). Since instability had already been ruled out as a possible cause of the low values, a new analytical method was

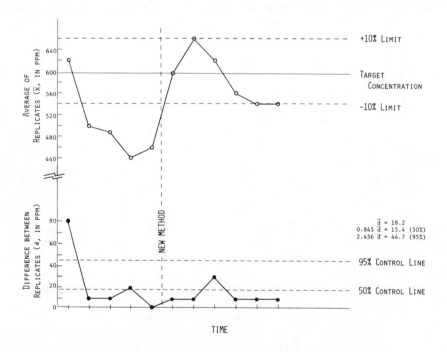

Figure 15–5.   Control chart: Organometallic fungicide in feed.

developed. The original method was colorimetric and relied on a rather inefficient and nonselective extraction procedure. In addition, there is some reason to believe that spiked sample recoveries may have been higher than recoveries from actual samples, perhaps due to a weak binding of the organometallic to feed components in aged samples. The new method, a fairly direct atomic absorption procedure, improved matters considerably, although three of the six averages are still right at the $\pm 10\%$ limits, so the new method is still only barely adequate in this concentration range. With the exception of the first sample, reproducibility between replicates was quite satisfactory by either method. This simply demonstrates that $\bar{x}$ and d provide complementary information on the system, and both should be included in dose formulation control charts.

Volatile Organic in Corn Oil

Figure 15–6 is for formulations of a constituent of certain essential oils that is used as a flavoring agent and in perfumes. This chemical was administered by oral gavage as a solution in corn oil. Concentration units here are percentage weight-to-volume. The first three sets of samples were analyzed by direct injection of the corn oil solutions into the gas chromatograph. For subsequent samples, a method modification involving prior extraction of the chemical into methanol seems to have improved the

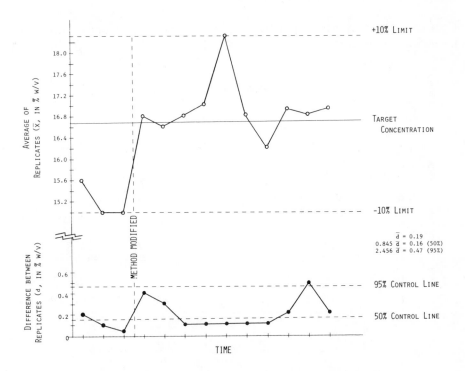

Figure 15–6.   Control chart: Constituent of essential oils in corn oil (gavage).

agreement of the results with theory. The single high average concentration at the
+10% limit later in the study was probably a mixing error since the replicate precision
was excellent for this mixture. The single replicate difference above the 95% control
line toward the end of the study may be normal statistical variance, although the fact
that the last three values were above the 50% control line suggests that control of the
system may have been beginning to slip again.

Water-Sensitive Monomer in Corn Oil

Figure 15-7 is a second gavage formulation, a monomer that reacts very readily with
water. There is no completely satisfactory way of performing a chronic toxicity study
on this material. The concentration is fairly low, and adventitious moisture plays
havoc with these samples. Consequently all of the sample concentrations are below
the target level, and only five of fourteen samples are within 10% of theory. The lower
95% confidence limit for this set of data, as shown in Figure 15-7, is in fact only 72%
of the target concentration, whereas it was almost 90% for the chemical in Figure
15-6. Still, some improvement in the analytical concentrations was achieved when
the workup procedure was revised. Replicate agreement also improved somewhat,
with most of the values falling around or below the 50% control line.

Low-boiling Monomer by Inhalation

Control charts are even more powerful tools for following inhalation studies, where
the concentration of the test chemical in the chamber air is monitored continually

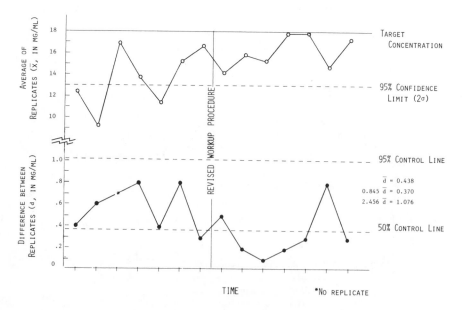

Figure 15-7.   Control chart: Reactive monomer in corn oil (gavage).

during each exposure period. In Figure 15–8 each point on the average concentration line is the mean chamber concentration of the test chemical over a 6 hr exposure period; each point represents one exposure day, so the thirteen points here cover a two and a half week period with five exposure days per week. Between four and ten samples were drawn from the chamber and analyzed each day during this period. The lower graph in Figure 15–8 plots the standard deviation for the chamber concentration measurements each day. Because we are now dealing with standard deviations, a more appropriate statistic for the control limits is some multiple of the standard deviation of the sampling distribution of daily standard deviations for a given number of samples (n) [3]. Thus, for each value of n samples measured per day, a distribution of the daily standard deviations exists for which a new standard deviation can be calculated. Traditionally, control limits are assigned as three times this new standard deviation, the so-called 3σ control limits. Since these control limits must vary as a function of n (the smaller the number of samples, the wider the limits), the upper and lower control lines are stair stepped rather than level. If the same number of samples were taken each day (the ideal case when all systems are functioning properly), the control lines would be level. Roughly 99% of the daily standard deviations should fall within the 3σ control lines, so when a value falls outside these limits, it is very likely that there is a serious problem.

In the case in Figure 15–8, a major excursion in the mean chamber concentration occurred on day 6. The interesting point is that this excursion was foreshadowed

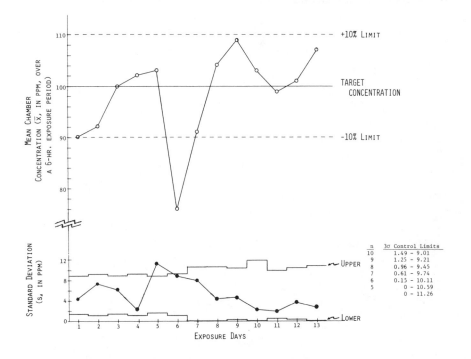

Figure 15–8. Control chart: Low-boiling monomer by inhalation.

by a standard deviation far above the 3σ limit the day before, although the mean for that day was fine. What was happening was the technician was having problems with the photoionization detector (PID) and with bubbles in the line delivering this low-boiling monomer to the vapor generator at the chamber, resulting in large fluctuations in the chamber concentration. It was only fortuitous that the mean was within tolerance limits on day 5 because the individual readings that day ranged from 82 to 120 ppm. The second day the standard deviation was still quite high, and the combination of the two technical problems made it impossible to stay within tolerance limits. With a new PID and corrective action to eliminate bubbles, the system returned to a state of control. A system cannot be considered to be under control unless both the mean and some indicator of the reproducibility of the measurements (in this case, the standard deviation) are within appropriate limits.

Reactive Monomer by Inhalation

In Figure 15–9 the mean chamber concentrations remained within ±10% during the two and a half week period; however, a notable excursion in the standard deviation well beyond the control limits occurred on day 8 when polymer buildup temporarily plugged the line to the generator, resulting in a drop in chamber concentration. When the plug was cleared, the concentration quickly rose above the +10% limit and then returned to normal. On this exposure day the system clearly was not in a state of statistical control, although the mean chamber concentration was right on target.

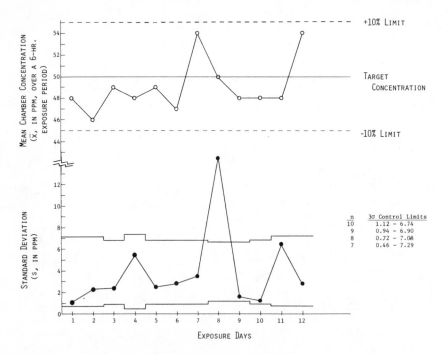

Figure 15–9.   Control chart: Reactive monomer by inhalation.

SUMMARY

The evaluation of analytical chemistry data generated in support of toxicology studies was discussed from the perspective of management and the laboratory chemist. Management must ensure that the proper channels of communication and interrelationships between chemistry and toxicology are established and are clearly defined so that the close coordination necessary for a successful study is achieved.

Control charts based on actual samples rather than reference materials offer a simple means of monitoring the accuracy and precision of dose formulation and analysis and of identifying undesirable trends in the data as potential problems. A number of examples of control charts for different routes of administration were given.

CONCLUSION

In summary, control charts provide a simple and highly graphic means of monitoring the quality of the analytical data and indeed the quality of the entire dosing or exposure system in a toxicology study. These charts can reveal by inspection real or potential problems that may be difficult to pick out in the raw data. They also offer a readily interpreted display to demonstrate good quality control to laboratory management, upper management, or the study sponsor. If the data output is computerized, charts can be updated automatically with simple programs. The application of control charts based on actual samples rather than reference materials is a practical and powerful tool in the analytical toxicology lab for data evaluation and management.

REFERENCES

1. Taylor, John K. "Quality Assurance of Chemical Measurements," *Anal. Chem.* 53(14): 1588A–1596A (1982).
2. Youden, W.J. and E.H. Steiner. *Statistical Manual of the Association of Official Analytical Chemists* (Washington, D.C.: AOAC, 1975), p. 40.
3. American Society for Testing and Materials. *ASTM Manual on Presentation of Data and Control Chart Analysis,* Special Technical Publication 15D (Philadelphia, Pa: ASTM, 1976).

CHAPTER 16

Evaluation of Dosage Analysis Data from a Problem-Solving Point of View

Joseph E. Tomaszewski
National Toxicology Program, Westwood Towers Building, Room 818D, 5401 Westbord Avenue, Bethesda, Maryland 20205

Linda M. Scheer
Carltech Associates, Inc., Suite 355, 6101 Montrose Road, Rockville, Maryland 20852

Perhaps one of the most important aspects of a properly conducted toxicological study is the correct formulation of the chemical/vehicle (c/v) mixture for administration to the animals. The individual responsible for this task must make certain that great care is taken to disperse the chemical uniformly throughout the vehicle, whether it be feed, corn oil, water, acetone, air, etc. For this reason, considerable effort is expended in the National Toxicology Program (NTP) before the start of a study to devise formulation procedures that will accomplish this task. It is also equally important to develop analytical procedures that will accurately reflect this fact. With the development and validation of these formulation and analytical procedures before the onset of a study, all problems theoretically should have been solved. However, in practice we know this not to be the case for a variety of reasons. It is the aim of this chapter to point out the reasons for these and the solutions that were developed to solve these problems.

ANALYSIS OF PRECISION

A way in which mixing and/or analysis problems can be detected during a study is by performing an evaluation of the precision and accuracy of the c/v data generated at each of the bioassay labs. The precision of each analysis is of obvious concern, since imprecise measurements generally signal problems in the methodology (sampling, extraction, and analysis) and cast doubt on the reliability of the data. With the routine use of internal standards or spiked standards to correct for recovery, problems are normally easier to pinpoint. For well over a year, Tracor Jitco has been formally calculating and reporting the variance between replicates for each c/v analysis conducted at the bioassay laboratories (inhalation data are not included in this analysis). With some minor exceptions (Table 16–1), the data collected during the past year were very consistent month after month. On the average, only 6.7% of the replicates varied from one another by more than 10%[1].

At first it was not clear why there were so few exceptions. As a general rule, analyses that vary from the theoretical level by more than 10% are considered to be out of specifications in the NTP and the formulation must be remixed. This $\pm 10\%$ was considered to be the maximum tolerance limit for the variance between replicates before additional analyses would be required. In Figure 16–1, this limit is designated as Lp [2]. The confidence limits, Cm, which encompasses the uncertainties in the measurement, can be estimated initially in most cases from the variation that the analytical subcontractor experienced in the development of the procedure. However, the quantities B and s, the systematic and random errors, respectively, that are associated with each laboratory, i.e. their instruments and analysts, only become known when the bioassay laboratory puts the procedures into use. If the systematic and random errors committed by the bioassay labs are greater than those of the analytical subcontractor, then the estimated value of Cm will probably be too low. Some other variables must come into play when the replicates vary by such wide margins—i.e., $Cm > Lp$. It was necessary to analyze the data from as many points of view as possible in order to pinpoint the specific problem areas.

Table 16–1. Measure of Precision, by Month

Month	No. of Analyses	Each $\bar{c}$ the Other (%)		
		<5	5–10	>10
January	245	66.3	27.2	6.5
February	240	82.1	12.9	5.0
March	211	78.5	10.1	11.4
April	257	81.3	11.3	7.4
May	235	80.6	12.5	6.9
June	322	75.1	16.8	8.1
July	301	74.6	16.3	9.1
August	150	84.3	11.2	4.5
September	287	84.0	9.8	6.2
October	192	73.3	20.3	6.4
November	273	80.5	14.7	4.8
December	178	78.8	16.3	4.9
Average		78.3	15.0	6.7
SD ($\pm$)		5.2	5.0	2.0

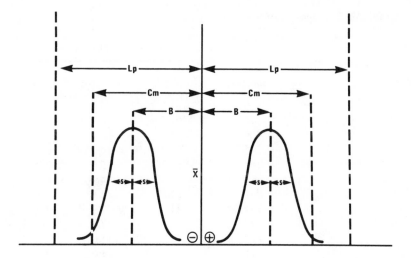

Figure 16-1.   Graphical representation of an analytical measurement's tolerances and errors.

The data from each laboratory were analyzed first to determine if the problem was strictly lab related. The results of this analysis are tabulated in Table 16-2. It is obvious from these data that some of the laboratories experienced considerable difficulty with the procedures. This does not appear to be a workload-related problem, although the lab that performed the greatest number of analyses had the largest percentage of analyses out of specifications and vice-versa. On closer scrutiny, the problems appeared to be related more to the nature of the chemical and the type of formulation prepared rather than specific analytical problems, although these did exist. Generally there was no clear effect related to the vehicle or the analytical method. There were some problems that seemed to indicate that the systematic and random errors being committed by the labs were exceedingly large. These appeared to be due to inexperienced analysts, incorrect calculations of chemical and/or vehicle requirements, and the use of methods with very high and/or variable blank values.

MEASURE OF ACCURACY

In the course of this monthly analysis of the c/v results, an examination of the accuracy of the measurements allowed mixing and/or sampling problems to be detected. The data in Tables 16-3 and 16-4 reflect the accuracy of each analysis, as well as that of the average of the duplicates versus theory. By comparing these data with those in Table 16-1, it is evident that the analyses appear to be more precise than the formulations are accurate. While, on the average, 10.4% of each of the analyses were out of specifications, only 6.5% of the average values were out. It was fortuitous that almost 40% of the individual values were brought back into specifications when averaged with the respective duplicate result. This generally occurred when the precision

Table 16-2. Measure of Precision, by Lab

	No. of Analyses	Each $\bar{c}$ the Other (%)		
		<5	5-10	>10
	30	93.3	6.7	—
	72	91.7	8.3	—
	309	94.3	3.5	2.2
	245	83.2	14.3	2.5
	163	81.3	15.8	2.9
Average	—	79.6	14.1	6.3
	241	80.5	12.4	7.1
	249	74.8	17.7	7.5
	498	75.0	17.2	7.8
	220	79.7	11.0	9.3
	101	72.0	18.6	9.3
	111	57.9	25.4	10.1
	703	71.6	18.3	16.7

between the analyses was poor. As with the evaluation of the method's precision, the accuracy of each lab's formulations was examined. These results are presented in Tables 16-5 and 16-6. Here we find a somewhat different picture than that seen in Table 16-2. An evaluation of the data in each of these tables indicated that precision and accuracy do not necessarily go hand in hand. The lab that performed the most precise analyses (30 analyses) fell to well below average in accuracy, and a lab whose analytical precision was below average (241 analyses) turned out to be the most accurate in formulation.

COEFFICIENT OF VARIATION

The overriding question concerning these data is why 6 to 7% of the formulations prepared each month were out of specification, i.e., vary from theory by more than ±10%. In an attempt to answer this, the generalization proposed by Horwitz, et al. [3,4] for an interlaboratory analysis program (see Figure 16-2) was examined to determine if it could be used to answer some of the questions concerning the NTP c/v analysis data. Briefly, Horwitz, et al. [3,4] found that the reliability of the results from analytical operations could be represented (in an oversimplified fashion) by a plot of the determined coefficient of variation mean versus the concentration.

The former was expressed in powers of 2 and the latter in powers of 10. Simply stated, the lower the concentration, the higher the coefficient of variation. While this generalization may hold for a set of data from interlaboratory analyses, it certainly did not hold for this type of program as one might have expected. When the coeffi-

Table 16-3.   Measure of Replicate Accuracy, by Month

Month	No. of Analyses	Each $\bar{c}$ Theory (%)		
		<5	5–10	>10
January	245	57.9	29.0	13.1
February	240	64.0	26.5	9.5
March	211	44.2	29.7	26.1
April	257	66.5	25.2	8.3
May	235	61.5	27.4	11.1
June	322	64.9	26.5	8.6
July	301	64.9	29.7	11.1
August	105	62.2	29.8	8.0
September	287	66.9	24.2	8.9
October	192	72.8	20.6	6.6
November	273	66.4	23.8	9.8
December	178	71.2	24.7	4.1
Average		63.6	26.4	10.4
SD (±)		7.3	2.9	5.4

Table 16-4.   Measure of Overall Accuracy, by Month

Month	No. of Analyses	Average $\bar{c}$ Theory (%)		
		<5	5–10	>10
January	245	64.4	26.4	9.2
February	240	65.8	26.7	7.5
March	211	58.3	35.5	6.1
April	257	72.0	24.1	3.9
May	235	60.9	30.6	8.5
June	322	66.3	26.3	7.4
July	301	65.4	27.4	7.2
August	105	68.8	26.1	5.1
September	287	72.8	21.9	5.3
October	192	62.3	29.9	7.8
November	273	70.3	22.5	7.2
December	178	76.4	20.8	2.8
Average		67.0	26.5	6.5
SD (±)		5.3	4.1	1.9

Table 16–5. Measure of Accuracy of Each Analysis, by Lab

	No. of Analyses	Each $\bar{c}$ Theory (%)		
		<5	$5-10$	>10
	241	71.9	24.2	3.9
	72	59.6	36.3	4.1
	249	62.4	33.2	4.4
	245	69.7	25.4	4.9
	163	64.8	29.0	6.2
	498	66.2	26.5	7.3
Average	—	59.3	29.9	10.7
	309	65.2	23.9	10.9
	220	53.4	33.5	13.0
	30	48.3	38.3	13.3
	703	57.9	27.3	14.8
	111	46.8	34.6	18.5
	101	45.5	26.8	27.7

Table 16–6. Measure of Overall Accuracy, by Lab

	No. of Analyses	Average $\bar{c}$ Theory (%)		
		<5	$5-10$	>10
	241	81.2	18.4	0.4
	72	60.3	37.0	2.7
	249	66.8	30.1	3.1
	245	74.0	22.8	3.2
	163	65.7	30.3	4.0
	498	75.0	20.6	4.4
Average	—	63.5	28.3	8.2
	309	66.1	25.0	8.9
	30	50.0	40.0	10.0
	220	60.7	28.7	10.6
	703	60.2	29.2	10.6
	111	55.7	32.1	12.3
	101	45.9	25.7	28.4

cients of variation were calculated for each chemical and compared with other chemicals at the same level and other levels, a great overlap occurred between the various levels with no correlation possible. This tended to confirm that the underlying reasons for the problems seen in the NTP c/v analysis program are rooted in the laboratories and specific chemicals rather than the program as a whole, which is generally very successful.

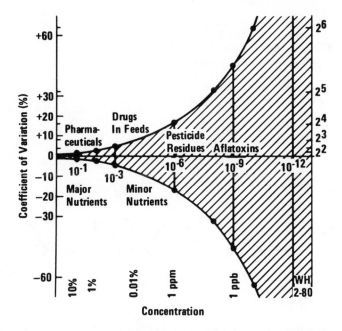

Figure 16-2. Relationship of an analysis's coefficient of variation with change in concentration from an interlaboratory analysis program.

SOURCES OF ERROR

Insofar as the sources of error (systematic and random) that arise at the lab are concerned, each laboratory must take a much closer look at their procedures with the help of the program in an attempt to reduce them as much as possible. The problems with specific chemicals have been dealt with in the past and should continue to be dealt with in the future on a case-by-case basis. Some specific examples of these problems and how each solution was approached and achieved will be discussed in the following sections.

Tolylene Diisocyanate

Tolylene diisocyanate (TDI), a mixture of the 2,4- and 2,6-isomers, is a very moisture-sensitive chemical. The chemical reacts with water as shown in Figure 16-3 to produce the amine, which can then react with another molecule of TDI to form a urea derivative [5,6,7]. TDI was formulated in corn oil for a chronic gavage study. While soluble at the dose levels used, analyses of the formulations were consistently low and out of specifications for the most part. The fact that the urea derivative was formed in corn oil formulations indicated that great care was necessary to protect the chemical and the formulations from exposure to moisture. However, this proved not to be enough. In a study conducted at the analytical subcontractor[8], it was learned

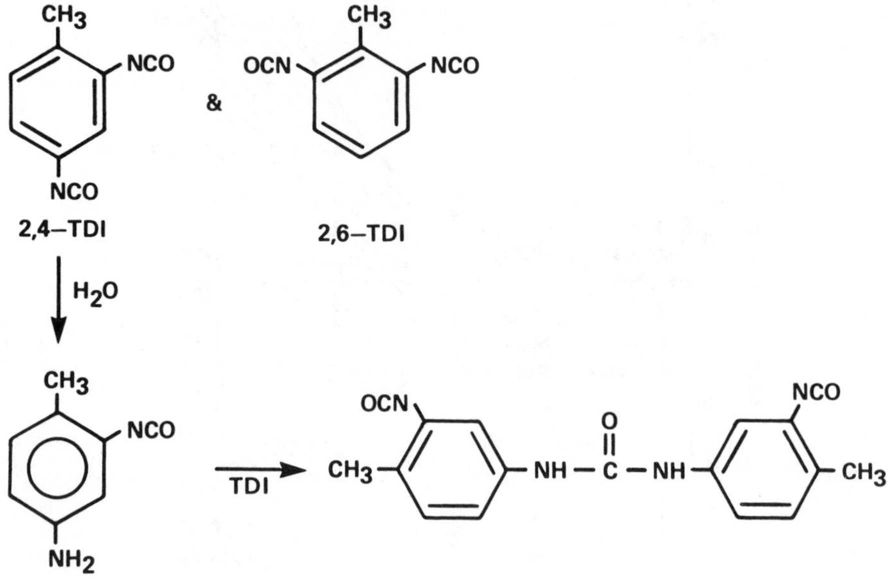

Figure 16-3.   Reaction of tolylene diisocyanate (TDI) with water. Reaction is shown only for the 2,4-isomer even though chemical is a mixture of the 2,4- and 2,6-isomers.

that normal corn oil used in the laboratories contained approximately 0.05% water. While small, this amount of water was enough to react with 12 to 98% of the TDI present (see Table 16-7). The results from a stability study [8] confirmed this result but also indicated that TDI reacts with certain components of corn oil, which in itself should not be surprising since corn oil contains numerous fatty acid glycerides, sitosterols, waxes, and peroxides [9]. This fact is borne out more graphically when one examines the stability of TDI in corn oil that had been dried (see Table 16-8)[8]. It is not known whether the drying process may have produced other components in the corn oil, such as greater quantities of peroxides, that would be far more reactive toward TDI. At any rate, through careful handling of the chemical and the formulations, the bioassay laboratory was able to supply the animals over the course of the two-year study with formulations that were on the average [10] 77 to 91% of theory, depending on the dose.

Table 16-7.   Normal Corn Oil

Dose		% TDI That Reacts with Water	
mg/ml	(μmol)	Theoretical[a]	Actual[b]
9.0	(51.7)	98.3	79.5
36.0	(206.8)	24.6	48.9
72.0	(413.6)	12.3	27.4

[a]Calculated, based on normal corn oil water content of 0.05%.
[b]Reported by MRI 1/8/80 after 7 days at room temperature.

Table 16-8.   Dry Corn Oil

Dose		% TDI That Reacts with Water	
mg/ml	(μmol)	Theoretical[a]	Actual[b]
9.0	(51.7)	10.4	52.0
36.0	(206.8)	2.6	32.1
72.0	(413.6)	1.3	19.3

[a]Calculated, based on dry corn oil water content of 0.0053%.
[b]Reported by MRI 1/8/80 after 7 days at room temperature.

4,4'-Diphenylmethane Diisocyanate (MDI)

MDI suffers from the same problems as does closely related TDI, but to a lesser extent. However, another variable confounded the stability problem, a difficulty with formulation. To eliminate this as a problem, the bioassay lab heated the chemical to melt it and then added it to warm corn oil to prepare the formulations, which remained as solutions throughout the dosing period. Since heat should only accelerate the reaction of MDI with water and corn oil, it was not known with any certainty what dose the animals received in the subchronic study. To solve this problem, the analytical subcontractor was directed to prepare formulations both at room temperature and heated as at the bioassay lab and determine the amount of MDI present in the formulation after 3 hr, the time period in which the formulation would generally be used at the lab for dosing animals. The results are shown graphically in Figure 16-4. Midwest[11] determined that at zero time, 5.0% of the MDI in the heated formulation had already reacted with the water/corn oil. At the end of 3 hr, 86.1% of the MDI remained in the mixture. Therefore the animals received on the average 91.3% of the dose. These data were used to set doses for the chronic study. In another stability study, Midwest[12] found that only 80.5% of the MDI formulated with corn oil at room temperature remained fourteen days after mixing when the mix was stored at ambient temperatures, whereas 90.1% remains when it was stored at 5°C (Figure 16-5). With these data and a recommendation to use doses for only one week with storage at 5°C, we were ready to start the chronic, confident that the animals could be dosed within specifications. Unfortunately the chronic study was cancelled.

Glycidol

Glycidol, 2,3-epoxypropanol, is a chemical that also reacts with water at room temperature and is even more reactive than MDI or TDI. It was surprising to learn that the toxicology study was to be conducted by gavage in aqueous solution. A Midwest stability study [13] indicated that this would not be a problem since this reaction could be easily controlled by storage at 5°C, such that 95.4% of the dose remained after fourteen days (Figure 16-6). The study is proceeding with no incidence of misformulation or decomposition.

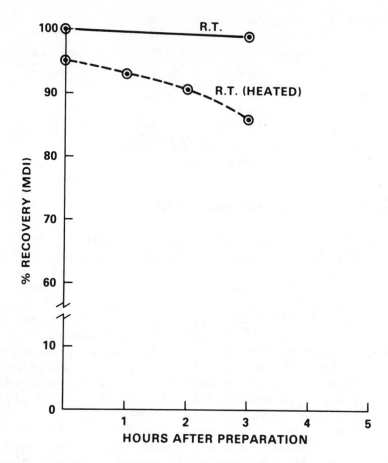

Figure 16-4. Stability of MDI/corn oil mixtures for 3 hr after preparation at room temperature with a Polytron (o—o) and after heating to ~45°C to melt MDI followed by dissolution in corn oil (o---o).

Dichlorvos

The pesticide dichlorvos, or DDVP, is a volatile organophosphate compound. This volatility coupled with the low doses used in the subchronic study created significant formulation problems. Formulation was initially based on wt/vol and then a wt/wt basis; however, it was not until formulation was based on a vol/vol basis with the use of positive displacement pipettes for dispensing the chemical that the situation was brought under control. The major problem with using weight was that the balance used was not sensitive enough. The amount of time needed for this operation allowed evaporation to occur. It can be readily seen from the data in Table 16-9 [14] that the number of mixes out of specification was reduced to just 2% of the total formulations mixed in contrast to 28% before the switch to the pipettes. Both the standard deviation and the coefficient of variation were nearly cut in half in the process.

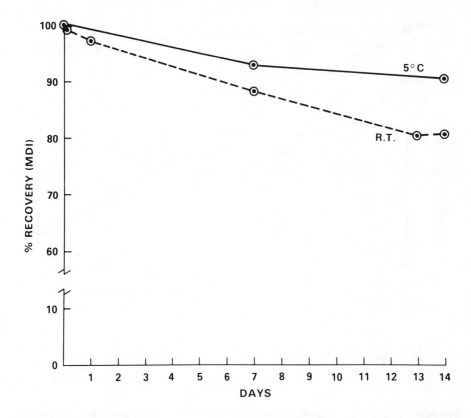

Figure 16-5. Stability of MDI in corn oil after storage for up to 14 days at 5°C (o—o) and room temperature (o---o).

Table 16-9.   Dichlorvos C/V Dosage Analysis

	Formulation by	
Average accuracy (%)	*Weight[a]*	*Pipet*
<5%	41.7	59.6
5–10%	30.5	38.5
>10%	27.8	1.9
No.	36.0	52.0
Mean	104.8	100.8
S.D.	±9.9	±5.6
Range	89.3–131.0	90.0–112.3
C.V.	9.5	5.5
Concentration range (%)	0.04– 1.6	0.09– 0.44

[a]Does not include one analysis that was 308% of theory.

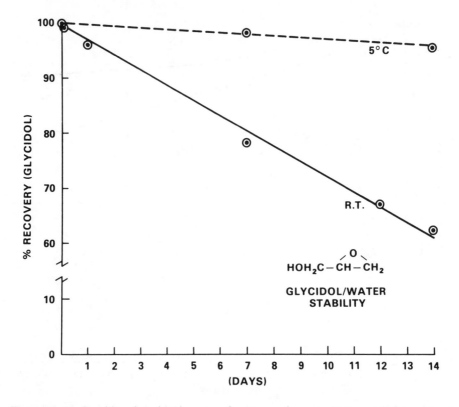

Figure 16–6. Stability of glycidol in water after storage for up to 14 days at 5°C (o---o) and room temperature (o—o).

ANIMAL ROOM SAMPLING

Specific examples of problems such as those just discussed can be dealt with rather easily; however, the situation becomes much more serious when a group of studies is affected with a common problem. Suspensions tend to create the most problems. To help alleviate this problem, homogenizers such as a Polytron® have been put into general use to produce particles of a uniformly small size that suspend and stay suspended more readily. Dose levels have been lowered to eliminate the use of formulations that have the consistency of wet concrete. The use of stirrers to keep the chemicals suspended in the animal room has been recommended, and the formulation of larger amounts of these suspensions has been encouraged such that the last animal to be treated will receive the same dose as the first. Finally, the laboratories have been urged to take special care in the sampling of the mixes in order to eliminate this as a further source of error. For a discussion on the importance of sampling in chemical analysis, see the recent study by Kratochvil and Taylor[15].

In an effort to uncover problems in the animal room, analysis of samples pulled in the animal room was instituted to determine whether the animals were receiving the proper dose after a great deal of effort had been expended to ensure a homogeneous formulation. Table 16–10 [16] lists the results for suspensions on test. In some cases, the limited number of data available make it difficult to form any definitive conclusions. However, it is evident that the chemists are doing a better job of sampling the suspensions for analysis than the formulators and animal room technicians are since the analytical precision is generally much higher than the accuracy of the formulations. It is also evident that the animal room technicians are having the most difficulty in handling suspensions. While the record is much improved over the past, there is still more room for improvement.

Sampling of dosing mixtures in the animal room was not limited solely to suspensions; skin-painting solutions as well as volatile and viscous gavage formulations were also included. The results from those studies in which the volatility of the solvent is the key element are shown in Table 16–11. Again, an animal room problem can easily be discerned; however, it is generally limited to those in which volatile solvents like acetone and ethanol are employed as the vehicles. As the volatility of the solvent decreases, so do the problems. The number of animal room samples is still too few to reflect any improvements made at the labs to correct for evaporation problems. Finally, the high viscosity of the chlorowaxes and the volatility of dichlorvos also placed them into this special category, and the results from their analyses are shown in Table 16–12. These three chemicals follow the same trend as with suspensions and studies with volatile solvents. The results from all of these studies point to the need for proper instruction of animal room personnel when suspensions or volatile chemicals are used for dosing animals. It is simply not enough to formulate properly and then act as if the problem were only associated with formulation and analysis.

It was also of interest to see how well the labs fared in these situations compared to what the analytical subcontractor experienced in the procedure development and in the referee program [17], i.e., was the estimate of Cm based on the MRI method development accurate? These results are displayed in Tables 16–13 through 16–15. The one fact that emerges from these tables above all else is that with the majority of the chemicals, the coefficients of variation in the Midwest referee analyses were appreciably greater than that originally experienced in the development of the method. This occurrence does not appear to be due to the fact that the methods were developed at concentrations significantly different from those employed in the chronic study. In fact, most of the concentrations used for method development fall within the range of the chronic doses. Since the methods are developed by a group different from the one that performs the referee analyses, the errors committed by this latter group may be of a different origin from those of the method development group and therefore could account for the discrepancy. Another possible difference is the method by which the error is computed for the c/v referee analyses. This fact needs to be explored in greater detail. Taken in this light, then, the results from the bioassay laboratories do not seem to be as bad as they first appeared.

Table 16-10. Corn Oil Suspensions-Formulation versus Animal Room Samples

Chemical	Source[a]	No.[b]	Precision (%)			Replicate Accuracy (%)			Average Accuracy (%)		
			<5	5-10	>10	<5	5-10	>10	<5	5-10	>10
Acid Orange No. 3	F	76	93.4	2.6	4.0	66.4	21.1	12.5	68.4	26.3	5.3
	AR	10	90.0	10.0		50.0	25.0	25.0	50.0	30.0	20.0
2-amino-4-nitrophenol	F	21	75.0	15.0	10.0	70.7	22.0	7.3	71.4	28.6	
	AR	7	33.3	50.0	16.7	66.7	16.7	16.6	71.4	28.6	
2-amino-5-nitrophenol	F	23	65.2	30.4	4.3	66.7	33.3		82.6	17.4	
	AR	6	33.3	66.7		61.5	30.8	7.7	50.0	50.0	
Ampicillin · 3H₂O	F	15	78.6	21.4		76.7	23.3		86.7	13.3	
	AR	1	100			100			100		
H.C. Red No. 3	F	49	82.0	10.0	8.0	58.4	23.8	17.8	63.3	22.4	14.3
	AR	8	100			56.3	25.0	18.7	50.0	37.5	12.5
Mercaptobenzothiazole	F	21	95.7	4.3		88.1	9.5	2.4	95.2	4.8	
	AR	3	100			50.0	50.0		66.7	33.3	
Penicillin VK	F	21	100			69.0	26.2	4.8	66.7	28.6	4.7
	AR	1	100			100			100		
Phenyl butazone	F	10	100			95.0	5.0		100		
	AR	4	100			89.3	10.7		92.9	7.1	
Succinic anhydride	F	47	76.1	15.2	8.7	46.5	34.3	19.2	55.3	34.1	10.6
	AR	33	75.7	15.2	9.1	33.3	23.6	43.1	39.4	24.2	36.4
8-Methoxypsoralen[c]	F	18	77.3	22.7		52.8	41.7	5.5	50.0	44.4	5.6
	AR	2	100			100			100		

[a]F = formulation room sample, AR = animal room sample.
[b]Number of samples analyzed.
[c]Predissolved in acetone before addition to corn oil.

Table 16-11. Solvent Effect-Formulation versus Animal Room Samples

Chemical	Source[a]	No.[f]	Precision (%)			Replicate Accuracy (%)			Average Accuracy (%)		
			<5	5-10	>10	<5	5-10	>10	<5	5-10	>10
Diesel fuel marine[b]	F	34	94.2	2.9	2.9	76.5	16.2	7.3	73.5	23.5	3.0
	AR	3	100			33.3	33.3	33.3	33.3	33.3	33.3
1,2-Epoxyhexadecane[b]	F	60	86.2	10.3	3.4	69.0	31.0		75.0	25.0	
	AR	9	77.8	22.2		60.0	40.0		55.6	44.4	
Navy fuel JP-5[b]	F	42	86.8	5.3	7.9	72.4	13.1	14.5	78.6	9.5	11.9
	AR	8	100			81.3	18.7		75.0	25.0	
p-Nitrophenol[b]	F	4	100			77.8	22.2		75.0	25.0	
	AR	4	100				55.6	44.4		50.0	50.0
o-Phenylphenol[b]	F	7	71.4	28.6		92.9	7.1		85.7	14.3	
	AR	4		100			16.7	83.3			100
2,3-Dibromopropanol[c]	F	49	84.4	15.6		69.7	22.5	7.9	69.4	26.5	4.1
	AR	1	100			100			100		
2-Butanone peroxide[d]	F	33	69.7	18.2	12.1	65.2	24.2	10.6	69.7	30.3	
	AR	8	75.0	12.5	12.5	68.8	31.2		87.5	12.5	
Chlorpheniramine[e]	F	40	95.0	5.0		77.5	22.5		75.0	25.0	
	AR	1	100			100			100		
Malonaldehyde[e]	F	24	75.0	16.7	8.3	72.9	27.1		83.3	16.7	
	AR	1	100			100			100		

[a] F = formulation room sample, AR = animal room sample.
[b] Solvent: acetone.
[c] Solvent: ethanol.
[d] Solvent: dimethyl phthalate.
[e] Solvent: water.
[f] Number of samples analyzed.

Table 16-12. Volatile and Viscous Corn Oil Solutions-Formulation versus Animal Room Samples

Chemical	Source[a]	No.[b]	Precision (%)			Replicate Accuracy (%)			Average Accuracy (%)		
			<5	5-10	>10	<5	5-10	>10	<5	5-10	>10
Chlorowax 40	F	167	88.4	7.3	4.3	68.4	28.1	3.5	68.9	28.1	3.0
	AR	13	100			53.1	46.9		53.8	46.1	
Chlorowax 500C	F	99	81.2	9.9	8.9	67.5	23.7	8.8	65.7	31.3	3.0
	AR	3	100					100			100
Dichlorvos	F	36	85.3	11.8	2.9	53.8	38.5	7.7	63.9	30.6	5.5
	AR	10	20.0	60.0	20.0	55.0	35.0	10.0	60.0	40.0	

[a]F = formulation room sample, AR = animal room sample.
[b]Number of samples analyzed.

Table 16–13. Comparison of Precision on Analysis of Corn Oil Suspensions

Chemical	Source[a]	No.[b]	Precision (%) <5	Precision (%) 5–10	Precision (%) >10	Original MRI Precision (%)	MRI Referee Precision (%)
Acid Orange No. 3	F	76	93.4	2.6	4.0	3.0	0.4 – 8.2
	AR	10	90.0	10.0			
2-Amino-4-nitrophenol	F	21	75.0	15.0	10.0	2.2	2.3 – 9.2
	AR	7	33.3	50.0	16.7		
2-Amino-5-nitrophenol	F	23	65.2	30.4	4.3	1.0	0.6 – 4.7
	AR	6	33.3	66.7			
Ampicillin · 3 H$_2$O	F	15	78.6	21.4		0.9	0.6 –14.1
	AR	1	100				
H.C. Red No. 3	F	49	82.0	10.0	8.0	4.0	0 –10.4
	AR	8	100				
Mercaptobenzothiazole	F	21	95.7	4.3		1.6	0.3 – 2.5
	AR	3	100				
Penicillin VK	F	21	100			0.9	0.3 – 5.2
	AR	1	100				
Phenylbutazone	F	10	100			1.0	0 – 0.7
	AR	4	100				
Succinic anhydride	F	47	76.1	15.2	8.7	2.0	2.3 – 2.9
	AR	33	75.7	15.2	9.1		
8-Methoxypsoralen[c]	F	18	77.3	22.7		1.0	0.07– 1.0
	AR	2	100				

[a]F = formulation room sample. AR = animal room sample.
[b]Number of samples analyzed.
[c]Predissolved in acetone before addition to corn oil.

Table 16-14. Comparison of Precision on Analysis of Formulations with Solvent Problems

Chemical	Source[a]	No.[f]	Precision (%)			Original MRI Precision (%)	MRI Referee Precision (%)
			<5	5-10	>10		
Diesel fuel marine[b]	F	34	94.2	2.9	2.9	5.0	1.0 – 6.0
	AR	3	100				
1,2-Epoxyhexadecane[b]	F	60	86.2	10.3	3.4	2.0	0.4 – 0.6
	AR	9	77.8	22.2			
Navy fuel JP-5[b]	F	42	86.8	5.3	7.9	5.0	0.4 – 3.8
	AR	8	100				
p-Nitrophenol[b]	F	4	100			0.5	0
	AR	4	100				
o-Phenylphenol[b]	F	7	71.4	28.6		0.2	0.4 – 2.5
	AR	4		100			
2,3-Dibromopropanol[c]	F	49	84.4	15.6		4.0	1.6 – 5.9
	AR	1	100				
2-Butanone peroxide[d]	F	33	69.7	18.2	12.1	0.6	0.2 – 1.3
	AR	8	75.0	12.5	12.5		
Chlorpheniramine[e]	F	40	95.0	5.0		1.0	0 – 3.9
	AR	1	100				
Malonaldehyde[e]	F	24	75.0	16.7	8.3	4.0	0.2 – 7.5
	AR	1	100				

[a]F = formulation room sample, AR = animal room sample.
[b]Solvent: acetone.
[c]Solvent: ethanol.
[d]Solvent: dimethyl phthalate.
[e]Solvent: water.
[f]Number of samples analyzed.

Table 16–15. Comparison of Precision on Analysis of Corn Oil Solutions with Volatile or Viscous Chemicals

Chemical	Source[a]	No.[b]	Precision (%)			Original MRI Precision (%)	MRI Referee Precision (%)
			<5	5–10	>10		
Chlorowax 40	F	167	88.4	7.3	4.3	3.0	0–0.4
	AR	13	100				
Chlorowax 500C	F	99	81.2	9.9	8.9	3.0	0–4.2
	AR	3	100				
Dichlorvos	F	36	85.3	11.8	2.9	1.8	2.3–4.7
	AR	10	20.0	60.0	20.0		

[a]F = formulation room sample, AR = animal room sample.
[b]Number of samples analyzed.

CONCLUSION

While the analytical portion of the NTP Bioassay Program has made great advances over the past six or seven years, there still appears to be room for improvement. A few programs could be instituted that might produce further improvements. One such program was initiated in recent months and perhaps should become a standard part of the program. This involves having one group from the analytical subcontractor or another lab prepare a formulated mixture of a chemical whose analyses are in question at the bioassay laboratory. The formulation will then be analyzed by the bioassay lab alone or by both the bioassay lab and the c/v referee group of the analytical subcontractor. The purpose of this procedure is to define exactly where the problem lies—with the formulation or analysis procedures—and to detail the steps that need to be taken to resolve the problem. A second possibility is to set up an interlaboratory analysis program similar to those used by many other agencies such as the Environmental Protection Agency to certify labs or the Food and Drug Administration for food contaminant analyses. The analytical subcontractor could prepare a mix, analyze it, and then send samples to each of the bioassay labs for analysis to serve as a measure of their proficiency with a particular type of analysis, formulation, or chemical class. A third possibility is one that has been used only to a very limited extent in the program but is extremely helpful in illustrating difficulties that arise during the course of a study—the use of control charts. While these have not been used at Tracor Jitco or in the NTP, the concept has been used and is extremely effectual in detecting problems. The overriding concern in all of these analyses and procedures is to produce data that are of the highest caliber such that no doubt exists concerning the concentration of chemical to which the animals were exposed.

REFERENCES

1. The data presented in Tables 16-1 through 16-6 were calculated from the c/v analyses submitted by the following laboratories in their monthly reports to Tracor Jitco as part of the requirements under the NTP prime contract in the calendar year 1981: Battelle Columbus Laboratories, Bioassay Systems Corporation, Gulf South Research Institute, Hazleton Laboratories of America, Litton Bionetics, EG&G Mason, Microbiological Associates, Papanicolaou Cancer Research Institute, Physiological Research Laboratories, Southern Research Institute, Springborn Institute for Bioresearch and SRI, International.
2. Taylor, J.K. "Quality Assurance of Chemical Measurements," *Anal. Chem.* 53:1588A–1596A (1981).
3. Horwitz, W., L.R. Kamps, and K.W. Boyer. "Quality Assurance in the Analysis of Foods for Trace Constituents," *J. Assoc. Off. Anal. Chem.* 63:1344–1354 (1980).
4. Horwitz, W. "Evaluation of Analytical Methods Used for Regulation of Foods and Drugs," *Anal. Chem.* 54:67A–76A (1982).
5. Campbell, G.A., T.J. Dearlove, and W.C. Meluch. "Humid Age Compression Set in High Resilience Polyurethane Foam," *J. Cell. Plas.* 12:222–226 (1976).
6. Campbell, G.A., T.J. Dearlove, and W.C. Meluch. U.S. Patent No. 3,906,019, "Di(isocyanatotolyl)urea" (September 16, 1975).

7. National Toxicology Program Analytical Report. "Special Report on Tolylene Diiso-cyanate" (Midwest Research Institute, September 6, 1979).

8. National Toxicology Program Analytical Report. "Special c/v Report on Tolylene Dii-socyanate" (Midwest Research Institute, January 8, 1980).

9. *Merck Index: An encyclopedia of chemicals and drugs,* 8th ed. (Rahway, N.J.: Merck and Co., 285–286 1968).

10. National Toxicology Program. "Tolylene Diisocyanate Chronic Gavage Study Mate-rials and Methods Final Report" (Litton Bionetics, April 1981).

11. National Toxicology Program Analytical Report. "Special c/v Report on 4,4'-di-phenylmethane Diisocyanate" (Midwest Research Institute, July 14, 1980).

12. National Toxicology Program Analytical Report. "Special c/v Report on 4,4'-di-phenylmethane Diisocyanate" (Midwest Research Institute, March 19, 1980).

13. National Toxicology Program Analytical Report. "Bulk Chemical Report on Glycidol" (Midwest Research Institute, September 26, 1979).

14. Analyses of c/v mixes of dichlorvos were performed at Southern Research Institute.

15. Kratochvil, B. and J.K. Taylor. "Sampling for Chemical Analysis," *Anal. Chem.* 53:924A–938A (1981).

16. The data presented in Tables 16–10 through 16–15 were calculated from numerous monthly reports of all of the labs listed in reference 1 with the exception of Bioassay Sys-tems and Hazleton.

17. The Midwest Research Institute data reported in Tables 16–13 through 16–15 were calcu-lated from numerous reports issued by Midwest on these chemicals for the NTP.

CHAPTER 17

Management of a Repository for Chemicals Used in Coded Toxicity Testing

D.R. Boline and L.H. Keith

Radian Corporation, 8501 Mo-Pac Boulevard, Austin, Texas 78766

Douglas B. Walters

National Toxicology Program, P.O. Box 12233, Research Triangle Park, North Carolina 27709

The National Toxicology Program (NTP) maintains a chemical repository of compounds selected for testing in various studies. In order to ensure consistency throughout the evaluation of a substance, a bulk quantity from a single sample lot is purchased. Then aliquots of the chemical are shipped to testing laboratories, and the remainder is stored in an environment designed to retard degradation and prevent contamination.

The repository also serves a second function in the NTP studies. In order to minimize bias of the results, the compounds are tested without the identity being known by the testing laboratory personnel. Coded samples are shipped from the repository, and the identity of the substance is not revealed until testing has been completed. In order to protect the people testing these compounds, a safety and handling document accompanies each test chemical submitted for testing. This document contains data obtained from a thorough literature search for physical, chemical, and toxicological properties of the chemical.

An emergency procedures document is placed in a sealed envelope and is also included with each test chemical. This envelope is to be opened only in the event of a spill or accidental exposure of laboratory personnel. First-aid and other emergency procedures to be followed are included in this document. Opening this envelope invalidates the test, and the chemical is withdrawn from the laboratory and resubmitted for testing at a later date, usually at a different location.

The NTP repository also provides a variety of support services to the testing program. These include:

- Acquisition of test chemicals.
- Maintenance of accurate computerized inventory and shipping records for each compound.
- Assignment of random number aliquot codes and filing of sample identity by code number, name of the chemical, and other unique identifiers.
- Decoding the sample on completion of the study.
- Conducting chemical analyses to determine the purity of selected compounds and to identify major and, occasionally, trace-level contaminants present.
- Conducting solubility studies at five levels in four solvents for each compound.
- Determination of the twenty-four-hour stability of chemicals in solvents required for the testing program if this information is not available in the published literature.
- Conducting flash point, vapor pressure, and density measurements on selected compounds.
- Conducting glove material permeation measurements on selected compounds if this information is not in the published literature.

A project director has overall responsibility for coordination of the technical aspects of the repository operation. He is assisted by three task leaders who manage the following functions: repository laboratory operations, literature search and computer services, and chemical analysis and testing. Each task leader is assisted by a staff of chemists and chemical technicians.

The management of this repository requires the close coordination of efforts and accurate transfer of information between these task groups. A computerized data base with multiterminal access was developed to meet this need, and all information about each compound is stored in a multitiered, interactive system.

Data Base Content

On notification of the selection of a compound for addition to the NTP repository, a search for sources of a high-purity sample of the chemical is initiated by the task leader for laboratory operations. Simultaneously a literature search is conducted, and all available information is entered into the data base catalog record. The information in the catalog record includes: the primary name (defined as the NTP-preferred name); Chemical Abstracts Systems (CAS) registry number, catalog record number; synonyms (which may range in number from one to over thirty); chemical formula; Wiswesser line notation; physical description; molecular weight; density; melting point; boiling point; solubility in six selected solvents; flammability; reactivity; stability; National Institute of Occupational Safety and Health (NIOSH) registry number; acute and chronic toxicity data; proper shipping name (Department of Transportation, DOT); hazard classification (DOT); uses; acute hazards; recommended protective clothing, recommended glove materials and respirator; storage conditions and special precautions; procedures for cleanup of spills or leakage; first-aid procedures for skin contact, inhalation, eye contact, ingestion; recommended fire extinguisher; procedures for disposal of excess or waste chemical; and literature references.

This information is first recorded on a form completed by a member of the literature search team. It is checked for consistency and accuracy by the task leader and entered into the data base. The information can then be retrieved by entering any key identifier, the most commonly used identifiers being the compound name, synonyms, or CAS number.

The physical properties and safety-related information is completed prior to receipt of the chemical. Thus, these data are available to laboratory personnel prior to unpackaging and storage of the compound. A remote terminal located in the laboratory enables the technician to review all properties of the substance, recommended handling procedures, and storage requirements.

All compounds are repackaged prior to being stored in the repository. This step is necessary to achieve consistency in the size containers and to ensure proper containment for long-term storage. Chemicals that are unstable in the presence of air or moisture are repackaged in a dry, inert atmosphere.

The inventory record of each chemical is initiated by an entry in the repository log book. This record contains an assigned two-letter prefix to designate the repository and a six-digit number for identification of the chemical. In addition to the primary name and CAS number of the substance, the source, purity, quantity received, date, and initials of the person making the entry are recorded. This log book is kept in the laboratory. A separate inventory log sheet is completed and transferred to the data center where the information is entered into the computerized data base inventory file. The log sheet is retained as an additional hard copy record. The log sheet contains the storage location and a physical description of the chemical in addition to the information in the repository log book. On assignment of the inventory number, the list of key identifiers is complete. These key identifiers are the descriptors that can be used to access information from the computerized catalog.

Data Base Levels

The procedures followed to enter a chemical into the repository are shown in Figure 17-1. The data base is divided into three hierarchical levels of multitiered access to provide the flexibility and degree of security required to manage the operation and maintain the integrity of the data. These three levels are the catalog record, the inventory file, and the aliquot file. The catalog record is at the highest access level of the program. Information can be obtained by entering the inventory number of a chemical or any other key identifier. Thus information about a chemical is readily available to anyone who may need it.

The inventory file is at a sublevel to the catalog record. Access to this information is also obtained by first entering a key identifier. If this identifier is other than the

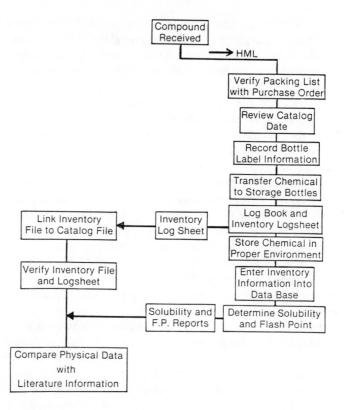

Figure 17–1. Procedures for placing a chemical in the NTP Repository.

inventory number, a list of all inventories of the compound is displayed. Entry of the desired inventory number will provide access to the information required. This feature permits separate repositories to share a common catalog file but still maintain individual inventory records. The inventory file contains information about the source, purity, and amount of chemical in the repository. The quantity remaining in the inventory is automatically updated by the computer each time an aliquot is removed for analysis or testing.

The aliquot file has the most restricted access. Only authorized personnel are provided the sequence of operations that must be performed to obtain information from this file or enter data into it. On selection of a chemical for shipment, the computer is instructed to generate a random six-digit aliquot number, automatically determined to be unique and rejected if duplication has occurred. Once a unique number is obtained, it is assigned an inventory number. Additional information regarding the chemical to be shipped and destination is entered, and an aliquot data sheet is printed and sent to the laboratory. The information it contains is used to prepare labels for the sample bottles and shipping containers. Additional information, including a physical description of the chemical and the amount shipped, is recorded on the form by laboratory personnel. The aliquot data sheet is then returned to the task leader for computer services. All information is checked and verified prior to shipment. The amount of chemical shipped is recorded in the aliquot file and automatically subtracted from the current inventory.

An interactive program has been found to provide the simplicity of operation required for routine use and yet allow access to the multitude of data available for each chemical in the repository. On accessing the program, the operator is provided with a list from which the desired type of information or operation to be performed can be selected. The operator is then prompted to select the desired repository record and identify the compound by entering its CAS number, primary name, a synonym, or its inventory number. The desired information can be displayed on the screen, or a hard copy printout can be obtained. All computer functions can be accessed from the remote terminal in the laboratory in addition to those in the computer center. Access to the edit or data entry modes is limited by security codes. Thus authorized personnel can update inventory records or check aliquot data without leaving the laboratory. This feature is important for efficient time management.

Shipping Documents and Procedures

The sequence of events required for preparation of a chemical for shipment is shown in Figure 17-2. This diagram illustrates the coordination required to ensure the accuracy and completeness of each shipment.

The safety and handling document, which accompanies each coded test chemical, contains the information required to prepare a solution of the chemical and use it safely. The information fields contained in the document are:

- Personal protection: Recommendations for minimum protective clothing, recommended glove material, and type of respirator are included in this section.
- Acute hazards: These are identified based on published information.
- Spills and leakage: Procedures for cleaning contaminated areas are recommended.
- Storage precautions: Environmental conditions required for safe storage and retardation of degradation of the chemical are recommended.
- Chemical and physical properties: The physical description, melting point, boiling point, and solubility in selected solvents are provided.
- Flammability: The probability of fire hazard is identified.
- Stability: Decomposition in solvents or as the result of shock or contact with other materials is explained.
- Toxicity: Available toxicological data are included.

This information, used in conjunction with the general NTP guidelines for laboratory procedures, enables testing laboratory personnel to conduct experimentation on coded samples with minimal risk.

In the event of an accident involving a coded test chemical, laboratory personnel have immediate access to the emergency procedures document. A label attached to the sealed envelope has the same identifying six-digit code assigned to the test

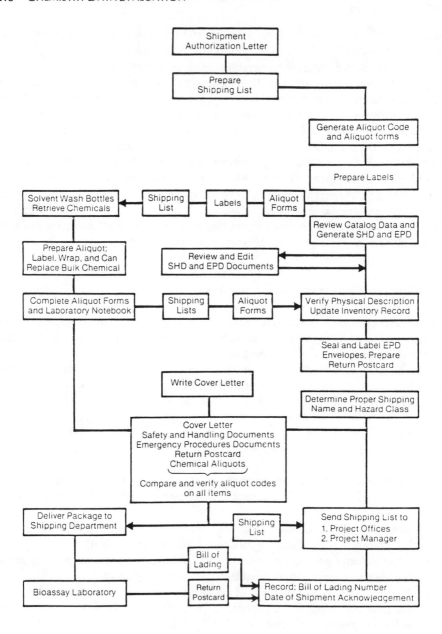

Figure 17–2. Preparation of shipment of chemicals from NTP Repository.

chemical. The information in this document includes: the primary name of the chemical, CAS number, repository inventory control number, synonyms, acute hazards, symptoms of exposure, recommended first-aid procedures for skin contact, inhalation, eye contact, and ingestion, and spill and leakage cleanup procedures.

All information contained in these two documents is stored in the data base catalog file. It is reviewed periodically and updated as additional information becomes available.

A postcard is included with each shipment of test chemicals. This card is imprinted with the code number for each sample in the shipment. Verification of receipt of the shipment in proper condition is made by return of the signed card to the repository.

On completion of testing, a letter requesting decoding of the samples is sent to the repository. The aliquot file is used to match the code number to the identity of the chemical. This information is then provided to the NTP.

Analytical Support

Purity assay of selected compounds is performed on request. Each assay consists of analysis by two methods. The most commonly used techniques are high performance thin layer chromatography, gas chromatography using capillary columns, high performance liquid chromatography, gas chromatography/mass spectrometry, inductively coupled plasma emission spectroscopy, atomic absorption spectroscopy, and ion chromatography.

A purity assay report specifying the method used, percentage purity of the chemical, and major contaminants identified is prepared for each substance analyzed. Quality assurance audits on blind samples are also performed each year to validate the methods being used in the various analytical laboratories.

The coordination of all activities associated with the repository requires timely communication between the NTP project officer, the project director, task leaders, and supporting technical staff. Weekly staff meetings are held to discuss progress, scheduling, and problems encountered.

Management and Communications

Monthly reports summarize all repository activities. More detailed semiannual reports are written to track milestones achieved, document problems encountered and their resolution, and project future activities. These reports include tables that contain complete inventory, shipment, and decoded aliquot information. Experience has shown these reports to be invaluable records for management of the repository. The computerized data base provides the speed and versatility required for daily operations. The written records are useful for review of the overall progress of the project and serve as ready references for all of the repository activities for the various testing phases of this large and complex program.

The NTP repository has been active for several years. During this time, periodic evaluation of management needs has occurred [1,2,3]. The continual growth in number of compounds being tested and additional functions to be performed has created a need for a flexible management system.

REFERENCES

1. Harless, J.M., K.E. Baxter, L.H. Keith, and D.B. Walters. "Design and Operation of a Hazardous Materials Laboratory," in *Safe Handling of Chemical Carcinogens, Mutagens, Teratogens and Highly Toxic Substances,* Vol. 1, D.B. Walters, Ed. (Ann Arbor, Mich.: Ann Arbor Science, 1980), pp. 79–100.
2. Walters, D.B., L.H. Keith, and J.M. Harless. "Chemical Selection and Handling Aspects of the National Toxicology Program," in *Environmental Health Chemistry,* J.D. McKinney, Ed. (Ann Arbor, Mich.: Ann Arbor Science, 1981), pp. 575–592.
3. Keith, L.H., J.M. Harless, and D.B. Walters. "Analysis and Storage of Hazardous Environmental Chemicals for Toxicological Testing," in *Environmental Health Chemistry,* J.D. McKinney, Ed. (Ann Arbor, Mich.: Ann Arbor Science, 1981), pp. 575–592.

CHAPTER 18

Effects of Good Laboratory Practices on Chemistry Requirements for Toxicity Testing

Charles K. Grieshaber and Carrie E. Whitmire

National Toxicology Program, P.O. Box 12233,
Research Triangle Park, North Carolina 27709

Scientific management is one of the critical facets of animal toxicology testing activities. Once the experimental design is completed, a protocol developed and operational, and methodological procedures set in place, the accuracy of data collection must be verified to ensure that the studies are technically and managerially sound. Quality control measures to control errors and quality assurance that protocols are being adhered to are the essential features of the verification process. A number of federal regulatory agencies have recognized this aspect of animal tests and formalized some of their concepts into Good Laboratory Practices (GLP).

The Food and Drug Administration (FDA) has formally issued these basic principles as the FDA Good Laboratory Practices to ensure the quality of toxicology studies intended to support applications for permits for regulated products. The GLP Regulations promulgated by the FDA in the Federal Register of December 22, 1978 (21CFR, Part 58, 43FR59986, December 1978), became effective on June 20, 1979[1]. These regulations were amended on April 11, 1980.

The National Toxicology Program (NTP) formally adopted a modified version of the FDA/GLP regulations as procedural guidelines for all NTP-sponsored animal toxicology testing studies performed after October 1, 1981. In contrast to the test results from studies performed for the FDA, the test results from the NTP-sponsored studies are not used in support of marketing or research permits, but the data are often used to predict and assess the possible adverse effects of a chemical compound on the health of an exposed population. Test results may also support regulatory agency standards for control of the use and manufacture of the tested chemical.

The analytical chemist as a member of the study team and analytical chemistry as a critical discipline in the study are subject to the GLP requirements. Essentially the requirements address procedures, equipment, and management practices. To conform to GLP requirements, the analytical chemistry laboratories must be aware of a number of general managerial elements, each of which is based on administrative insight and common sense. Included in these elements are maintenance of records, a quality assurance unit, the analytical procedures to be used, final reports, and archives. It must be borne in mind that GLPs as described here need not, and in fact do not, rule out flexibility or restrict the use of judgment or impose unnecessary expenses.

The entire GLP regulation should be reviewed and considered by analytical chemists involved in toxicology studies. The document sets forth the requirements for GLP compliance for all aspects of such studies. Subpart D (Equipment) and Subpart F (Test and Control Articles) should be carefully considered because these sections contain essentially all requirements of immediate concern to the analytical chemist.

ADMINISTRATIVE REQUIREMENTS

Record Maintenance

The major recording requirements for GLP compliance include maintaining and monitoring personnel files regarding training, experience, and position description for individuals engaged in each of the chemistry operations. These files should be maintained by the study director for the analytical chemists. An established set of standard operating procedures for all routine chemical operations, including instrument calibration and maintenance and standard sample preparations, must also be maintained. Additionally, all approved analytical chemistry protocols for each specific compound under test must be retained in a readily accessible file.

Quality Assurance Unit

The Quality Assurance Unit (QAU) functions as a source of information and expertise for planning phases of a study, as a record keeper, and as an auditor to document deviations from GLP procedures and quality standards. During the conduct of a study, the QAU focuses particularly on the GLP operational provisions, which support the acquisition of quality data.

The analytical chemist must be receptive to and responsive to the institutional QAU. This unit monitors each study and each discipline's contribution to the toxicity study to assure management that all practices conform to the GLP requirements. This unit does not provide scientific advice but serves to verify the accuracy of data collection and recording. The personnel in the QAU are entirely independent from the scientific administration charged with toxicology testing. This unit must have a direct line to upper-level institutional management. QAU personnel must have a knowledge of the particular discipline's role and involvement in the toxicology study that is being audited, but a complete understanding of the scientific intricacies is not needed. In addition, the QAU must also have its own set of Standard Operating Procedures (SOPs) for its audits and inspections.

Certain elements of a toxicity study are considered critical and must be audited and inspected for accuracy by the QAU for the test chemical in each phase of a study. The QAU inspects critical technical and managerial phases to document discrepancies between the protocol and laboratory procedures. These critical parameters include chemical-specific protocols and all amendments and deviations from these protocols, chemical analyses of test and control articles, dosage preparations, and dosage analyses. For chronic (two-year) studies, these critical phase inspections should take place quarterly.

The analytical chemist must be aware of the duties and responsibilities of the QAU. Those items that relate to the responsibilities of the chemist and are retained in the QAU files are as follows. Schedules, both master for the entire testing laboratory and compound specific for each test phase, are retained in the QAU files. Copies of all SOPs for the chemistry laboratory are also included in the files. These SOPs are essential to the QAU's inspections to ensure GLP compliances, as are all analytical protocols including amendments. QAU records of inspections and data audits including inspection date, studies inspected, and names of the individual performing the inspection must also be retained, as are all QAU audit reports including responses to the report. Reports prepared by QAU auditors are forwarded to institutional management relating audit findings and remedial actions.

TECHNICAL REQUIREMENTS

Standard Operating Procedures

SOPs are the most critical element on which the QAU auditors rely to define routine procedures and practices within the chemistry area. The SOPs remain virtually unchanged and refer to routine procedures. These routine procedures are written and followed for analytical procedures that will directly effect the quality and integrity of the data generated by the chemistry laboratory. For example, SOPs describe the methods and schedules for routine maintenance, calibration, and standardization of instruments and equipment. All reagents and solutions in the chemistry laboratories must be labeled indicating identity, concentration, storage conditions, expiration date, and disposal information.

SOPs for inventory control are also required to ensure the test material is handled only by authorized personnel as well as monitoring the quantity of material required or being used in order that the stock is not depleted before the study is completed. GLPs require periodic analysis of test and control articles. Operating procedures describe the time of these analyses and refer to compound-specific protocols for the precise analytical methodology.

Compound-Specific Protocol

Documentation of the identity, purity, and composition of each batch of test compound as well as the compound/vehicle mixture is required with documentation prior to the initiation of the animal testing phase of a toxicity study. All methods must be documented in the chemistry protocol for each compound. Storage conditions and stability of test material and the test material/vehicle mixture must also be documented prior to the beginning of the study. Periodic analyses of the test compound and the test compound/vehicle mixtures are required to document the concentration of the compound/vehicle mixtures. These analyses provide a quality control check verifying stability of the compound and that proper formulation and mixing procedures have been followed. The frequency of these analyses depends on the physical properties of the test compound and is a matter to be determined by the chemist and the study director prior to initiation of testing. Tolerance limits and detection limits should be determined, from which permissible deviations in measurement error may be established [2].

In the NTP, the test chemical is procured by an NTP contract analytical laboratory prior to initiation of testing. Quality control procedures are established to control errors; quality assurance activities verify that the system is operating acceptably. As part of quality control measures, the NTP analytical contractor determines the identity, purity, stability, and best procedure for analysis. Quality control and quality assurance activities for analytical chemistry continue throughout the duration of the study. For example, the testing laboratory determines the purity of bulk chemicals every four months. The laboratory analyzes the dose preparation on a regular basis, and referee analysis is carried out by an independent analytical contractor on paired chemical/vehicle samples to ensure that the dose preparations are properly prepared and analyzed.

Adequate record keeping is essential to the quality of the chemistry program. Assurances that records are accurate permit the chemist to submit accurate and interpretable reports. Interim analytical reports generated during the course of a study are sent to the QAU for review. The QAU examines the reports to confirm that the results accurately reflect the raw data and that unforeseen changes or planned changes in the methods that would affect the data are noted. After the toxicity study is completed, a final report on all aspects of the study is required. This report should include all chemistry data acquired during the study, using the original protocol as a guide to the chemistry data presentation.

A final report must be prepared that includes stated objective and procedures in the specific protocol; characteristics of the compound, including strength, purity, and composition; stability of bulk material and dosage mixtures; and a description of all circumstances affecting the integrity of the data. The final report results are examined to verify that they accurately reflect the raw data and that the methods and standards operating procedures are accurately described. An important aspect to discuss in the final report is the detection limits of the methodology. Frequently this item is not mentioned in GLP requirements, however; guidelines for the evaluation of data established by the American Chemical Society Subcommittee on Environmental Analytical Chemistry include limits of detection [3]. Archival storage of study reports, raw data, specimens and project protocols are also required to comply with GLPs.

SUMMARY

GLPs are based on principles to ensure that all phases of a toxicology study are sound. It is our experience that one of the reasons a study is deemed inadequate is because of animal death due to overdosing with improperly formulated or mis-handled dosing mixtures. Conversely, a study may be considered inadequate due to unavailability of the test compound to the animal due to decomposition, insolubility, binding, and so forth. Following GLP requirements does not guarantee these problems will not occur. However, these scientific management practices should provide for more accurate and reliable chemistry data, thereby solidifying the in vivo or in vitro toxicology results.

REFERENCES

1. "Nonclinical Laboratory Studies: Good Laboratory Practice Regulations," *Federal Register* 43 (247):59986 (1978).
2. Taylor, J.K. "Quality Assurance of Chemical Measurements," *Analytical Chemistry* 53:1588A–1596A (1981).
3. "Guidelines For Data Acquisition and Data Quality Evaluation," *Analytical Chemistry* 52:2242–2248 (1980).

INDEX

227